Church of England Record Society

THE HISTORY OF A HISTORY MAN

OR, THE TWENTIETH CENTURY VIEWED FROM A SAFE DISTANCE

THE MEMOIRS OF PATRICK COLLINSON

Patrick Collinson, *c.* 1988

THE HISTORY OF A HISTORY MAN

OR, THE TWENTIETH CENTURY VIEWED FROM A SAFE DISTANCE

THE MEMOIRS OF PATRICK COLLINSON

Patrick Collinson

THE BOYDELL PRESS

CHURCH OF ENGLAND RECORD SOCIETY

The right of Patrick Collinson to be identified as
the author of this work has been asserted in accordance with
sections 77 and 78 of the Copyright, Designs and Patents Act 1988

First published 2011

A Church of England Record Society publication
Published by The Boydell Press
an imprint of Boydell & Brewer Ltd
PO Box 9, Woodbridge, Suffolk IP12 3DF, UK
and of Boydell & Brewer Inc.
668 Mt Hope Avenue, Rochester, NY 14620, USA
website: www.boydellandbrewer.com

ISBN 978–1–84383–627–8

ISSN 1351–3087

Series information is printed at the back of this volume

A CIP catalogue record for this book is available
from the British Library

The publisher has no responsibility for the continued existence or accuracy
of URLs for external or third-party internet websites referred to in this book,
and does not guarantee that any content on such websites is,
or will remain, accurate or appropriate.

Papers used by Boydell & Brewer are natural, recyclable products
made from wood grown in sustainable forests.

MIX
Paper from
responsible sources
FSC® C013604

Printed in Great Britain by
CPI Antony Rowe, Chippenham and Eastbourne

Contents

List of Illustrations

Frontispiece: Patrick Collinson, *c*. 1988

Colour plates are between pages 118 and 119

Black and white illustrations

Acknowledgments

I am indebted to my former publisher, Martin Sheppard, who worked painstakingly on an earlier version of these memoirs to produce something more user-friendly. I am no less in debt to my daughter, Helen Collinson, and to her partner, Julian Elston, for turning the memoirs into a privately printed edition, and to all my children and grandchildren for presenting them to me as an eightieth birthday present. Special thanks to Stephen Taylor for his editorial work with this volume. Others have contributed, and I must single out Esther Moir, whose memories of times past have often corrected my own. I feel bound to apologize to those many people, most of them no longer with us, whose appearance in these pages approaches caricature. I do know that Clement Attlee was a remarkable prime minister and not totally devoted to the consumption of pink ices and champagne; and that the duke of Edinburgh has done many good things for the University of Cambridge. A cartoonist was one of the things that I almost became, and I am afraid that that has affected many of the occasions when these people, great and small, have found themselves floating across the little span of my own life. All errors, of fact not less than of appreciation, must be attributed to myself alone.

Why?

A once famous bishop of Durham, Herbert Hensley Henson, published, in the mid-twentieth century, his autobiography: *Retrospect of an unimportant life*. It ran to three volumes. I am not capable of so much false humility. Such self-knowledge is too wonderful for me. It is high, I cannot attain unto it (Psalm 139). But don't get me wrong. As a child, I too longed to be famous. Being driven from Islington to Ipswich, through Walthamstow, there was a little factory, proudly proclaiming itself to be COLLINSONS SCREWS. That was a source of great encouragement. Clearly some Collinsons had made it. Later the 'S' dropped off the sign, which now claimed COLLINSON SCREWS. That was either defamatory or at least excessive. Later the entire building disappeared, to make way for something else: a kind of emblem of my unimportant life.

So why should I embark on this sufficiently obscure memoir? At seventy-eight I am not these days considered to be all that 'old,' whereas in the sixteenth century, where much of me belongs, to be sixty was 'ancient'. But there can be no doubt that almost all of my life is behind, not ahead. The demographics of another psalm, Psalm 90, attributed to none other than Moses, are not easily faulted: 'The days of our years are threescore years and ten; and if by reason of strength they be fourscore years, yet is their strength, labour and sorrow, for it is soon cut off and we fly away.' The prophet Zephaniah pronounced that God had been indignant against Jerusalem 'these threescore and ten years'. Has that been my experience? Has God been indignant? My daughters chose to celebrate my seventieth birthday by taking me to the National Theatre to see *Look back in anger*. But the answer is, no, not at all. God has been good. I am happy to appropriate these lines, an adaptation of Psalm 104:

> Frail children of dust,
> And feeble as frail,
> In thee do we trust,
> Nor find thee to fail;
>
> Thy mercies how tender!
> How firm to the end!
> Our Maker, Defender,
> Redeemer, and Friend.

But of course there have been shadows, and there are regrets. Those who know the music of Gabriel Fauré may recognize the mood of his last piano composition, written at the age of seventy-six, the reflective and regretful but also angry Nocturne No 13 in B minor, especially in what has been called 'the chain of suspensions' with which it opens: music more personal, even more private, than Elgar's no less elegiac Cello Concerto, written two years earlier, at the age of seventy-two. The Fauré would be my choice, for a posthumous Desert Island Discs; that and the great six-part Ricercar from Bach's Musical Offering (BWV 1079), which would do for a memorial service.

Looking back, with nostalgia rather than anger, I am reminded that most of the people I have known and have cared for, in some cases dearly, are dead. This memoir is punctuated throughout by deaths, and that cannot be avoided. My father died fifty-five years ago, and yet few days go by without my remembering out loud, 'as my father used to say'. He was a non-eminent late Victorian (getting on for fifty when I was born), who never went outside without a trilby hat, which he raised to passing ladies, even strangers, and he sometimes wore spats. My mother, who was the love of my life, followed him twenty years later, confident that she would be reunited with her husband in Heaven, but for me she is still present. There is one troubling memory. On her deathbed, with only a day or two to live, leaning against me, she said: 'Do you love me more than the other?' I did not know and shall never know whether that other was Liz, my wife, or my father's first wife. She perhaps imagined in her woozy state that I was my father.

And then there was my half-sister Hilda, exactly four years older than me. Hilda died of cancer, more than twenty years ago. I am not sure that that needed to happen. Hilda and I had fought tooth and nail as children. Later we had cycled around the Suffolk countryside, drinking fizzy lemonade in pubs (one publican called across to us – 'you don't want to drink that old stuff, you oughter drink Cobbold's beer, that keep yer bowels open! in't nothin' worse in this world than constipation!'). As evacuees in wartime Huntingdon, I was the go-between in Hilda's assignations with more than one boyfriend. When as a missionary nurse in Nazareth she rather unexpectedly married a quite elderly Swiss husband with a grown up family (and a geriatric and deranged mother) I wrote to say that I desired her happiness more than that of anyone else I knew. My elder sister Marjorie, much beloved, died two years ago, aged ninety-one.

By now the ghosts are gathering around in a tight circle, demanding to be remembered rather than exorcised. No need to ask. They too are ever present: Michael Apps, one of my closest friends as an undergraduate at Pembroke, who became Father Bernard as an Anglican Franciscan, and who died this year; Mike Farnell, one of my mountaineering friends of a lifetime ago, a victim of cancer, who left all his climbing gear to my son; Dick Marsh, with whom I climbed in the Alps, who had a ready flow of bad language (for a clergyman) when I was too slow on the Zinal Rothorn – killed on Dow Crag more than forty years ago (and thirteen friends whom I climbed with were killed climbing); another, more celebrated clergyman, David Sheppard, the cricketer and bishop of Liverpool, with whom I had sat in the same classroom in Cambridge and whose ministry I had shared in Islington in the 1950s; Jock Morrison, who introduced me to Liz in Khartoum and who was my best man, but who drowned off a Hong Kong beach, again more than forty years ago; Francis King, writer of numerous books on the occult (was he or was he not the natural child of Aleister Crowley, whose biography he wrote?), the most amusing and perhaps the most learned friend I ever had, victim of an incautious lifestyle, for all that he drank Tizer at parties before going over to scotch at midnight. The most learned? Have I forgotten Jeremy Maule, my colleague at Trinity, who knew more than it was decent to know about Renaissance literature, the classics, theology and history, whose quite unacceptable death in his early forties happened nine years ago? I think that I was lucky to be in Africa at the time of his funeral (which Jeremy himself scripted), and so missed Dido's lament, sung to a harpsichord accompaniment. Remember me! People found it hard to take. Another very dear friend among historians was quite unlike Jeremy. The Australian George Yule had a heart considerably larger than his head, often writing the story of, as it might be, Martin Luther or the English Revolution as he would have liked it to have been rather than how it was.

My teachers and mentors in Tudor and Reformation history are all dead, of course: giants they seemed to us dwarfs who perched on their shoulders: the London Tudors, S. T. Bindoff, A. G. Dickens, G. R. Elton (transplanted to Cambridge), Joel Hurstfield, J. E. Neale; and, in Oxford, Christopher Hill and Hugh Trevor-Roper. R. H. Tawney, the Christian Socialist whom Elton called a very good man and a very bad historian, departed first. I read my first paper in his seminar and he slept soundly throughout. The best of my schoolteachers, the indefatigable Muriel Arber, died aged ninety in May 2004. We arrived at the King's School Ely on the same day in January 1942: odd to think that she was then only twenty-eight, for she didn't seem to be in the least young – almost old!

In the same month, May 2004, my Khartoum colleague John Ingledew died in Jamaica, where he had lived and taught for most of a lifetime. John and I had had some improbable adventures in the Ethiopian highlands in 1957, and he had taught me to drive, early in the morning in the suburban streets of the Sudanese capital. A year later, Richard Gray was dead. Richard was a fine African historian. We had shared an office in the University of Khartoum and Richard, too, had been with me to Ethiopia. Soon, a tight circle dating from my years in London in the early fifties, 'the crowd', was broken when Ian Orchardson, another Africanist, and Cedric Lazaro, a talented pianist from Burma, died within months of each other. You don't make such friends again. Unless you are exceptionally good at it, old age is bound to be increasingly lonely.

Most memoirs, especially those written by authors who are not very distinguished in themselves, are sustained exercises in name-dropping. Few of these ghosts in my life are household names. I have not known many famous people, let alone any of those who are famous for being famous, today's so-called celebrities: although, come to think of it, I have been a friend of such notorious media dons as Lisa Jardine and the three S's, Simon Schama, David Starkey and Sir Roy Strong. An exception among my mainly non-famous (but surely not infamous) friends, and what an exception he is, is Archbishop Desmond Tutu who as a student attended my lectures in Church History at King's College London in the 1960s, and more than once has been kind enough to remember me as 'one of my teachers!'

I was twice presented to the late Queen Mother, once as a visiting professor from Australia. 'Oh Sydney!' she said, 'that's a very gay place!' I bit my tongue and managed not to say that that was not my scene. The next time I was introduced as the Regius Professor of Modern History at Cambridge. 'Ah Cambridge! I was there just the other day, at All Souls College!' More tongue-biting was called for. I was once given a dressing down by Prince Charles at Highgrove for my distressingly liberal ideas about education. I can claim to have seen in the flesh Charles's mother and father, Winston Churchill, Anthony Eden, his nemesis Gemal Abdel Nasser, Haile Selassie, Tito, Nikita Kruschev, Pope John Paul II and Louis Armstrong. I once spent a long evening with the late Michael Foot while he expounded how *Guilty men* was written, and many other things besides. But in the background there was very loud music, it being the Sheffield History Society annual ball, and I could only see his mouth opening and shutting. The next morning I was at a wedding in Foot's constituency of Merthyr Tidfyl, the only time I have ever been there. I saw Clement Attlee twice, once in the House of Lords dining room, eating pink ice cream, once at a publisher's party at the Tower of London, sipping champagne. I can honestly say that whenever I saw Attlee he was either eating a pink ice or drinking champagne. Historians have to remind themselves every day that they do not necessarily know everything about those people who are their subjects, or even the most important and typical things about them. Even Henry VIII might have been fun to have known, on one of his good days. By the same token, the reader must not expect to learn everything about me from these memoirs. A few things have been deliberately omitted, and, it is certain, many more inadvertently.

Places can be ghosts too: my childhood London home, 106 Highbury New Park, N5. '106 to 106' my father used to say when asking for a report on the day's excursion. Twice bombed in the war, with us inside at the time, 106 was later bulldozed to make way for a primary school. There is a sadder story to tell of Great Blakenham, the Suffolk farm where I spent long periods of blissful childhood, riding the backs of immense cart horses, joining in the harvest before the days of combines, mucking out the pigs, snaring rabbits, fishing in the Gipping. The farm is no more. Chalk pits have eaten up most of the fields and the rest have been built over. The barn in which we played is still there in a shattered state, a pitiful reminder of what once was. But what the twentieth century did to Great Blakenham is about to be surpassed by the twenty-first. An outfit called SnOasis is to spend £350m converting those chalk pits into the world's largest indoor ski slope, with facilities for fourteen other winter sports, outdoing Ski Dubai. All this will be contained in a giant refrigerated building the height of Nelson's column. In John Steinbeck's *The Grapes of Wrath*, the Oklahoman folks asked, as they prepared to pull out for California: 'How will we know it's us without our past?' – and that past was as much spatial as temporal.

The question about the past, a question about identity, is one which I hope my children and grandchildren will ask, and which this book is an attempt to answer. Looking back should have some purpose. My children may want to know what happened to me, and to their mother, Liz. And whether they are interested or not, they should be told something about my father's family of twelve, my mother's of ten, even if they will be spared most of those countless cousins. And then there has to be a record of the tragic events in Kenya in 1934, when Liz's parents were charged with murder and her father died before the trial, which continued in his absence. And what about her name-dropping, Eminent Victorian ancestry? Thomas Arnold of Rugby a great great grandfather, Thomas Arnold the younger her great grandfather, Matthew Arnold a great great uncle, Mrs Humphry Ward a great aunt, Aldous and Julian Huxley her father's first cousins. So this is a book which Janus might have written, looking both ways.

I don't know how it might feel, at seventy-eight, to be a single person without any family. I am fortunate to have the companionship of my wife of forty-seven years, my four children all with partners whom we love as much as them, and (so far) nine grandchildren. This book is for them, and for anyone else in the future who might want to learn about my not unchequered past.

Shaldon, Devon,
December 2007

1

My Mother

Come with me and my mythical memories to the east of Scotland, and to the little kingdom of Fife, reached across the all so silvery Forth by that amazing bridge: the most exciting journeys of my childhood. Emotion is still aroused by the litany of station names as the steam train chugged eastwards, hugging the coast: Inverkeithing, Aberdour, Burntisland, Kinghorn, where a medieval Scottish king plunged to his death over the cliffs; and then Kirkcaldy, the home town of Gordon Brown, where I sucked in the heavy fumes of the linoleum factories long before that son of the manse and prime minister was born. And then, before the days of Dr Beeching, on to Leven, the upmarket golfing hotels of Lundin Links, the extinct volcano of Largo, where Alexander Selkirk (aka Robinson Crusoe) was born, Elie, Kilconquhar (Kilconker – but to the locals 'Kinnochar'); and so into the East Neuk, to St Monans ('Sent Minnins'), and to the proud and prosperous ports of Scotland's middle ages, Pittenweem, Anstruther, Crail, royal burghs now reduced in media perception to the status of 'fishing villages'; out to sea the distinctive shape of what the English call the Isle of May but Fifers know as 'May Island', and, far across the widening Firth, the Bass Rock and North Berwick Law.

Fifers claimed that their railway was mentioned in the Book of Genesis, when the Lord created 'all creeping things'. In its early days an old countryman, accustomed to hitching a lift into town on a cart, was affronted when asked to pay for his ticket. 'But the train was going onyway.' An Anstruther woman said she wanted a ticket for Florence, and when the clerk advised her to go to Edinburgh, where she could make further enquiries, she said: 'Edinburgh? She's only going tae Pittenweem.'

My mother was a native of Anstruther. Like other fishing communities, Anstruther has had its share of disasters and tragedies. Not to be sure on the scale of Eyemouth, far across the Firth to the south, where on a black Friday in October 1881 129 fishermen lost their lives, leaving 93 widows and 267 orphans: a now forgotten tragedy of epic proportions. Unlike Eyemouth, Anstruther had rebuilt its harbour, where my great grandfather was in command. But in the early 1900s a Pittenweem boat, the *Morning Star*, took on a miraculous draught of herrings, too many, and sank within sight and earshot of Anstruther's west pier, drowning all but one of those on board. And then on 26 October 2006, one of the last three trawlers working out of Anstruther foundered in the Norwegian Sea. The crew of four were all lost.

And here is another sad Anstruther story. In the early autumn of 1904 my mother, aged nine, was tucked up in bed with her nearest siblings, Willie, a year or two older, Rita, a year or two younger, and perhaps three-year-old John. Suddenly there was a great commotion downstairs. Willie said: 'That's my feyther deid and I'll need tae get a job.' Father, Alec (or Alex) Patrick, had been missing for six weeks, and his body had just been discovered in a ditch in East Anglia. Alec was a fishbuyer, and routinely carried a revolver to protect the considerable sums of money for which he was responsible. On the way to Lowestoft for the autumn herring fishing, he fell ill (perhaps from a brain tumour) and was told that he would never work again. Convinced that he would now become a burden on his wife and ten children, he went out for a walk and never returned. The coroner found that Alec Patrick had died instantly 'from revolver bullet wound in the head, self inflicted while in a state of temporary insanity'.

The suicide was as irrational as it was depressive in its motivation. Alec's death left Agnes Pringle (Patrick) without a penny. Willie did get a job, with the local butcher, and brought back meat on a Saturday night. Any of the Patrick children seen down by the harbour were given fish to take home, leaving my Auntie Rita with a lifelong aversion to anything fishy. A brother, 'oor Tam', who had emigrated to South Africa and had prospered (I remember my rich Pringle relations), sent his sister money to buy a smart little villa at the posher end of town, Anstruther Wester, called 'Algoa' in honour of the South African connexion. There my mother grew up and there I spent my summer holidays, wholly devoted to catching the fish which my aunt could never abide. And here it should perhaps be explained that 'Anstruther' was really three communities, indeed three royal burghs: from east to west, Kilrenny with Cellardyke, the heart of the fishing community, Anstruther Easter (where my mother was born, at Haddfoot Wynd) and Anstruther Wester.

My mother's background was a dichotomy between 'guid living' and 'ill living'. In that part of the world you either drank to excess or never touched a drop, or a dram. Old ladies who visited the local pub to purchase a dram would say, if challenged, that they were just looking at the time on the town clock, since their own clocks had stopped. Alec Patrick was a converted drunkard who preached to the tinkers in their caravans on the country road to Kilrenny, but religion had not cured the depression which had perhaps driven him to the drink.

There was a third strand in my mother's genetic inheritance: brains. Alec Patrick's mother, who was far from 'guid livin', gave birth to her son in 1859, when her husband had been away at sea for a long time. This was at Buckhaven, in West Fife, and there was uncertainty about the true father. But my great grandmother was clever and unabashed, 'canny' they would say in that part of the world. When Granny died in 1956, aged ninety-five, Alec's birth certificate was found, which established that his mother had registered Alec not in the name of Patrick but in her own maiden name of Cooper, which as a Scot she still used. So my mother was not really entitled to the name 'Patrick', nor I to my Christian name, which is simply my mother's (supposed) maiden name. Perhaps this never was a secret. My mother's birth certificate gives her father's name as Alexander Henderson Patrick Cooper, as does her marriage certificate of 1928. But the family went by the name of Patrick and 'Cooper' was explained with a story that my grandfather had been apprenticed to a cooper when he first came to Anstruther.

Alec Patrick had started off in a coalpit, but got himself out of the mines at the age of sixteen and walked eastwards along the Fife coast, looking for employment. He struck lucky when he got to Anstruther and found an opening, first as an apprentice cooper, then as a cod liver oil maker, and finally as a fishbuyer. He also found Agnes Stewart Pringle. Agnes's grandfather, who lived in that third Fife which is farming country, had been pressganged in the Napoleonic wars. According to family tradition, he died in a French prison, leaving his widow as destitute as Agnes would be after Alec's suicide 100 years later. But James Pringle seems to have fathered David Pringle, my great grandfather, in 1819, a little after the end of those wars.

1 The Patrick family, *c.* 1903 – *back row*: Lizzie, Nettie, Chrissie, Jim; *front row*: Alec Patrick, Annie, Willie, Dave (in army uniform with John, the youngest, in front of him), Belle (my mother), Rita, Agnes Pringle (Patrick). Photographic studio, Shore Street, Anstruther.

David Pringle was taught to read and write by the son of the laird while he looked after the kine in the fields. The fact that he had a brother called Anstruther Pringle may explain how this happened, since Lieutenant-General Anstruther of Airdrie was that laird. (An Anstruther Pringle was born in 1767 to Alexander Pringle and Christian Corstorphine.) David Pringle soon set off for the coast, and by 1841 was living in Cellardyke. He rose to be clerk to the Harbour Commissioners ('Collector of Harbour Dues') of Anstruther. He was also a prolific poet, mainly in the cause of temperance. (The Pringles had his book of poems and I hope that someone still has it.) So Anstruther harbour brought Alec and Agnes together. Thirteen-year-old Agnes was cheeky enough and ran after sixteen-year-old Alec, with his mass of auburn curls, shouting 'carrots'! He chased her and gave her a good drubbing. But the next day Agnes fell seriously ill with scarlet fever, and Alec was filled with remorse. Five years later they were married, on 1 October 1880.

The whole family was photographed, perhaps a year before Alec's death. The elder five children, Jim, Dave, Chrissie, Lizzie and Nettie are almost grown up, Jim with an impressive moustache, Dave in army uniform. Jim became an electrical engineer and lived in Edinburgh. Dave had run away to become a soldier when his father tried to put him behind the counter of a shop. He would not be seen for many years, but then he came back to rediscover his old mother, and he taught me most of what I know about sea fishing and told many stories. In the trenches there had been word of a barrel of beer in a captured German dugout. While Dave and the others were drinking the beer, a shell landed on the trench which they had just

2 Auntie Rita, Granny Patrick and Uncle Dave, *c.* 1952

vacated. 'Now if that was one of your Sunday School stories, the shell would have hit the dugout with the barrel of beer.' Dave knew what he was talking about. I have four of his illuminated Sunday School 'certificates of merit' dating from the early 1890s. In 1892 the subject was 'The Suffering and Risen Saviour', in 1893 'Nehemiah, his Character and Work', in 1894 'Abraham, the Friend of God' and in 1895 'The Miracles and Teaching of Christ'. That was something which died for millions in the First World War.

The elder girls all married and had children, Chrissie and her husband (the married name was Grierson) in Canada where they had emigrated. Willie also made his life in Canada and brought his five boys over to see us in May 1932. Later Roy and Moffatt were drowned in a lake in northern Canada on a fishing and hunting trip, leaving widows and children. Nettie's husband was an auctioneer called Dowie, and my cousin Dave Dowie, who died in July 2006, carried on that business. He helpfully contributed to this reconstruction of the Patrick family history. Lizzie became Lizzie McEwan, and Kenneth, one of her three children, started a new branch of the family in New Zealand.

There was something of a gap between the elder five and the younger five. When his mother wanted John she would shout 'Annie, Willie, Bella, Rita, JOHN!' Annie too married and became Annie Forbes. She had two children, down in Lancashire, the elder a girl called Agnes for her grandmother, now a widow of over eighty. But Rita was to live with her mother for much of her fifty-two years of widowhood. In the group photo Dave has little John between his knees. John was badly spoiled by his mother and was destined to lead a sad life which ended with his head in a gas oven. The farm girl whom he had married when he got her pregnant never complained although he had walked out on her and never sent her any money. No Child Support Agency at that time, nor would stone-deaf Auntie Nan have made use of its services if there had been. I was once close to the children of that unhappy marriage, Billie and Lexa, whose husband Doug was the sole survivor of a British ship lost in the Battle of the Coral Sea; and especially to Lexa's four children. Such were the Patricks. In my generation, I count sixteen cousins, but perhaps there were more; and what about the next generation? 'I will multiply thy seed as the stars of the heaven, and as the sand which is upon the sea shore' (Genesis 22.17).

But I may not have said enough about the widow of Anstruther, my Granny. She spoke in a foreign language, so far as my English father was concerned. A typical complaint: 'Ach, dinnie mak sic an opery aboot a'thing!' ('Oh, do not make such an opera about everything' – how impoverished is English English by contrast!) Brattizani's, the ice cream parlour down by the harbour operated, as in so many Scottish towns, by an Italian family, she denounced as 'the Deil's ain Sawbath skill' ('the Devil's own Sunday School'). She was a godly old lady in her seventies, eighties and nineties when I knew her, poring over a large-print Bible with the aid of a magnifying glass. 'Curses on Babylon! Curses on Babylon! chy should I strain my een reading curses on Babylon?' 'Yon Paul was an awfie man to argie!' When news came in 1943 that the bombers called Mosquitoes had raided Berlin, she called out: 'Rita, listen to this, it's the Lord's hand this time richt enough! There's moskeetees raiding Berlin!'

My mother added the piety of the Pringles to the brains of the Patricks. She was the child of a series of religious revivals which regularly engulfed Anstruther in her early lifetime, brought in by the 'pilgrims' of the Faith Mission. Her second name, 'Hay', which we have passed on to our elder daughter, was the name of a pilgrim lodging with the Patricks at the time of her birth. The Patrick family worshipped with the Church of Scotland, the 'Auld Kirk', at Cellardyke, which was not especially evangelical, but for an accidental reason. Cellardyke kirk needed a precentor. Alec Patrick had a good tenor voice. And the pay was equivalent to the annual rent for his house. So the family left the Baptists and were led past the door of the 'Dippie Kirk', only a few yards away from their home, where the deacons, Alec's old friends, stood outside and said: 'There goes Alec Patrick, takin' his wife and a' his bairns tae Hell!' This must have happened soon after my mother's birth in 1895, since Dave Patrick's Sunday School certificates are all from the Baptist Sunday School.

As a child my mother played a game in which you had to indicate what you wanted to be when you grew up with the first letter of some profession or other. Her initials, which no one ever guessed, were always 'M' and 'A': M for Missionary and A for Authoress. In the early 1960s she wrote a book, *Recollections of East Fife fisher folk*, which was belatedly published in 2003, nearly thirty years after her death. Belle Patrick was a writer of real merit, and she had both an eye and an ear for every aspect of a way of life which has by now entirely vanished. In the early 1920s she had published stories in the *Weekly Scotsman*, modestly signed 'B.H.P.': 'Cupid's Apprentice', 'Tammas's Proposal', 'Tammas's Wedding'. The first story paid three guineas, more than half a year's salary when she had first started work. Belle had lived among the fisher folk, 'but I was not of them, and that, I think was an advantage. I saw things as an onlooker.' Her book was also written out of deep affection for the fisher folk, and it ends with this sentence: 'Even if it means that

3 My mother, Belle Patrick, *c.* 1920

I shall be condemned as having become completely English, I must use one four-letter word which is, or was in my young days, completely barred in speech if not in writing, and leave them all my love.'

But my mother was not Dylan Thomas, whose account of Cellardyke might have resembled *Under milk wood*, with its caste of curious characters. The curiosity, which fluctuated between genius and madness, came from excessive inbreeding. Almost every family had someone 'up the stair' who was never seen. I remember 'Poetry Peter', Cellardyke's own McGonagall, who when not writing his verses went to the creels (which is to say that he was a crab and lobster fisherman, a somewhat despised occupation – but his house in Cellardyke bears a plaque in his honour); and his son who left a promising career as a mathematician in St Andrews to join his father at the creels. Then there was Kate McRuvie, 'Auntie Kate', who was what my father used to call a human flypaper, 'aye postit' as they say in Fife; and, a pillar of the local church, Mrs Pratt, who had a luxuriant moustache, and made life difficult for James Robert Lee, the minister, the victim of many cruel stories. At a Sunday School outing Mr Lee was in the lavatory with the door locked. Mrs Pratt, assuming some child was inside, pulled at it violently, shouting 'ye should have gone before ye cam' oot!' (But the minister was the minister, and when he called on a house where everything was not in apple-pie order, the wifie would be 'black affrontit'.) When, in my twenties, I joined the Church of England, Mrs Pratt exclaimed: 'Me, I dinnae like the likes of yon! Yon's hauf road tae Roman Catholic!' And how could I forget Provost Carstairs, of the same generation as my mother, a prominent member of the Chalmers Memorial Church, which was to burn down in somewhat mysterious circumstances; and owner of the local oilskin factory, where the workforce were rumoured to constitute his harem. Queen Elizabeth II conferred on Carstairs the OBE, and when the newspaper photograph showed him bending down to kiss the royal hand, people said that OBE stood for 'Oh the Back End!'

Belle Patrick's brains won her a scholarship to the Waid Academy in Anstruther, and then a bursary to St Andrews University. But her mother insisted that instead she get a job, which paid £5 a year, less than the university bursary was worth, rising to a giddy £12 10s after four years. Her employers, for whom she worked as a short-hand and typing secretary, were the local banking and legal firm of Mackintosh and Watson. Mr Mackintosh was town clerk of the neighbouring fishing village (actually yet another royal burgh), Pittenweem, and in the First World War Belle Patrick virtually ran the little town on Mackintosh's behalf, dealing with licences, ration books, exemptions from military service and many other things of that kind, while collecting the rates and balancing the books. When she applied for an administrative post in Roxburghshire, Mackintosh in his reference described her as a woman 'possessed of exceptional parts'.

But Mr Watson had other ideas. He knew that in the post-war world women, besides securing the vote, would be eligible to qualify as lawyers. In August 1920, Belle Patrick was formally apprenticed to Mackintosh and Watson as a trainee solicitor. She read her law books early in the morning and five years later passed all her legal examinations and was admitted a 'Law Agent to practise in all the Courts of Scotland, Supreme as well as Inferior'. Was she the first woman lawyer in Scotland or only one of the first? The politician and wife of Aneurin Bevan, Jennie Lee, who came from a mining community in West Fife (and therefore at the opposite end of the political spectrum from my mother) qualified at about the same time; and so, I believe, did the mother of Tony Weir, himself a lawyer and a Fellow of Trinity

College Cambridge. I have all my mother's examination papers, written in both shorthand and longhand. She found them easy.

But perhaps she had an even easier ride in the oral part of the examination. The first learned gentleman before whom she appeared reminded her that he had often taken her on his knee when he had visited her father's home in Colinton outside Edinburgh. 'Surely you remember me?' 'I have never lived in Colinton and my father died when I was quite a small child.' 'I have no further questions.' In the waiting room was another young woman who, my mother told her, was about to meet an old friend. The next examiner was an expert on the Court of Session and was delighted to learn that my mother had read his book on the subject. But he had just one question. 'I am very interested in cockatoos, and as you come from Anstruther perhaps you can tell me what happened to a bird which used to belong to Mrs Gourlay?' Now Mrs Gourlay was an elderly newsagent who liked fine her wee dram, and when you came into the shop the cockatoo would call out: 'Mrs Gourlay! Mrs Gourlay! Mrs Gourlay's drunk.'

But my mother chose not to be enrolled on the Register of Law Agents and never practised law in the Scottish courts, high or low, not for a single day. On the day after she was told that she had passed her exams she booked a passage for Algiers, where she was to be amanuensis to a remarkable lady and missionary, Miss Lilias Trotter. In her words, it was to be 'the Gospel instead of the Law'. Religion was the spur, and for Belle Patrick always had been. In her *Recollections* she tells us how she spent whatever time was left from running Pittenweem, reading law and writing stories for the newspapers. A serious illness in 1919 made her confront the fact that in all probability her life would be short. Soon she was leading prayer meetings for children in Pittenweem, and, in Cellardyke, a children's club and class which grew to 200 members. There were scenes reminiscent of the film *The King and I*. When Belle walked along Shore Street, she was surrounded by children, and the older women remembered that this was 'Alec Patrick's lassie'. Her dealings with these children and their families supplied her knowledge of a now lost way of life.

In 1924 my mother attended a convention of the Faith Mission in St Andrews. It was there that she met Lilias Trotter, 'a very austere figure, tall and dignified', and it was then and there that my mother became Miss Trotter's secretary, taking down in shorthand her replies to a mountain of correspondence.

Lilias Trotter was a talented painter and pupil of John Ruskin. When she left him for Algiers, Ruskin said: 'What a waste!' But Miss Trotter continued to execute and publish exquisite water colours and pastels in books with titles like *Between the desert and the sea*. The Algiers Mission Band, which she founded, was dedicated to converting not just the women of Algeria but the entire population. My mother's first task when she arrived in Algiers was to type the text of a book aimed at hundreds of thousands of Islamic mystics, the Sufis. The Band consisted of English ladies, whose home base was the fortress of a former Barbary corsair, Dar Naama, in an eastern suburb of Algiers, El Biar. There were also English *women* of a somewhat lower class, who looked after the housekeeping, much like the lay brothers in a medieval monastery. No one knew quite where to place my mother in this little hierarchy. Lilias Trotter, much like Florence Nightingale and other eminent Victorian women, had by now taken to her bed, or couch, from which my mother took dictation. She wrote one enthusiastic letter after another to Anstruther: 'That dear daughter of yours', 'I do look on her as one of God's most special gifts to me of late.' My mother, guessing what was being said, wrote: 'Please remember she's English and like all of them here is apt to gush a bit.' The terms of my mother's appointment were board and lodging and a personal allowance of £25 a year, most of which would be sent home to Granny in Anstruther.

My mother was not exactly a missionary. Indeed, after her first year, Lilias Trotter told her that she never could see her as a missionary, 'at least not yet'. My mother's letters report a quite conventional life in the Algiers of the twenties. When the British fleet put into port, the officers were entertained at Dar Naama and returned hospitality, on board. Belle was now intended to represent the Band in England, specifically in Croydon, living with the general secretary of the Band, Mrs Brading, mother of Lella Brading, who was Miss Trotter's nurse and housekeeper. Belle was to link the groups supporting the mission in various parts of the country.

But first she was sent off on one of the *tournées* undertaken by the mission in the interior, the purpose of which was to distribute tracts among the local population. The railways made this possible, but often sandstorms got in the way. Once, Belle and the other ladies were stranded on a train for two days, without anything to eat or drink, but with many Arab fellow passengers who were glad to share their company. At Khanga Sidi Naji, an oasis town deep in the desert, where there were no Europeans, a place with a famous mosque and a devout Islamic tradition, the ladies were closely watched and escorted at all times by the eight sons of the all-powerful Caid. The sanitary arrangements consisted of a hole on the top of the flat roof of the Caid's palace, in full view of the market square, so a biscuit tin was put to an unaccustomed use, and all the more necessary in that the ladies were locked into their room at night, to make sure that they would not proselytize their infidel beliefs. My mother was, understandably, an object of some interest. How old was she? Was she married? Why not? What was wrong with her that no one had offered for her? Was she rich? When one of the sons tried to slip some bracelets on to my mother's wrist in the suq, she knew she was in trouble, for this was equivalent to an offer of marriage.

This was perhaps the only notable incident which Belle failed to report in her frequent letters to her mother, which otherwise read like chapters from *Beau geste*. By the time she got back to Algiers she was at death's door with dysentery and pneumonia. Her always fragile health had collapsed. The doctor who examined her ordered an X-ray, convinced, like all other doctors who had ever seen my mother, that she was suffering from pulmonary tuberculosis, and he recommended that the quicker she could be got out of Algeria the better for all concerned. Back in London, another doctor pronounced that she would be 'pretty much of a crock' for the rest of her life.

2

My Father

In February 1927, Belle Patrick, writing from Algiers, had sad news for her mother. 'Mr Collinson, our Deputation Secretary, lost his wife this week and he is left with four little children. It is very sad for him. He is such a very nice man.' Indeed William Cecil Collinson, my father (known as Cecil) was a very nice man; people, especially ladies, often referred to him as a 'gracious' man. His children, destined to be my mother's stepchildren, were not all 'little'. Marjorie (who died in 2005 aged ninety-one) was already rising fourteen and had childhood memories of zeppelin raids in the war. Gerald was ten and Bernard seven, but Hilda not yet two.

My mother had met Cecil Collinson in Algiers twice, and it was intended that she would work closely with him in mission deputation. So, when she was still too ill to be out of bed, she took a quick peep, and 'as I looked at the gaunt, colourless face, I thought that at least I did not look as ill as he did'. As he left Dar Naama, my father approached Mrs Brading, Lella Brading and my mother, and said that he hoped later in the year to be able to drive the three of them in his new car to that annual evangelical festival, the Keswick Convention. Belle Patrick was not sure that she was to be included in the party. But it soon became clear that she was, and in July 1927, the three ladies travelled by train to Ipswich, and to Mr Collinson's new house, to meet the family; and to be driven the next day to Keswick in a newly acquired Standard Park Lane Saloon, via King's College Chapel in Cambridge and sundry other architectural gems.

At Ipswich Station, my mother got into a back seat of the car. My father indicated that she was to sit in the front. She proceeded to climb over the seating into the front, whereupon my father said: 'It's conventional to use the doors.' When my father's sister-in-law heard about that she said: 'That's the one then, you mark my words.' After a few days Mrs Brading suggested that Belle should not be seen so often in company with Mr Collinson. People might talk and the reputation of the Algiers Mission Band would suffer. My mother told her that she needed to see something of Mr Collinson since he had just asked her to marry him, and she scarcely knew him. The proposal had happened on a little walk to Friars Crag, on Derwentwater. This was a shock for Mrs Brading, who had assumed that Lella would be the widower's choice. It was even more of a shock for my mother, who for thirty years not only had no expectation of marriage but what she called 'a very definite intention not to marry'. It had amused her as a law student to learn that three classes of person were incapable of taking legal action: infants, idiots and married women. There was a great deal, indeed almost everything, that my parents, needed to know about each other. They had met on perhaps a dozen occasions, which was only enough to discover that they shared the same birthday, 22 August. A great deal of ground was covered in three hours of one afternoon at Castle Crag in Borrowdale.

Looking back at the age of seventy-two, my mother wrote: 'Though I could not claim to be head-over-heels in love as he undoubtedly was, I could at least offer him in return sincere respect and growing affection.' Marriage and motherhood were not what she had intended for herself, but she believed that her life was determined by a higher power. She wrote in 1967: 'So soon as I got my hands on business books and papers I knew instinctively what to do and how to do it, and when I worked out a financial problem or any other complicated transaction I had a sureness of touch which I never had in the kitchen, baking a cake.' But the kitchen and all the other chores which went with being a housewife were what the future was now to consist of.

On 28 April 1928 my parents were married in Darling's Hotel, Waterloo Place, Edinburgh, by James Robert Lee, the minister of Cellardyke. It was a very private affair, only my Granny, Auntie Rita, my father's schoolmistress sister Aunt Margaret and the best man (who was he?) in attendance; although my mother wore a conventional white wedding dress with a veil and all the trimmings, and my father held a top hat. Belle now had what some unkind souls in Anstruther called her stuck-up English man.

It is time to explain what had happened to W. Cecil Collinson, as he was always known, before that day in July 1927. The Algiers Mission Band may have consisted exclusively of English ladies, but the committee at home was, like so many worthy and highminded committees at that time, a largely male affair. In 1924 my father had taken his ailing wife, Hilda Quant, on a Mediterranean cruise, and from that came firsthand acquaintance with the fringes of the Islamic world and an interest in the conversion of Muslims which transformed his life.

In the spring of 1926 my father was in Palestine, Egypt and Algeria, took many photographs (he was a great photographer), and wrote the text of many a lantern slide lecture. (I am not sure how it was possible to be so far away from home for two months. Hilda, my sister, was six or seven months old and Hilda, his wife, had less than a year to live.) Just like my mother, later in the same year, my father undertook a taxing tournée in the deserts and oases of Algeria beyond the mountains, distributing tracts. ('1131 books sold, 688 given away. Value of sales 481 francs.') His travelogue is full of excited reactions to exotic landscapes and scenes, and is more exact and observant than my mother's account. 'The graves in the burial grounds are covered with old bottles, empty marrow shells and skin water buckets. Water gathers in the skins and marrow shells for the birds to drink out of, and thus evil spirits are propitiated. Candles are lighted and set in the jars and bottles on feast nights.' At El Hamel, near Bou Saada, there was a sacred stone into which a local saint was supposed to have put his finger. 'As we look and hear the story, two men on donkeys draw near, alight, put their fingers in, kiss their fingers, and pass on.'

My father now sold up his business, became secretary of a society called the Fellowship of Faith for the Muslims, and joined the home committees of more than one missionary enterprise, including the Algiers Mission Band and the North Africa Mission (with which the Band would later merge).

How had this come about? Why was evangelical religion the spur for my father, as it was for my mother? She was, formally, a Presbyterian, a member of the Church of Scotland; he a Quaker, a member, like all his family, of the Society of Friends. In neither case did these denominational affiliations matter a scrap. My parents were not so much undenominational as antidenominational Christians. Both were powerfully motivated by a fervent evangelistic and second-adventist imperative. Today they might be called 'fundamentalists', but that expression has American

4   My parents' wedding, 1928

(let alone Islamic) resonances which do not quite fit. They were saints in St Paul's language, 'godly' as they would have described themselves if they had lived in the sixteenth century. Everything that my father said and did was, so far as he could manage it, 'God honouring'. He saw to it that two relationships into which my sister entered, and which might have developed into marriage, were terminated. 'Be ye not unequally yoked together with unbelievers' (2 Corinthians 6.14). 'Can two walk together, except they be agreed?' (Amos 3.3).

My father's father was Samuel Collinson, a native of South Cave near Beverley in the East Riding of Yorkshire. There were many Collinsons in both South Cave and North Cave, grocers, druggists and Quakers; my father's mother, Samuel's second wife, was Alice Blanche Lean, a member of a notable Quaker dynasty. The only child of Samuel's first marriage, Mary, married Norman Penny, a distinguished historian of Quakerism, editor of George Fox's Diary, and Librarian at Friends' House. The endless ramifications of these almost incestuous Quaker alliances were all contained in the heads of one of my elderly maiden aunts. She was scandalized when, in the late 1940s, the film director David Lean, some sort of cousin, got divorced.

Samuel Collinson had moved from Yorkshire to Ipswich, where he opened a grocer's shop. There were twelve children, if we include Mary and another daughter, Winifred, who died in childhood. They lived first at 170 Woodbridge Road and then at 13 Corder Road, in a genteel suburb where all the roads were named for Suffolk painters, Gainsborough Road, Constable Road and so on. Here the maiden aunts held court in later years. There were four adult sisters, apart from Mary. Sophie married a certain Mr Brown, and in the thirties and forties we regularly saw 'Uncle Percy Brown' (so named to distinguish him from my siblings' Uncle Percy Quant) and his daughters, who lived in Luton, when all that went on there was the manufacture of hats. The other sisters never married. Aunt Margaret, a severe schoolmistress, died in 1940. Rosalind, Auntie Rossie, died in the same year, unnecessarily, of peritonitis. She was not supposed to be ill. Kathleen, the family's mental archive, was thought to be delicate, but she went on living at Corder Road until the mid-1960s, by which time she was in her nineties, making life hell for a succession of unfortunate companions, who included, for many years, my sister Marjorie. She pulled intellectual weight with these poor women, for she had been a governess in the Cadbury family in Birmingham, where she had met Edward Elgar, and she was bookish. The pictures on the walls of Corder Road were the prints you would find in any Quaker house, such as the bored child in a Quaker meeting, looking at a sparrow on the floor, and Elizabeth Fry visiting the prisoners in Newgate; but also Dante and Beatrice on the bridge, and Dante's dream. These pictures were imprinted on my consciousness by many a sticky Sunday afternoon tea party.

Howard was the eldest son, and he too lived into post-Second World War Britain, another nonagenarian. He was a founder member of the Ipswich Permanent Benefit Building Society, where he was succeeded by his son, Norman, my favourite cousin, a man of extraordinary kindness, a talented photographer and involved in all sorts of societies and clubs dedicated to the preservation of rural Suffolk. After his father died, Norman, already about fifty and lodging, temporarily, with my mother said: 'I suppose that now I ought to get married, but it will have to be a Quaker, and the trouble is they're all so plain.' But in 1961 he married Jan, a spirited and not at all plain Quaker of about his own age. The wedding took place at Old Jordans Meeting House in the Chilterns on a golden October day. Norman's brothers, already married with children, were Edward, a solicitor, and Hugh, a talented painter and art teacher (he and Muriel adopted their children). Howard's wife, Auntie Cathie, was a Pease, another Quaker dynast. After the death of her cousin Constance, she was heard to shout into the ear of Kathleen at a family party: 'I'm wearing Constance's coms.'

Gerald, for whom my elder brother was named, was a bookbinder by trade, who died of liver cancer at about the time that my father made his first marriage in 1911. Gerald was an active evangelist, and founded a tabernacle in one of the poorer parts of Ipswich, the Gipping Mission, where his portrait hangs to this day. His widow, Auntie Carrie, a Salvationist, was a poor thing, cold-shouldered by her brothers-in-law. Eric and Arnold moved far away from Ipswich, to the north-west, and we heard little from them, although I visited Uncle Arnold, his partner and my cousin John at Wallasey, when I was serving in the RAF.

My father was number eleven of this large family, born in 1881, so he was four-teen years older than my mother. He was in every sense a late Victorian, and wore a top hat when he went to Quaker meeting. Once he even saw Queen Victoria, a small globular lady bobbing up and down in a coach in Hyde Park. He was in meeting when someone came in to announce that the old queen was dead.

The youngest of the family was Frank, who also made his career in the Ipswich Building Society, and who was the last to depart, again in his early nineties, in 1976. We have remained in Christmas card touch with the children of Uncle Frank and Aunt Edith and their families: Ruth, David, a geophysicist, who died in October 2007, and Elizabeth, close to me in age. Norman, David and I had a wonderful week of walking in the Lake District at Easter 1950, based at Buttermere – all at Norman's expense.

It will be seen that these Collinsons were on the whole a less colourful and interesting crowd than the Scottish Patricks. Ipswich was a town where you either went to work or to business, and the Collinsons, especially Howard and Frank, defi-nitely went to business. They respected wealth and spoke of this or that person as a 'warm man'. They disapproved when my brother Bernard married the daughter of a railway clerk who lived on the wrong side of the Ipswich tracks. They were conven-tional in their Quakerism, and their memorial is the room in the Ipswich Meeting House called the Collinson Room. My father was very quakerly to his dying day, at least in speech, theeing and thouing my mother. ('Have thee got thy gloves?') But what took him out of this conventional environment was the Young Men's Christian Association, at a time when it was still thoroughly Christian, and evangelical; and also an evangelical Quaker agency called the Friends Evangelistic Band. Frank, too, was part of this evangelical movement, and the brothers cycled around Suffolk, spreading the word. But Frank soon gave up, whereas my father stayed in the reli-gious hothouse. He ceased to attend meeting, especially after marrying a Baptist wife, Hilda Quant. Presently his brothers wrote him out of membership, which he much resented. But it was no doubt a reasonable thing to do. When we lived in north London, Uncle Howard happened to mention that he often passed the end of our road. My father said that he ought to call and see us. Howard said: 'Oh no.'

My father went to a Quaker school in Yorkshire, Ackworth (whereas Howard and later his sons were educated at Bootham). I have his first letter, written from school and dated 24 January 1890, when he was eight, no doubt one of those Sunday after-noon letters which all of us who have been at boarding school remember writing:

Dear Papa and Mother, I still like being here very much and I am very happy. This afternoon some men came to do things in the gymanaseym and we are going to watch them. Please will you send me a button hook as soon as you can I cannot have my button boots on yet because I havent got one. I have not had any punishments yet a lot of the boys have. How is papa and baby [Frank] I hope they are better give baby five kisses for me. Now I must stop I remain your loving son Cecil.

After leaving school, Cecil was apprenticed to an Ipswich clothier called Arthur J. Ridley. He went home with his fellow apprentice Percy Quant and met his wife, Hilda, when she was just fourteen. In due course he had his own tailor's and outfitter's shop in Bury St Edmunds, selling, amongst other items, horse blankets for the racing stables, at Newmarket, where he opened another branch of the business. A degenerate aristocrat came in every week to purchase bottles of eau de cologne. My father knew that they were bought to be drunk, but said that he had no choice but to sell them. Marjorie, Gerald, Bernard and Hilda were all born in Bury, Marjorie, Gerald and Bernard at a house on the edge of town called Sunny Hill, Hilda at 78 Risbygate Street, which was home from October 1923. It was from there that their mother Hilda Quant was taken to the hospital where she died, in February 1927. Soon after this, in April, the family moved back to Ipswich, and to 62 Tuddenham Road, called 'Melverley', a stone's throw from Corder Road. Grandma Quant moved in to manage the children, but it was mismanagement, which was why my father needed a new wife.[1]

A few other things should be said about my father. He detested (not too strong a word I think) the Church of England, and all set forms of prayer and worship. But in spite of that the greatest enthusiasm of his life was medieval ecclesiastical architecture, all those ruined abbeys and cathedrals. In the early 1900s he cycled all over England carrying a heavy plate camera and other photographic gear with which he took, and processed, superb images which deserve to be published. These photographs were the stuff of many lantern lectures, with titles like 'Minster 'Neath the Mendips' (Wells) and 'A Petrified Pageant of Periods' (Ely), all written out in an impeccable copperplate hand. By 1914 he was a motorist, having acquired a Swift Cycle car for £115, which cost £58 2s 2d to run in its first year. In 1919 he drove 2,585 miles for £23 0s 11d. (His Quaker mother, born in that other world of the 1840s, used to ask: 'Have thee got enough petrol?')

Another interest was stamp collecting. In 1919 the collection was carefully valued, from the Stanley Gibbons Catalogue, at £492 13s 10d, in 1920 at £872 13s 0d. My father then bought a collection from an ex-officer, down on his luck. It consisted of many hundreds of Victorian stamps from the West Indies. If he had not later disposed of this unique philatelic archive we might all be rich. And then there was botany, a hobby inherited from his father Samuel, who had a little chest of specimens. As children we were given a halfpenny for every wild flower we could name; and a whole penny for learning to spell one of the more difficult words in the botanical lexicon, 'Eschscholtzia' (Iceland poppies to you and me).

Although deeply devout, my father, like many a Puritan, had a strong sense of humour, and a great repertoire of funny rhymes and recitations. Many repartees were prefaced by 'as Uncle Frank would say', for Uncle Frank was even more humorous and given to parodying hymns: 'Blessed be the tie that binds/My collar

---

[1] It would be mischievous to remember what an Elizabethan clergyman wrote in his diary under the heading: 'Inconveniences If My Wife Should Chance to Die: no. 1 'Necessity to Marry Again'.

to my neck' 'Change and decay in all my teeth I see.' Here is my father at his most typical: 'I well remember my poor old father carving the Christmas turkey for the whole family, and then sitting down to a dish of rice pudding. [Pause] Which as we now understand was the worst thing he could have eaten.' When Daddy did the rounds first thing, emptying the chamber pots into a slop bucket, he called them 'Pochefstrooms', an echo of the Boer War. There were also earlier Victorian memories, recalled with a good sense of irony: 'Since wishing will neither procure nor prevent, I must strive to remain in my state of content.' 'Now and then a pleasant day, long in coming, soon away.' When I refused to eat my dinner I was told, again with tongue in cheek: 'You deserve to eat candles in a mine.' But my father was stern enough with it. Without a trace of irony, he often asked me: 'Why don't you do something constructive?' The constant reiteration of that 'work ethic' no doubt had something to do with what became of me.

My father was generous to a fault. When he was a little boy, an old man approached him and asked: 'Have you got such a thing as a bit of cold pudding about you?' My father at once withdrew all his savings from the Post Office and presented the man with two quarts of gooseberries. In later life, he was always a soft touch for what he called 'ticket of leave men', those recently released from prison. These were quakerly instincts. But when in the 1930s tramps came asking for bread and dripping, that was precisely what they got, and it was usually thrown back over the hedge. The mysterious chalk marks made on the pavement outside our gate no doubt read: 'Don't expect to get any money here.'

Daddy was also impulsive, impulsive enough to propose to my mother whom he scarcely knew. Coming back from the seaside he would suddenly drive into a field, go round it two or three times, and then back on to the road. In August 1940, on the eve of the Blitz, we drove to Tottenham and came back with a whole set of live chickens in the back of the car, which no one had intended when we set out. The rest of the evening was spent in frantic efforts to provide the birds with suitable accommodation. As the bombing intensified, I subscribed to *Poultry World*, kept a careful account of all the eggs laid, and slaughtered the poor birds without any compunction when that became necessary: something I simply could not do, in Australia, more than thirty years later.

I wish that I had known my father when he was younger. He always seemed to me old, and I never saw him in anything but a suit and the kind of collar which was detachable and had to be sent off in a box to the laundry to be washed and starched. I think that during the Second World War he may have been one of the very few people in Britain never to have listened on the radio to the comedy show ITMA. One of the catchphrases in Tommy Handley's programme was 'After you Claude; no, after you Cecil!' At the time my parents were running a canteen for servicemen in the Cambridgeshire fens. When a soldier, going out of the door, said to my father: 'After you Cecil!', he was horrified.

My father died on 9 November 1952, at 62 Tuddenham Road, where my parents had returned after the end of the war. I find it odd to think that I have already outlived him by seven or eight years. He had hypertension and I suppose died of renal failure, a problem which probably dated from his service with the Royal Army Medical Corps in the war of 1914–18. I share some of the same symptoms, but they are well controlled by drugs which were not available fifty years ago. Three things appeared to precipitate my father's final illness: the death of the king in February 1952 (he always stood for the National Anthem on the radio); my winning first class honours at Cambridge; and a visit from two Mormon missionaries, whom he was unwise enough to invite in, earnestly arguing the theological toss with them for three or four hours.

I suppose my father, too, could have been a 'warm man'. He had a sharp business sense, and always managed to talk down the price of anything he bought. But his estate was worth just £7,993 5s 7d, before funeral expenses of £55 18s 0d. I suppose that we have to put a nought or two after that. His legacy included shares with the firm of A. J. Ridley worth £1,000, which, in the late 1960s, brought in just £88 2s a year. In 1969, when my mother emigrated to Australia, her total assets were worth £7,415, most carefully husbanded. My father would have been worth much more, but for what he called 'The Lord's Work'. He always claimed that, in the days when Puritans gave their children fancifully meaningful names, there was an unfortunate man called We-Brought-Nothing-Into-This-World-And-It-Is-Certain-We-Shall-Take-Nothing-Out Jones. My father's favourite text was Romans 8.28, which is inscribed on his gravestone: 'All things work together for good to them that love God, to them that are called according to his purpose.'

3

A Strange Little Boy

On 3 July 1929 Auntie Rita came down from Anstruther and stayed in Ipswich for a month. When she went back on the train, she took Gerald and Bernard with her to sample the delights of fishing at the end of the pier and to be entertained by Uncle Jim from Edinburgh. I was the reason for these movements. I was born at 62 Tuddenham Road at 4.45 p.m. on 10 August. Dr Williamson was not in attendance, since a few minutes earlier there had been a fatal road accident where Tuddenham Road meets Valley Road. I weighed seven and a half pounds, recovered my birth weight in a fortnight, and allegedly smiled at one month (probably wind). On 22 February 1930, with two teeth through, I could say 'Ta' and 'Dadda', and I stood unaided at eleven months.

All this I owe to my father's compulsive record keeping. What he failed to mention was that I was born with a large birth mark (nevis), covering the whole of my left cheek. It must have been a great shock, and sorrow, to my parents. In the early baby photographs the birth mark has been airbrushed out. I do not think, although I cannot be sure, that the disfigurement ever caused me much distress. Years ago, small children used to point and ask questions. I find that they no longer do that, which is interesting and indicative – of what? But I think it likely that my Cain's mark is the reason why I am by nature non-combative, fearful of many things, and even, as some would say, nice. Nature (a lack of fluid in my mother's womb) had decided that I could not afford to be anything but nice. But I suppose that the birth mark could have made me nasty. I do not think that I was any part of my father's plan when, aged forty-six, he married my mother. He needed a mother for his growing family. I was in the bath when I told my mother what terrible people stepmothers were, in all the fairy stories I had been told. My mother said that she was not so sure about that. 'After all, I'm Hilda's stepmother.' A moment's reflection led to the pronouncement, on which my parents dined or rather tea-partied for some time: 'Oh, I see, those stepmothers were the ones who didn't love the Lord Jesus.' Wanted or not, I was dedicated to the Lord Jesus from birth, destined, along with my siblings, to be an evangelist and a missionary. My nurse, Sister Ridley, used to bounce me on her knee, saying 'Don't let them make you a missionary.' It seems to have worked.

The most important thing to have happened to me in those early years was the arrival on the scene of Olive List, a young woman from the village of Tuddenham who was recruited to be my nursemaid and mother's help. There were other girls around the house, 'maids' who rarely lasted very long. One 'had to go' when it was found that she had amassed several dozen cans of a substance called Ronuk in order to obtain coupons with which to secure silk stockings. But Olive was different. Yet she too almost had to 'go'. Wagging tongues reported that she was seen chatting up young men in the park. Challenged with this evidence, Olive said that of course she had spoken to those men, who were all from her village and all out of work.

5   Patrick Collinson as a baby: my birthmark has been carefully airbrushed out

So Olive stayed, but soon she married a farmer, Gene Hood, who had taken over a farm at Great Blakenham, five miles out of Ipswich. That became my second home (my parents were often overseas) and Olive my second mother. She and Gene had no child of their own until 1942, when Robin was born. But they loved children and filled the rambling old farmhouse (which dated from the fourteenth century) with a whole lot of us. There was a wet day when it was suggested that we should all play at nudist colonies, a matter of prurient interest in the 1930s. I ran upstairs and reappeared starkers, to find that I was the only one to have done so. Once when I came back from the farm, my mother said, 'I think that you love Auntie Olive more than me.' I found that suggestion surprising and redundant. 'Of course I do.' Olive died in her early nineties in December 2004. Long before that, the farm was gone, and with it her life, so much of it given to others. One negative memory of those happy times: there were no books at Tolgate Farm, Blakenham, or rather 'books' meant magazines, like Farmer's Weekly. When I began to spend my saved-up pocket money on real books, especially books about birds, Olive gave me a piece of her mind. It was unnatural. In retrospect, it reminds me of Maggie Tulliver in *The mill on the Floss*. If Tulliver had not chosen to take that parcel of books against a bad debt, what then?

I was an odd little boy. As both an only and a youngest child, I longed for a little baby sister or brother. For some time I thought that such a sibling could be bought, in Woolworths. One day my mother told me that there would be a great surprise when I came back from school at dinnertime. ('Dinner' in our lower-middle-class home was in the middle of the day.) Of course that could only mean a baby. But when I got home, full of excitement, it was only a roast turkey. I was also obsessed

6 Olive Hood ('Auntie Olive')

with the problem of how you got married. I thought that you had to go up to a total stranger in the street and pop the question. How could you do that? Twenty years on, I realized that finding a lifelong partner was a little more complicated than that.

Most of my education was in private schools of one kind or another. I never met the greater part of mankind until I began my National Service, at the age of eighteen. First there was a dame school called Park House in Ipswich, to which I was admitted at the age of three and a half. From the word go we learned French, the names of animals and other things, but no grammar. At break time we had to choose between milk and a ferocious homemade ginger beer. In the basement there was a central pillar which was crying out to be swung around, although we were assured that that was very likely to bring the whole place down. I must have been insecure, perhaps because of the birthmark. I had an imaginary friend, 'Patent'. One day I went to school having decided that my name would henceforth be 'John', and everyone called me John until breaktime. Then they said (and one can almost hear Joyce Grenfell's voice), well that's the end of that, now you're Patrick again. On another occasion the children invited to a birthday party were to stay behind until they were collected. I knew that I had not been invited, but stayed all the same, until the inevitable humiliation came upon me. When the time came for my family to move to London, a little girl said: 'I suppose you'll be living in the suburbs.' I said, yes of course, having no idea what suburbs were.

We lived not in the suburbs but in Highbury New Park, once upon a time the better end of Islington, but close to the ethnically and socially different Stoke Newington (Green Lanes). Highbury New Park had been millionaires' row in the 1890s. There had been gates at either end, the road sanded, and on Sundays the carriages were stacked up outside St Augustine's Church, next door but one to our house, but which in our time had a congregation of six. By the 1930s most of the houses were in multi-occupation, but not by the kind of people we knew. Highbury New Park had taken a nosedive. But our house, no. 106, built by a margarine millionaire, was all ours. There was a lift. There was a large coach house (for us, the garage), a tackle room and loft above (my refuge), loose boxes and a stable yard, which is where those chickens had to be housed in August 1940. There was a long garden with the kind of pear trees which infested north London, grown so tall that the pears could not be harvested and, as they fell, they either knocked you out or squashed into a pulp. My sister Hilda and I kept rabbits and tortoises. The Indian doctor next door and his family, the Mottaframs, were friendly, and we could climb their large mulberry tree and enjoy the clothes-staining fruit.

How did we come to be living in such a place? 106 Highbury New Park was the London headquarters of the Egypt General Mission. (The concentration of evangelical missionary agencies in that part of London was something which went back well into the nineteenth century.) In 1935 the general secretary of the EGM, Douglas Porter, was returning from the Keswick Convention (again that convention played a part in my destiny) when he was killed in a car crash at Brough, where the road from Scotch Corner meets what is now the M6. My father succeeded Douglas Porter and we moved to Highbury, not long before the death of George V (I can still see the headlines). But for that road accident, my life would have been entirely different.

No. 106 was a house on three storeys, four if you count the basement, where, for safety, we lived during the war. The ground floor was mostly occupied by the mission offices, a large room for the secretarial staff, who included, of course, my mother; a study at the end of the passage for my father; with, on the right of the

7   Patrick with Hilda at 106 Highbury New Park, *c.* 1938

passage, a rather gloomy drawing room rarely used except for my sister's hated piano practice. You went down from that level to the garden via an elegant wrought iron stair, heavy in summer with the scent of a luxuriant jasmine. We lived on the next two floors. I shared a bedroom with my brother Bernard, who was to become a missionary, but who was then working as a nurseryman at Perry's of Enfield, becoming in due course an expert on ferns. I hero-worshipped Bernard, not least when he served as a medical commando in the Second World War. Gerald I liked less, and he me. Asked to put something in my autograph book, he wrote 'You Little Twerp!' No doubt a fair comment. In more recent years we have got on well. He too is now over ninety.

There was a crisis when I was eight, in January 1938, when the problem which had made me sickly for years was diagnosed as appendicitis. Before I went into the Mildmay Mission Hospital, I was committed to the Lord at a little service in the drawing room. We sang 'Safe in the arms of Jesus'. The surgery was barbaric, the anaesthetics procedure more so, but I survived, to wake up in an adult ward in which, a day later, the man in the next bed rather noisily died. I remember his family coming to collect his clothes.

Naturally, the affairs of the mission dominated our lives. The EGM, like the Algiers Mission Band and the North Africa Mission, was a 'faith' society, which meant that the missionaries were not on regular stipends (as with denominational societies) but dependent on 'allowances', which varied with what faithful supporters contributed, from month to month. The Americanization of many of these societies in the second half of the twentieth century has transformed their material prospects, but in the 1930s life was hard for everyone, including me. Once I was given the lead rôle in the school play, the part of a king who required appropriate robes and a crown. My father said that he could not possibly justify that expenditure when the missionaries in Egypt were on half allowances. So I was obliged to take on the non-speaking part of a slave, which required only a white sheet and some cocoa. The boy who got to play the king was called, appropriately, Duncan, although the play was not *Macbeth*.

'School' was another little dame school, a few hundred yards down the road: Arundel House, it was called. Miss Fulford and her assistants did a magnificent job. We learned to spell and to count, multiply and divide, and we spent a whole term on the Wars of the Roses, which might have put me off history for life but didn't. I received high praise for my capacity to write a good précis, which was perhaps indicative of what I would later be good at. In my first surviving letter, to Auntie Rita at the age of six, I wrote:

> Mummy and all of us send our special love. This is the longest letter I have ever written, first of all I am going to tell you about our new schools. I am going to say the names of some of the teachers. [The names of my teachers and Hilda's follow.] I hope You and Granny (Mrs PATRICK) are ever so well. Goodbye to telling you things about London I want to ask you how Scotland is getting on. Now I only have a few more words to say. Now only one more sentence A Hotel opposite always has chimney fires. love Patrick.

I have not needed to correct any of the spelling. On Friday afternoons we had country dancing, in the only large room in what, after all, was only a private house. We also gathered there for assemblies. I always remember Miss Fulford telling us that 'Oh God our help in ages past' was a very good hymn, because it had no specifically Christian connotations. Clearly there must have been many Jewish children in the school. There were also two German refugee boys, not Jewish I suppose because they could not have been more Aryan: tall, slender and almost white-haired. Once we all had to sit in Miss Fulford's study to hear a live broadcast covering the state visit to London of President Lebrun of France. So it was that the terrible events of the 1930s in the world outside came within our narrow consciousness.

One of the deficiencies of my early, and for that matter later, education was that I was never taught to know and love the English poets. To this day, thanks to a gifted French teacher at sixth-form level, I have more French poetry in my head than English. But in earlier years, hymns made up in part for the lack of canonical poetry. I still carry around a vast repertoire, sung silently as I plod up mountain paths. And some hymns were a window on to a sunnier world than Highbury in the gritty 1930s. 'Summer suns are glowing, over land and sea.' 'Fair waved the golden corn / In Canaan's pleasant land, / When full of joy, some shining morn, / Went forth the reaper-band.' 'As pants the hart for cooling streams / When heated in the chase, / So longs my soul, O God, for thee, / And thy refreshing grace.'

I had few if any friends. The Jewishness of our neighbourhood was part of the problem. We were a gentile minority. You needed to know when most of the local shops would be open or closed. I developed irrational fears not only of the rabbis with their black hats and sideburns, emerging from houses bursting at the seams with books, but of bread studded with sesame seed. (In the same way Islam may be a problem these days for lonely little boys growing up in certain parts of Bradford.) Nowadays Judaism has moved up market from Stoke Newington to Stamford Hill, and Green Lanes has been taken over by Turkish Cypriots and other Middle Eastern communities.

Our separateness was compounded by the extremity of the Christianity which my parents embraced and which was imposed on me. When, years later, I came to read Edmund Gosse's *Father and son*, there was much with which to identify. Friends outside the household of faith were not encouraged. And there were few within that household who were of my age and class: only a succession of missionaries who came to stay on their way to and from the mission field. There were prayer meetings morning and evening, readings from a conflation of biblical texts called *Daily Light*, intercessions for the work of the Gospel in every part of the Muslim world. I was supposed to proselytize, to enlist other children into Bible-reading fellowships and things of that kind. That has left me with a lifelong reluctance to persuade anyone to do anything. For many years my inner life was dominated by knowledge that I needed to be converted, that without that once-for-all experience I was not saved, not even a Christian. But in spite of numerous occasions in overheated mission halls, the gas competing with the emotion, when it might have happened it never did. But I probably pretended that it had, and so deceived my parents and half deceived myself. It's hard now to say.

On Sundays we attended an unaffiliated church called Derwent Hall, which met in Stoke Newington Library, ruled with a rod of iron by a man called Mr Hobbs, an evangelical city gent in black jacket and striped trousers, in appearance a little like Bristow, the cartoon character in the *Evening Standard*. There was a Sunday School in which I was inevitably enrolled, and in which my older siblings taught. The children smelt with an unwashed smell. They were forever being sick on the floor, and I had a great dread of that. Some of them were the children of Mrs Tovey, who washed and otherwise 'did' for us. It was the kind of family where there were uncles younger than their nephews. Mr Tovey had been gassed in the war, and the family lived on bread and dripping. One day Mrs Tovey arrived in tears. There had been a gas leak and there was a bill they had no means of paying. It was my father who was suspicious, my mother who insisted we must trust Mrs Tovey and pay her bill. In the war, the Toveys proved to be practical friends. They had moved out into the country and we often came home to find rabbits and fruit left on the doorstep.

It doesn't sound much fun, but it was all very evocative, a London which any American movie-goer would immediately recognize: fog, street singers, barrel organs, rag and bone men, plane trees; a London which no longer exists.

The result was a strange child. I had so far embraced the missionary spirit that I wrote and published (via my mother's typewriter) a little magazine linking together what I chose to call the Prayer Club for Adults. Copies went to the missionaries in Egypt and I published their replies; and a poem which I called 'Egypt Land':

> Far away there is a land,
> A land not led by God's dear hand,
> The streets are untidy and are not clean,
> The people are naughty and very mean.
>
> Let's go to a street, dirty I'm sure,
> There sits a Moslem outside his back door,
> Let us go to church, church there is none,
> Surely it's the queerest place under the sun.
>
> Here's an idea, let's preach them the Word,

> It will be the most wonderful story they've heard.
> Come all ye people and listen to me,
> Come I say, there is no fee.

It is clear that here was no future poet laureate. But my magazine also included a commentary on world affairs:

> A Talk on the World's Different Leaders. *Dictators*. In this time of war, the world's dictators are being heard of throughout the globe. At the time Hitler of Germany has somehow been stirring up something with Viscount Halifax. Between Italy and Abyssinia there was a war. Mussolini of Italy was considered rather terrible with the slaughter he was giving them. *King of Kings*. The most important of all leaders is JESUS, King of Kings, who made every other possible leader.

Vol. 1, no. 2 (July 1937) contained an article 'All About the lovely New Zealand': 'New Zealand holds about 1 1/2 million people and it is a little larger than Britain and Northern Ireland, while it is five weeks' journey from London.' But the focus was on Egypt: 'Egypt is a very ancient land of Gods, Pyramids, and the Sphinx, and these are what I want to talk about. As for the Gods, I will pass the remark that people should not worship them. Pyramids were built a very, very, very long time ago for storing Kings in.' Not bad for seven. But I must have got some of this from Arthur Mee's *Children's Newspaper*, to which my father subscribed on my behalf. I assumed that he must have been very keen on this publication, so my Christmas present to him in 1937 was a bound volume of selected pages, pasted on to cardboard sheets.

How far all this was internalized I cannot tell. That little boy is almost inaccessible. But I can say that what saved my bacon was my other life, on the Blakenham farm. It was a wonderful life. The cows came up the road early in the morning below the window of the little bedroom where I slept. We helped with the milking and cleaned out the sheds. Half way through every morning Gene Hood would say: 'Pat go up the road and get me a bar of Aero.' There was usually a halfpenny in it for me, enough for a sherbet dip or fountain. I worked mainly with the pigs, preparing the mash, helping with the nose-ringing and worming. The farmhouse (at first no electricity or even gas – oil lamps and candles, infested, I was sure, with ghosts) was full not only of children and the bachelor farm workers but lodgers from the local factory, who contributed to the fragile household economy. Often in the evenings guitars were brought out. Later one of the lodgers, Mr Rooney, made me a wire-netted eel trap, nine feet long. My daily routine then consisted of snaring rabbits, skinning and cleaning them, and using the guts for eel bait. No Italian Renaissance artist can ever have skinned an eel, because I have never seen that almost iridescent blue of the inside skin in any of their paintings. I could still draw from memory an accurate map of those 250 acres, with every path and clearing in the three woods, 'The Little Wood', 'The Big Wood', 'The Top Wood', all in their proper places. On the way to the Top Wood there was a shallow pond which swarmed with newts. Once I took a bucket of newts back to London and walked all the way to the Holloway Road in pouring rain to hand them over to a pet shop which paid me nothing for them, much to my parents' disgust.

The high point of the year was harvest, when we came with our sticks to surround the steadily shrinking square of corn. At first the odd rabbit ran out, but then suddenly there were rabbits everywhere. We rushed after them, tripping over the sheaves ('shoofs' in Suffolk), bringing the frightened animals down with ruthless efficiency. Greyhounds were set on the odd hare, and they died with child-like screams which sickened even me. Once a vixen and all her cubs came out of the barley. On a neighbouring farm we were allowed two rabbits each. I killed four and hid two in a ditch. When I came back later to fetch them I was met by a little posse of farm workers who advised me not to show my face on that property again. Threshing was a noisy, itchy affair: a steam roller, humming belts, men forking up the shoofs, others on top cutting the twine and dropping the corn into the dangerous machinery, bags filling with chaff, others with the corn. There were hundreds of mice to be killed as they seethed out of the diminishing stacks, rather like that prôleptic scene in *Tess of the Durbevilles*.

But it was not all killing fields. One year on Palm Sunday I listened to the church bells while picking primroses in the ditches. In May we gathered armfuls of bluebells. Come the autumn we harvested hazelnuts in the woods, and in the spring, when the wild cherries blossomed, we played at weddings. The butterflies still rose from the ground in swarms and we caught them in nets, disposed of them in killing bottles, and carefully pinned them out. We did a great deal of birdnesting too and soon I had a large collection of eggs. But I got into serious trouble at the farm when I robbed a robin's nest. That was worse than breaking a mirror or walking under a ladder.

We drove around to pubs (unheard of in my family) and sat in the car, eating crisps (you still needed to undo that little blue bag of salt) and drinking fizzy grapefruit juice out of distinctively shaped bottles. We went to the cinema (not allowed in my family) two or three times a week. On one glorious day, one of the farm workers was deputed to take me to Bertram Mill's Circus, where tribal women from Burma paraded around the ring with their giraffe-like necks. Then came a fish and chip tea, followed by a Hoppalong Cassidy programme at the Ipswich bughouse, Poole's Cinema. We went regularly to the Ipswich Hippodrome, which stood on the site of Cardinal Wolsey's birthplace where there is now a supermarket (there you have the history of Ipswich in eighteen words). Some of the comedians, especially Max Bacon, were a little close to the bone for that time. (A soldier is about to jump off the platform of a moving bus. Conductress: 'Do you want to get me into trouble?' 'Not now love, but when do you knock off?' 'Have you heard about the dwarf who married a big tall lady? His friends put him up to it.')

We sang all the best songs of the time, which I am sure were never heard at home: 'Red Sails in the Sunset', 'The Isle of Capri', 'It's a Sin to Tell a Lie', 'Love Is the Sweetest Thing', 'Somebody stole my gal / Somebody stole my gal / Somebody came and took her away / She didn't even, say she was leavin.' My sister dated her first serious boyfriend, a certain Jock Keble. Once my mother was alarmed to find that I had written in my diary: 'talked with some nice girls in the lane'. I can remember that at the time there were many bats fluttering over our heads, in the gloaming. But I was only nine or ten and there was nothing in it.

Hilda adopted one of the farm cats, tamed her and called her Cornelia. After seeing a film about a tiger in a circus called Satan, I renamed Cornelia and turned her into a raging fiend. I think a water butt was what I used. No wonder Hilda hated me at that time. Once, when my parents turned up by chance at the farm, I said: 'What are you doing here?' – a good question. This was in all respects another world. When I quoted one of my father's favourite sayings, 'foxes can't smell their own holes', I couldn't understand why the Hood family fell about.

8   Mummy, Patrick and a friend at the London Zoo

Anstruther, where I spent many summer holidays, was even better. The tides ruled the day. At low tide, we dug for lugworms, and towards high tide fished from the end of the pier for coalfish (the little ones were called 'dirgies', the herring-sized fish 'potleys') and flatties. When we got a bit older we went out on the skerries or on to what was called 'the back of the blocks', behind the breakwater, where we caught codling, 'red whore codling', since they came out of the kelp or 'whore', a brilliant coppery red. Nowadays little boys fish all day and catch nothing. The rock pools were another secret world, to which Philip Gosse had introduced the Victorians, with sad consequences for the ecology of rock pools. But in those days they were still full of life.

Whether it was the farm, or the sea, or the books I read, from Kingsley's *Water babies* to tales of hunting and trapping in the Canadian Arctic, or a children's programme on radio called *Romany*, I was now fixated on the natural world of living things, interested in little else. Of course I wanted to kill them, like any Victorian gentleman naturalist; but also to see them and to understand them. Once there was an epiphany on a Sunday morning, as we walked to those dreary Derwent Hall services along the New River, at that time crystal clear – and look, there was a little pike. London Zoo was tremendously important, and so was Alfred Waterhouse's cathedral, the Natural History Museum at South Kensington. Like all children, I fell for the dinosaurs. Once we went to some kind of religious rally at the Crystal Palace in Sydenham. We all noticed that a strong smell of gas and the many stuffed animals which had seen better days were a dangerous combination. Two weeks later the Crystal Palace burned down. We could see the glow from the back windows of our house in Highbury. On that afternoon visit I had wandered down to the lake, and there were those astonishing life-size dinosaurs, on all the islands and promontories; in improbable postures, imagined as they had been when Gideon Mantell and Richard Owen had feuded over fossils in the 1840s.

But my Philip Gosse-like father told me that it wasn't necessarily so. The so-called scientists who had put together those bones were making it up. The creation story in Genesis could not be made to square with dinosaurs, and whatever could not be made to square with the Bible could not be true. (My father was very keen on those archaeologists whose work had 'proved' the biblical narratives, and he had a little box of charred barley from Jericho, evidence that the city had been burned by the Israelites – I still have it.) This is where the small fissure opened up between my parents' world view and my own which would later become a chasm. And yet, outwardly, I stayed on board the evangelical, missionary thing for another fifteen or sixteen years before converting it into a rather more manageable and conventional form of Christianity. At the age of eighteen I even stood up in an emotional meeting in Perth and dedicated myself to missionary service. Why? The birth mark?

In September 1938 there was the Munich crisis. I was all prepared for evacuation, my gas mask in its square cardboard box, a rucksack (unheard of and exciting) packed with those thick bars of chocolate you could only find in Selfridge's food hall. Then Mr Chamberlain came back with his piece of paper. In Green Lanes people stopped to talk to each other for the first time in their lives, and I was deeply disappointed. A year later, I was at the farm when on 2 September three evacuees arrived. The rest of the day was spent filling sandbags outside the village hall. (What were they supposed to achieve?) On Sunday 3 September I went to church, hoping desperately that there would be a war. I got back to the farm to find that Chamberlain had made his announcement, and that there would be, indeed was, one. As I walked down the lane to the river with Leslie, one of the evacuees, an old man with a white beard caught up with us and told us in grave tones what the war would mean. I had never seen him before and never saw him again.

Two or three weeks later I was packed off to Goudhurst School for Boys at Curtisden Green in the Kentish Weald, otherwise 'Bethany', a boarding school intended at that time mainly for the sons of missionaries overseas. I arrived a week before term, and the teachers treated me in a friendly way, almost as if they were my parents. But of course I was homesick, and the homesickness was intertwined with the sickly sweet smell of roasting hops coming from the oasthouses. (The Londoners who picked the hops, the nearest thing they had to an annual holiday, were camped in the woods of Spanish chestnuts which backed on to the school.) Then the rest of the boys arrived and it was less cosy. But Bethany was a civilized sort of place and I was not bullied, as I would be later, at Ely. There was a village pond (now long since dried up), where I learned to fish for little tench and roach, and where, in March, hundreds of spawning toads made a deafening noise. But I had a dread of swimming baths, and in that school swimming was the main summer sport. The science master, known as 'Pharaoh', told me in an unwise moment that, come the summer term, I would be thrown into the deep end and left to sink or swim. First I broke my ankle, was admitted to the Kent and Sussex Hospital at Tunbridge Wells, and had excruciatingly painful surgery and treatment for an abscess and osteomyelitis. When both my parents came to see me, it was all very solemn and sad; but when my father came it was all laughter – his jokes! Then came the winter of 1939–40: memories of the sinking of the *Graf Spee*, and of cold so extreme that the water jugs at the end of the dormitory froze, and our flannels too. In May, I had to watch from my dormitory window while the swimming pool slowly filled. It took a week. But within days I had learned to swim and could not be kept out of the water. Swimming would be one of my greatest pleasures, and it was one of the few physical things I was good at, throughout my teens.

In June 1940 my mother and father sat at the edge of the cricket field, talking with the headmaster. I was impressed that that great man was deigning to speak to my parents, but I did gather that they were agreeing that we were living through momentous times, and that they were talking about the events in France. Whether this was before or after Dunkirk I cannot remember. But soon I left Goudhurst, never to return. The school was closed, in expectation of the impending invasion. I went back there forty-five years later, to give away the prizes, and found a rather different kind of school. My speech was all about the virtues of taking a gap year. But I was told that most school leavers, girls as well as boys, not bothering with university, went straight into the City.

Back in Highbury New Park we made the best of the summer (no question of the seaside, which in 1939 had been East Runton in Norfolk), buying those chickens in Tottenham and having picnics, swimming and picking blackberries at High Beech in Epping Forest. That was where we were on that terrible Saturday when all hell broke loose over the London skies. Bernard, already in the army, got us into a ditch, from which we could follow the dogfight overhead: two German bombers and two British fighters shot down as we watched. We persuaded ourselves that the British pilots had safely bailed out, the Germans, to our satisfaction, not. We were constantly diverted on the journey home by blocked streets, sirens, visions of fire. That evening, God knows why, my father put me in the car when he drove Bernard to Waterloo Station. I remember looking downstream from Waterloo Bridge to see the whole river on fire.

The Blitz followed. One morning, Mrs Tovey was in tears. She had come past a block of flats which had been set on fire by incendiary bombs, and many of the occupants had been drowned in the basement by water from the fire hoses. She had heard someone say: 'Well, what's all the fuss? They were only a lot of Jews anyway.' We too were now living in the basement. There was a naval pom-pom gun on a truck outside our house which opened up whenever German planes were overhead. I found it all very exciting (whereas the much less threatening air raids of April 1944 made me physically sick all day, convinced that I would not live to see the next). On Sunday evenings, the national anthems of all the Allied and invaded countries were played on the radio, before the nine o'clock news. Halfway through the Czech anthem, a stick of bombs landed on the houses which lay behind our (fortunately) long garden and the little gardens beyond that. In our house windows and ceilings were damaged. That was all. (In June 1944 a V1 'doodlebug' exploded on the cleared space those houses had occupied and no. 106 sustained much worse damage.)

Soon after this event, a letter came from Huntingdon, where my sister and her entire school had been evacuated early in the war. Would my parents like me to join Hilda in their relatively safe house? Within the hour, my father had packed me into the car and was driving me to Huntingdon, up the A10 in a ferocious early October gale. The letter had come from Mr Prior, who, with Mrs Prior, lived at Tennis Court Avenue. There were no children. Mr and Mrs Prior did not get on very well. After the latest row, upstairs, Mr Prior would come down and say: 'Don't ever get married, Hilda.' Mrs Prior regularly packed her bags and said that she was off to her mother, but after a night at the Women's Royal Voluntary Service, she always came back. She used to examine Mr Prior's collar for stray blonde hairs and on my fishing

9 Patrick with his brothers and sisters on the eve of the Blitz, 1940 – *standing*: Hilda, Barnard (in army uniform); *seated*: Gerald, Marjorie

expeditions to nearby St Ives, where he worked in a local government office, I was told to keep an eye on him. This was totally new in my experience. If my parents had ever exchanged a cross word, I never heard it. I sat quietly in the corner, reading *Nicholas Nickleby*, the first considerable work of English literature on which I had embarked. Mr Prior's mother, next door but one, gave me tea and, in the *Daily Mirror*, I encountered Jane: almost my first sexual frisson.

But the Priors were both kind beyond the call of duty, Mr Prior especially. When I arrived, in October 1940, he took several days off work to introduce me to the fishing on the Ouse. I simply supposed that he must have been very keen on fishing. Fishing took over. I did no homework and no one suggested that I should. From having been at the top of the class at every school I had attended, I slipped to near the bottom. We used to fish at the mouth of an open sewer, just below Huntingdon, and nasty things came up on your line. An old man used to hover around, charging a halfpenny to see a flying fish he kept in a box. Nowadays he would be suspect as an at least potential paedophile.

My day job was cycling through Huntingdon to attend Huntingdon Grammar School, where Oliver Cromwell had been an earlier alumnus. This was a mixed school, and if I had stayed there I might have developed a more healthy and balanced attitude to persons of the other sex. I even remember dancing with a rather pretty girl at a school party. But everything was about to change. Towards Christmas 1941, my parents were recruited to run a forces' canteen, under YMCA auspices, in the village of Littleport in the Cambridgeshire fens, reputed to be the largest village in England. The recruiting sergeants were a family called Martin, who ran the place, and seemed to own much of the fens. The Martins were evangelicals, no less fervent than my parents, whose family had broken away from the parish church and had founded an independent chapel where missionary-minded people like my father had regularly preached. The Martins told a couple of humble peasants, Harry Sallis and his wife, that they had to accommodate my parents and me, so that was where I was taken, just before Christmas 1941.

Hilda, meanwhile, remained in Huntingdon, but later left for Ipswich, where she lodged with Auntie Kathleen and her sister Marjorie at 13 Corder Road and found a secretarial position with a local clothing store. With a very ordinary sort of fiancé whom my father disallowed (he failed to attend her baptism by total immersion), Hilda would not then have known that she *was* destined to become a missionary, at Nazareth in Galilee.

Harry Sallis was an interesting man. My parents took him to Ely Cathedral to hear a performance of *The Messiah*, which he agreed was wonderful to hear, 'under the oxygen' (meaning the Octagon). A ruinous greenhouse behind the Sallis property contained a vast printing press, acquired God knew when or for what purpose. As you went down the garden, there were various animals, including a goat called Betty, which had a suitably goaty smell but which failed to reproduce. I shocked my mother when I sang a parody of that aria from *The Messiah*, substituting Betty's name. Sometimes we rode out over the fens in a pony and little cart, with a pig under netting in the back. There were naturally lots of rats, which I delighted to catch in utterly barbaric rat traps and which screamed before I finished them off. And I kept rabbits, mostly Flemish Giants, and I learned to cure the skins, thanks to a friendly aircraftman who came from Sheffield and whose trade in civvy street was to make gloves from such skins.

Fishing now took over almost to the exclusion of all other pursuits and interests.

10   Patrick Collinson's book token, devised *c.* 1942: to be found
in most of his early books

My parents' canteen provided any amount of scraps, which became ground bait with
which I cultivated several swims on the Ouse. I caught bream, which often weighed
as much as seven pounds, and which, while not the best eating, my mother baked in
the oven, as she would have baked a cod in Anstruther. During the war, steel workers
were brought down to Ely and Littleport on special trains for fishing holidays. They
fished, while their wives sat a few yards back from the bank and knitted. As I dealt
with my monstrous bream, the professionals came by: 'Killing fish on t'bank!' – the
first words of Sheffield English I ever heard.

The serious business in life was attendance at the King's School Ely, a foundation with a plausible claim to be the second oldest school in England (after the
King's School, Canterbury). It was founded in 970, and is the sixth oldest charity
in the country. The dean of Ely in my time loved to tell the story of the old Queen
Mary asking him how old the school was. 'Well, Ma'am, Edward the Confessor was
educated here.' 'I don't think that we need to go back any farther than that!'

To qualify for entry, I had to reach a certain standard in Latin, a language I had never previously encountered. My mother was my tutor over those Christmas holidays. Once I wrote in my notebook 'Oh Heck!' Mummy was horrified. Did I not know that that word was equivalent to 'Hell', which she knew I would never use lightly. On an early and very cold January day in 1942, my father began to drive me to Ely, where I was to attend as a dayboy. Halfway there the engine seized up (this I suppose was in the days before anti-freeze). My father never drove a car again and I completed the journey by bus. Thus began the next chapter of my life.

4

King's School Ely

In 1942 the Kings' School Ely (at that time the plural was deliberate and considered important, recording the refoundation of the cathedral school as a royal grammar school by Henry VIII) had 125 pupils, all boys.[1] In those wartime years, like so many minor public schools, it was a place of unspeakable barbarity. If Philip Larkin had been at school at Ely he would never have written that sex was invented in 1963, 'a bit too late for me'. There was plenty of sex both theoretical and practical, although, in the total absence of girls, the practice was somewhat one-sided and single-handed, the theory very shaky. Well into my twenties my own knowledge of female anatomy was no better than John Ruskin's. There was a good deal of violence too.

It was not too bad in that first year, being a dayboy (we were called 'day-bugs'). I travelled every day on the bus from Littleport to Ely with the brightest boy in the school, Derek Goozee, like me an exile from wartime London. Derek was well read, immensely sophisticated and very knowledgeable about sex. When he came to tea he told me that my father was a real Christian and that I ought to be aware of that, since they were very rare animals indeed. He was not a Christian himself. He took his Higher School Certificate in one year of sixth-form study and left a year before me. He should have had an outstanding career, but spent his shortish life in librarianship and the journalism of trade papers. He died aged forty-nine.

The school did its best with very limited resources to provide some sort of an education. The bursar, E. Crichton-Wodehouse, ran it on a shoestring, since in the 1930s the fees were £26 a term, full board and tuition, and dayboys paid only £6.

But in those days teachers can have been paid no more than £200 or £300 a year. There was a teaching staff of just ten, which included the headmaster, G. J. Cross, who was as much in the classroom as in his study. The only modern language on offer was French. Latin was taught but not Greek. Science meant Physics and Chemistry, no Biology. The only musical instrument one could learn was the piano. Many of the regular staff were away at the war and not all their replacements should have been in the teaching profession. On one occasion Mr Cross publicly thanked us for having made that point clear to a master who had departed after we had made his life hell.

Muriel Arber was something else. A large, big-boned woman, she walked up from the station to the school on her first day, which was also my first day, in January 1942. She will have started that day by walking down to Cambridge Station from

---

[1] Nowadays there are nearly a thousand pupils, girls as well as boys, and in 2004 the school appointed its first female head. It is now an altogether more distinguished and civilized place; or so I found in 1997, when I went back for the first time, exactly fifty years to the day after I left, to make the speech and give away the prizes in Ely Cathedral.

11 The sixth form, King's School Ely – *presiding*: Mr Osmond and Miss Arber; *seated on the ground*: David Bennet, Patrick Collinson, Mark Myers, Brian Eliott, Derek Goozee, Neville Cousins

the Huntingdon Road, as she did every day for decades, a distance of two miles. Miss Arber was a geographer who came from a family of some academic distinction, and if she had been born a generation later she would have been a don herself. Her special subject was landslips on the Dorset coast, and it was said that she had learned Russian only in order to read a certain book on that aspect of Geology. She taught us Geography, and when we got to the sixth form, English. When she took the part of Mistress Quickly (and also Doll Tearsheet) in classroom readings of *Henry IV Part Two*, the class was reduced to helpless laughter. 'Do, do, do you me your offices.' In our school 'do' meant only one thing. I suppose that Shakespeare was not unaware of that meaning. After the war Miss Arber lost her job and had to make her daily journey to an indifferent grammar school in March, farther out across the fens. It was a happy time to be studying those *Henry IV* plays. They were being done at the New Theatre by Olivier and Richardson, and if you queued up in the morning for a stool, you got into the gallery for 1*s* 6*d*.

F. W. Wilkinson, 'Wilkie', a cricketer who had played for Cambridgeshire and ran most of the sport in the school, taught me to write a good English sentence. Wilkie had joined the staff in 1922 and stayed well into the fifties. Goodbye Mr Chips! My history teachers, especially when it came to sixth-form studies, were excellent. And L. F. Osmond, the science master (the only one!) was a good teacher, kind and supportive. He and Mrs Osmond entertained the sixth formers to supper on Sunday evenings. How, with rationing, they were able to produce hotpot for all of us I have no idea. After supper we were made to sit down and to play bridge, on the grounds that it would help us to get on in the world. F. W. Burgess was a cleric who taught Maths and Music. He could never be persuaded that I could not and never would be able to do Maths, that I had no instinct for the subject. But he worked on me as a pianist until I could play with some fluency the last movement of Beethoven's

Moonlight Sonata. I wish I still could. But most of the lessons conducted in his tiny room, heated to extremity by a large gas fire, were given over to his own performances of Arnold Bax, a composer he loved. Burgess deserved better than to be teaching in that nest of Philistines. He was ragged mercilessly, and had many nicknames, including 'Sus' (abbreviated from 'halitosus' – he did have bad breath) and 'Lulu'. He made things no better for himself by addressing all of us in a plaintive whine as 'friend'.

None of us could have managed without 'Matron', the truly redoubtable Nellie Canham, who having arrived at the school in 1906 gave it fifty-two years of carbolic-scented service. Nor could life have been imagined without Stanley Gann, the handyman and self-made laboratory technician.

I began well, academically. G. J. Cross wrote after my first term: 'He has made a good start, and is obviously a boy of intelligence who is very ready to learn. He must become neater'; and at the end of the summer term: 'He is well up to, and in some cases ahead of the standard of his age. I hope he will aim at the highest scholastic attainments. It is always a pleasure to teach anyone so polite and interested.' The teacher of Religious Knowledge reported, unsurprisingly: 'His knowledge of this subject is amazing.' But by Christmas some of the gilt had worn off the gingerbread. 'Most of this is good, but the deterioration in Latin and Science is not, and he must work harder at the subject for which he does not care. Also his behaviour in the school must be less noisy.' But by Easter 1943: 'His behaviour in the School is just right. He knows how to combine helpful goodness with the fun of school life.'

'The fun of school life!' Little did Cross know what was really going on! Sex aside, there was a good deal of petty crime. There were mass break-outs from the school in the middle of the night, large quantities of sugar stolen from the local sugar beet factory and hidden under beds, to be passed on to unsuspecting parents with the assurance that they had been freely given by the Italian prisoners of war who made up the workforce. Boys' studies contained (besides pin-ups of big-busted Jane Russell in the straw in *The outlaw*) pieces of electrical equipment, unscrewed from grounded American aircraft in a field near Newmarket, where to be seen was to be shot on sight.

Cross (Winchester and New College), a good classicist and an athlete whose profile might have been lifted from a Greek vase, was born to a family which had made its pile in Lancashire cotton, a line of impeccable Gladstonian liberals, and, on his mother's side, a Phillimore.[2] His maternal grandfather was Lord Phillimore, son of Robert Phillimore, student friend of Gladstone, parliamentarian and ecclesiastical lawyer. Grandfather Phillimore, who had helped Gladstone to fell those trees at Hawarden, was a judge who was involved in setting up the International Court of Justice at the Hague, and for contributing ideas to the creation of the League of Nations. G. J. Cross was one of the five children (four brothers and a sister, a barrister, who died in 2008, just short of her hundredth birthday) of Francis Cross, who had settled into a Berkshire manor house and many acres. Francis was an athlete who, if the Olympic Games had been revived ten years earlier, would have been a gold medallist in the mile and half-mile. Cross's mother, Eleanor, 'honourable', given her father's peerage, appeared on speech days wearing the clothes, and

2   This paragraph, and some of what follows, is indebted to Michael Gray, a pupil of Cross's at Sutton Coldfield, who is writing his biography.

hats, of pre-1914. Cross was the author of *The triumph of Athens*, which I still possess, and of a book on Hegel, an unfashionably theological exposition of Hegel's 'whole doctrine' as nothing less than 'the truth'.

As a headmaster, Cross was enlightened and progressive. He disbanded 'the corps' and beefed up the Scouts, replacing rugger with soccer. When my father first called at the school, he thought that it was one of the older boys who answered the door. Well, Cross was all of thirty-one, having arrived earlier in the year from his first post, at Manchester Grammar School. Our Latin textbooks were his own, and they contained crossword puzzles and murder mysteries, in instalments. He succeeded an amiable canon and scientist called T. J. Kirkland, always known as 'T. J.'. T. J. had taught at Ely since 1906 and had been head for twenty-three years. Like so many of his headmasterly contemporaries (thinking of my wife's grand-father and uncle) he was an enthusiastic flogger. In spite of that there were many affectionate T. J. stories. 'Catch it, Gann', he once said, as he threw a bottle of hydrochloric acid in the general direction of his technician. T. J. cannot have made life easy for Cross. He remained a school governor, was president of the Old Eleans, and came back regularly to preach. Cross was never known, endearingly, as 'G. J.'.

What went wrong for Cross at Ely? Dean Lionel Blackburne was at first delighted with his acquisition (Cross was, after all, a Wykehamist), but increasingly the dean had his doubts. There may have been theological reasons for that. Cross wanted to become a lay reader, but was turned down by the bishop for his (Hegelian?) views. By 1943 there were quarrels with the dean, in December 'perhaps the worst so far'. By March 1946 Cross was writing: 'Unexpected and more or less open warfare suddenly flared up eleven days ago and there may be a stormy governors.' The dean had told him that 'the morals were all wrong'. Well, they were. But did that include Cross's own morals? Cross was perhaps rather too close to some of his boys, and he had his favourites. He even wrote about his 'failings' in that respect. I suspect that his inclinations were 'Greek', that he had homoerotic tendencies which were kept under firm control. His *Times* obituary might well have said: 'He never married.' How strange! The boys in his charge were indulging night after night in innocent bouts of mutual masturbation (I have no evidence that 'buggery' was ever involved). It never occurred to those (us?) boys that in the adult world there might be such a thing as active homosexuality. Our fantasies were all about those unattainable girls, on some other planet.

In the summer of 1946, as I approached my final year at the school, the dean and other governors (five out of the eight were clerics) seized their opportunity to get rid of Cross. The head boy, who had just left the school, became a whistle blower, and went public with some of the scandalous things which had been going on. In September all twenty-five sixth formers were brought before a kangaroo court in the head's study, where Cross revealed all that he knew, and how he had spent the summer taking the advice of his legal relations. We all had to write an account of what we had been up to. (I recall that my own confession was closely if uncon-sciously modelled on St Augustine of Hippo: only some scrumping in Ely orchards.) It was too late. In October the governors gave Cross the choice of resignation or the sack. So he resigned, but his resignation was followed by a storm of protest from parents. All to no avail. But Cross picked himself up, dusted himself down, and, after unsuccessful applications for as many as eight posts, succeeded in becoming headmaster of Bishop Vesey Grammar School at Sutton Coldfield, a rather larger responsibility than Ely. The authorized history of the King's School, published in

12 The King's Scholars with the headmaster, G. J. Cross, 1946

13 The King's School cricket team with their scorer and F. W. Wilkinson ('Wilkie')

2004, records of these events only that Cross had 'decided to move on', while admitting that under his leadership discipline had been 'very lax'. I suppose that if I had been a little more observant I might have drawn lessons about the limitations and perils of the kind of liberalism which Cross personified. But Cross was a success in the more secular climate of Sutton Coldfield, which I am glad about.

To go back four years: I can still remember where I was standing in the kitchen, towards the end of 1942, when my mother told me that she and my father were going back to London, and that henceforth I should have to board. The bullying began on my very first night, in a little dormitory at the top of the Priory. And it was not casual bullying. It was organized by a boy called Elliot, from Jesmond in Newcastle, who had boarded at the school since the summer of 1940. Several larger boys beat me up systematically, night after night, and told me every day what to expect. I wrote to my parents and told them that I intended to run away. All that happened was that my letter was sent to the headmaster, who had me on the carpet. I suppose that it could have been worse. It was perhaps an advantage not to be a pretty little boy. Brian Elliott went on to a blameless forty-year long career as a chartered surveyor in Newcastle before retiring to Morpeth. Even the bullies in *The lord of the flies* might have been nice to know, if they had made it into adult life.

Why was I so isolated and unpopular? The birthmark obviously made me different. I was no good at either football or cricket (played every Tuesday, Thursday and Saturday afternoon), and considered a 'weed'. Even G. J. Cross could see that this was a problem: 'I would like him to take a more enthusiastic part in the school games and sports, and show the team-spirit for his House' (July 1943). 'His greater need is to develop himself physically, to put more effort into his games, and to find the joy of comradeship in sport' (December 1944). With the passage of time the bullying stopped, but I was never popular. Apart from two Jewish boys, Neville Cousin and Mark Myers, who were friends, especially Mark, I was the only non-Anglican boy in the school. I never joined the Scouts, on which Cross was particularly keen. A taste for classical music was held against you, and to be always reading too.

But life became tolerable. I was made a King's Scholar, which I suppose helped my father financially, and which meant that once a month I had to process in Ely Cathedral, wearing a surplice. Often it was possible to slip away from the Tuesday, Thursday and Saturday sports parades to the Rex Cinema, to see Granger and Lockwood in *The wicked lady*, or Erroll Flynn in *Moon over Burma*. More and more time was spent out in the fens, fishing, with pike now the main quarry. Like anyone who has been exposed to that landscape, especially in winter and sharing only his own company, I was haunted by the vast flatness of the fens, those unattainable skies, and the straight lines of the little rivers known as 'drains'. I once turned up for Sunday lunch late, with a rather large live pike. Mr Cross made me bring it in to show everyone, and by the time I had finished my lunch it was swimming around in one of the changing-room baths. Cook later dealt with it.

I even came to terms with my deficiency in physicality: not that I learned to play cricket, but I did become the official scorer to the cricket team, and there are group photographs to prove it. I am standing in a double-breasted grey suit, holding the scoring book, alongside those white-flannelled heroes. As scorer one got to go to other schools, breaking out of what was virtually an open prison: Bury St Edmunds and Soham. I did a bit of rowing, which pointed to the future. But, best of all, my successes in the pool won me, in my last term, my Swimming Colours. G. J. Cross

14 With my parents, *c.* 1945: the war has taken its toll

was exultant: 'In swimming, where his feet do not handicap him [they were flat], he has been showing himself strong and keen.' The colours were on account of my prowess at something called the long plunge, which I fear no longer exists on the tariff of swimming events, from the Olympics downwards: a shame, since I was very good at it.

I became editor of the school magazine, the *Elean*. Did I increase my popularity when I announced, in the Christmas number of 1946, a new editorial policy (my own arbitrary policy – there was no committee)? 'Enterprise has never entered the some-what stilted pages of the school magazine. Our aim now is to introduce life into the magazine, which we are sure may be done without overstepping the bounds of tradi-tion.' The usual group photograph of the football team was deemed 'so poor as not to warrant admission to the magazine', and it was replaced with one of my father's stunning portraits of the interior of Ely Cathedral. There was a Literary Supplement, containing illustrated historical articles of some merit, by myself and Derek Goozee. Towards the end of my time I became a prefect, to everyone's surprise.

Meanwhile, of course, the war had been going on outside. The school had, in a sense, received a third foundation in First World War myths and memories. The four houses, which competed against each other on the playing field, were named for four alumni who had 'fallen': Boultbee (shot down by Manfred von Richtofen), Burns, Ingle (the Somme), Ivatt. Wilkie often told us that by being at the King's School we were destined to be 'leaders', and there was little doubt that that meant that we too were potentially second lieutenant material. In the summer of 1944 ceaseless waves of bombers flew low over our dormitory, and soon we were clustered around the radio to follow the news of D-Day. My RAMC brother was in the second wave of the landings, and I followed his progress through Normandy to Arnhem, where he was with the Somersets, who fought their way through to join up with the paratroops, only to be cut off themselves. When he came to see me, soon after the crossing of the Rhine, I was in seventh heaven. Ever since 1940 the war had jostled for atten-tion with other enthusiasms, and instead of drawing animals I drew planes in action, and maps with large arrows, as we advanced and retreated in the Western Desert.

I was at home in London for the air raids of the spring of 1944, which were very noisy (all that anti-aircraft firepower in Hyde Park), spending most of my days at the London Zoo, drawing the animals but sick with fear of what might happen that night. Then came the doodle bugs (V1s), which we laughed at in daylight. But it was a different matter at night, when you heard the engine cut out just above your house, not knowing whether it would drop like a stone (some did) or glide for a few more miles. I was at school, preparing for the School Certificate exams, when a V1 landed close enough to blow out all our windows. The V2 rockets which followed were terrifying, since the first thing you heard was the colossal bang, followed by the sound of the supersonic engine. Once, when walking Hilda to Liverpool Street Station, we were close enough to a rocket to see the flash of its descent and to be knocked to the ground by the force of the explosion.

As everyone living at that time knows, the years immediately after the war were the time of greatest hardship. There had never been much to eat. Many meals had consisted of suet puddings which we called 'boiled baby'. Now, with bread rationed, there was a sack of potatoes outside the headmaster's study, and you could go in of an evening and roast them on his stove. The winter of 1946–7 was savagely cold, and followed by a disastrous thaw, which caused the Great Fen Floods. We were lined up for games when word came that the school had to be evacuated within three or four hours to make way for refugees from the fens. I was in charge of a large dormitory of little boys, all of whom had to be packed up and ready to travel within that time. It was the first major responsibility which I had ever been asked to handle. Our train to London was diverted several times and we arrived in the early hours of the morning.

In spite of the danger of those later years of the war, and the privation which followed, in my late teens I was happy to be at home in London. You could even say that I was in love with London. At school I sat and drew maps of it. I would have been very good at the spoof contest on Radio 4, Mornington Crescent. I was still at the Zoo, two or three times a week, almost like the old white-bearded man who came every day to the bird house to chat up a talkative mynah. I went fishing wherever there was water, in the Regent's Canal hard by the Zoo, in the New River, in the lake in Finsbury Park. I remember a summer evening when I sat catching gudgeon and saw a mass migration of rats swimming across from the island, while the band played *Cavalleria rusticana*. I cycled all over London, which you could safely do in those days: up to Trafalgar Square and Piccadilly Circus, down to the docks. There were many visits to the Tatler Cinema in the Charing Cross Road and the news cinema, Studio Two, near Oxford Circus: not only newsreels but *The three stooges* and *Crime doesn't pay*. With Mark Myers, whose family kept a pub in Westbourne Grove, I went to the only professional football match I ever saw in my life: Queens Park Rangers versus I have no idea what team. Lyons Corner House, whether at Tottenham Court Road or Coventry Street or Marble Arch, was where all treats happened. At the Salad Bowl you could eat as much as you liked for half a crown.

But, above all, I discovered music, which was to become a consuming interest, far more important than religion, perhaps a religion in itself. It began with a school-mistress called Mrs Kent, who played wind-up records to some of us in her tiny room. Among the early pieces to come alive in that room was the cloying sweetness of Mendelssohn's Violin Concerto. But then came the Proms. I was there night after night, either standing in the arena or sitting in the gallery at the top of the Albert Hall. At first Beethoven (every Friday night!) was all important. I could play every symphony through in my head, and I could whistle all the great tunes. The Eroica and the Seventh, 'the apotheosis of the dance', were my favourites. Brahms came next, the symphonies, especially the third and fourth, with its majestic passacaglia, and the second piano concerto. I cannot now hear Brahms's St Anthony Variations without being carried back to the summer of 1947. I was in raptures over Schumann's First Symphony, thrilled by the exuberant third movement, and also in love with Schubert's Great C Major.

Bach, and the Baroque more generally, happened later. Bach would become the most important thing in my life, family and history aside. But no one was making any sense of Bach, in 1946. I began to try to play the 48 in 1949, and still do, but without making enough sense. I remember in that year a concert given by the Jacques Orchestra in the Felixstowe Pavilion. In response to calls for an encore, Reginald Jacques said, 'I'll play you the little Bach tune again': the Air on the G String. (The only alternative would have been 'Jesu Joy of Man's Desiring'.)[3]

---

[3]   Less than ten years later, the world discovered Rosalyn Tureck. When I went to Khartoum in 1956, all six of the LP records on which Tureck had played the Preludes and Fugues for the Brunswick label went with me, a present from my girlfriend, Esther. And then there was a hurricane: the brilliant, audacious Glenn Gould, who was not really bothered whether you were listening or not, as he

When I was seventeen, we moved back to Ipswich, and to part of the house in which I had been born, now 62a Tuddenham Road. Suffolk was so lovely in those days, seen from the saddle of a bike. At Ufford, near Woodbridge, it was not the spectacular late medieval font cover in the church that I remember but the roach and rudd in the still crystal clear water of the Deben. In the winter I caught sizeable cod in freezing conditions at Languard Fort, at the mouth of the Orwell. Little did I know that, forty years on, those shingle beaches would be Felixstowe Docks, still less that I would be a fellow of the college which owns those docks.

The School Certificate exams proved a watershed in my life. I was a born naturalist, who read and almost worshipped everything that Henry Williamson had written: not only *Tarka the otter* and *Salar the salmon* but the strange novels, and books like *Goodbye West Country* and *The story of a Norfolk farm*, for all that they were shot through with Williamson's pro-Nazi sympathies. As a teenager he was my favourite author by a long chalk, but Richard Jefferies too, to whom I was introduced by Williamson. It was my intention to become some sort of biologist, preferably a marine zoologist. I had read many more or less popular books on the subject. And it was possible to do Biology in the sixth form by joining classes in the neighbouring girls' school (which made it a popular subject). But now I was told to forget about any kind of Science and to take, for the Higher School Certificate, History, English and French. The reason was my Achilles heel, my almost non-existent Maths, a subject I had narrowly passed in the School Certificate exams.[4]

So it was that I was destined to become a historian. I had two teachers in this subject. There was Mr Saunders, an elegant, sceptical man, who urged me to model my style on the essays of C. V. Wedgwood (*Velvet studies*), and who wrote: 'Not only is his knowledge sound and comprehensive, but he is developing a sense of style and argument that promises well for the future.' Mr Gambles, a very young Oxford man, scarcely five foot tall, who the Cambridge bulldogs mistook for an undergraduate without a gown ('I am a graduate of the senior university'), wrote: 'He continues to produce work of first-class quality. He shows a ready understanding of historical problems and outstanding powers of literary expression'; 'it has been a privilege to teach him. He has, undoubtedly, a great future.' I am still in touch with Robert Gambles, now twenty years into retirement, and the recent author of *Breaking butterflies: a study of historical anecdotes*. I know of no autobiography or memoir by a historian which does not attribute his or her commitment to the subject to some gifted teacher. And, by the same token, when people tell you that they could never get on with History, they will invariably add that they were badly taught.

The comments which Saunders and Gamble made on my essays were shrewd, and some of them could well apply to things that I have written more recently. 'A tendency to include too much detail.' But, on another occasion: 'You must make sure that you support your ideas and arguments by facts, of which there are only about half a dozen in your essay. No matter how sound your ideas you must *support* them.' 'I would recommend the elimination so far as possible of "catch-phrases" and

---

masturbated Johann Sebastian. At last there appeared Angela Hewitt, the Pearl of Great Price. To be able to play like her, I would gladly sell all that I possess.

4 My school reports had seen it coming: 'His weakest subject' (Christmas 1942); 'this appears to be his weakest subject' (Summer 1943) – these the shrewd judgments of L. F. Osmond. But F. W. Burgess's reports had been absurdly optimistic: 'Excellent' (Easter 1944), 'his work improved greatly during the last month of the term' (Christmas 1944).

"clichés", and beware of anachronisms and far-fetched fantasies – e.g. "Communist" and Aristotelian comparisons' – this said about an essay on the unrest in Britain after Waterloo.[5] But on the whole I got alpha marks and such comments as 'A first-class essay. Very pleasing indeed.' 'Comment would be superfluous.' And, indeed, I find that the essays still read well.

In December 1946 I went to Cambridge to sit the scholarship examination, having been entered for King's College. Cambridge was dank and gloomy, and deeply impressive. Provost Shepherd passed around apples and desperately tried to learn all our names. I was badly prepared for the experience. When asked why I had opted for King's, I said that I was at the King's School so it made sense to apply to King's College. The general paper, sat like all the other papers in the top room of the old Divinity School, was intended for clever boys from even cleverer schools. The essay topics included: 'The Grand Manner', and 'We love a man that damns us and run after him again to bless us.' I scrunched up many sheets of paper. Interviewed by the Tudor historian Christopher Morris and, one of the last true eccentrics, John Saltmarsh, I was asked what I thought of Gustavus Adolphus. After I had offered a suitably cynical view of why he had intervened in the Thirty Years War, Christopher said (though in later years he always denied it): 'Well, of course, I am a Protestant and I thank God for him.'

It is a remarkable and not altogether comfortable fact that, at a time when less than 4 per cent of the population made it to any kind of university (and there were only ten), virtually everyone from my not at all distinguished sixth form made it to Cambridge (in most cases) or Oxford. Were we that good? Soon a telegram arrived informing me that I had won an exhibition to Pembroke. It had been a close run thing. It had always been my mother's ambition that I should go to university, something that had been denied her. My father was very suspicious of universities, which he believed were places where you Lost Your Faith, which had very nearly happened to a lifelong friend, Ronald Hodgkin, a member of another famous Quaker dynasty. The deal between my parents was that I would have one go at getting in. But my school had regarded this as a dry run. A lifetime later, Christopher Morris, who had become a friend, gave me a copy of his little history of King's College, inscribed 'with the author's profound apologies'. I understood him to have been apologetic that I had not been offered a scholarship at King's. But although I could never tell him so, I was very happy at the way things had worked out. I loved Pembroke, and am not sure that I should have been as much at home at King's.

---

5   Forty years on, I would be censured by an eminent historian, A. G. Dickens, not only for quoting the Mandy Rice Davies line in the Profumo affair, 'he would, wouldn't he?', but for finding room for Miss Rice Davies in the index. A later book, on the Reformation, would contain far too many 'Nine Eleven' moments.

5

History

Since history was to be my life, I had better explain what drew me to it, what kind of history I wanted to explore, to teach and to write, and, to anticipate much of what follows, what sort of historian I eventually became. There was no dramatic Damascus Road conversion from the schoolboy who had wanted to be a naturalist and biologist. It took a great many years for me to discover that I would never have been up to much as one of today's marine zoologists. Friends who worked in the marine laboratories in Plymouth offered to show me round and to explain what they were doing, and that was a full fifty years after I had been told to forget about science. I was excited by the prospect of meeting all sorts of exotic sea creatures. But all that there was to see was mussels – two whole floors of mussels, in trays, filtrating hundreds of different algae and other microorganisms while their efforts were monitored on computer screens. I suppose that mussels for marine biologists are what rats are for their terrestrial colleagues. That would never have been me. What I had wanted to be was the hunter-gatherer field naturalist of the nineteenth century, penetrating jungles and the unknown world of the deepest oceans, observing and describing, identifying and collecting new specimens and new species, reliving the experience of Sir Harry Johnson when, in the twentieth century, he discovered the okapi, deep in the Ituri rain forest: Gilbert White in the age of empire. Had I been born a hundred years too late? Perhaps not. David Attenborough would no doubt have found something that even I could do: as that favourite hymn of mine puts it: 'The earth with its store of wonders untold.'

The hunter-gatherer and explorer was the kind of historian that I grew into. My instincts and ambitions were primitive: to penetrate hitherto neglected archives, to lay my hands on manuscripts never seen before. I was very good at that, and made many discoveries of some importance in my own chosen field. That, rather than having any new ideas, was what constituted doing 'new', original work. This innate tendency was reinforced by exposure to the school of history which predominated in the University of London, where I did my postgraduate work and first began to take history seriously. Certainly this was the imprint of the Tudor school presided over by my supervisor, Sir John ('Jimmy') Neale, and that admirable teacher, S. T. ('Tim') Bindoff. I have heard it described as 'archival positivism'. Once I shared a class with Bindoff in which he spent the best part of an hour arguing that a mid-Tudor treatise known as the *Discourse of the common weal* had been written, not by a certain John Hales, but by the notable scholar and politician Sir Thomas Smith, something more or less established by one of his pupils and Smith's biographer, Mary Dewar. After all that, he asked the class why it might matter to determine the question of authorship. Various bold students suggested what it might signify that the author was Smith, not Hales. Sucking his pipe and scraping it out, speaking with excruciating slowness, as he always did, Bindoff said that that was all very well, but he supposed that if you had spent an hour determining that A rather than B had written C, you had not wasted your time, since you would have made an addition, however small, to the sum total of human knowledge.

If that was all that there was to it, then the study of history would be mere antiquarianism, a kindred discipline with which history has always had an uneasy relationship. A clever writer of the 1620s composed a caricature of the antiquary which fitted me to the tee, as an apprentice:

> A great admirer he is of the rust of old monuments, and reads only those charac-
> ters where time hath eaten out the letters. Printed books he contemns as a novelty
> of this latter age, but a manuscript he pores on everlastingly, especially if the
> cover be all moth-eaten, and the dust make a parenthesis betwixt every syllable.
> He would give all the books in his study for six lines of Tully [Cicero] in his own
> hand.

I remember a magical moment in the Northamptonshire Record Office where I was reading a correspondence concerning a proposed but ultimately abortive marriage between two county families, the Drydens and the Ishams. There came the time when the match-maker (a famous Puritan divine called John Dod) ceased to write numbers on the back of an envelope and allowed the two young people in question to correspond directly. And there, pinned to the page, was a lock of the young woman's hair, as pristine as if it had been cut only yesterday. So, yes, I am an antiquarian. But I take comfort in the fact that it was the dusty antiquarians of the sixteenth and seventeenth centuries, not the writers of what was deemed to be proper history (who, as Sir Philip Sidney cheekily remarked, authorized themselves for the most part on other histories), who in their time made the greater contribution to the appropriation and understanding of the past.

But to be sure, antiquarianism is never enough. What more is required? In my case, not what is called theory and sometimes 'grand theory'. I do not think that the study of the past can produce theory, for history never exactly repeats itself and cannot be studied in laboratory conditions. There are no Newtonian historical 'laws', not even what one theorist has called 'lawlike generalizations'. The greatest mistakes in history (some of it very recent history) have been made by politicians who have read the past into present crises, Eden at the time of Suez, Bush and Blair confronted with Saddam Hussein's Iraq; although, come to think of it, some knowl- edge of history might have helped to avoid their mistakes. Yes, history does have its limited uses. A preacher addressing parliament on the eve of the English Civil War pronounced: 'If you will not learn from history, God will make you the next history.' That seems a more sensible observation than the over-worked: 'The only lesson from history is that there are no lessons from history.' There are lessons, but they are like the lessons you learn from your parents, not like the laws of nature: do as you would be done by, not the first law of thermodynamics.

Nor do I think that history depends upon theory. Those who have thought and acted otherwise have written some very bad history. The bankruptcy of Marxism, not only in practical politics but in making sense of the past, is an example of what Karl Popper might have called, but didn't, the poverty of theory. The leading Marxist historian of 'my' period, Christopher Hill, was unkindly but all too justly indicted by the American J. H. Hexter for combining, with fatal results, the techniques of source-mining and 'lumping'. Sources were mined on to index cards, by a Marxist mentality, and were then lumped together to a tendentious end. The result was that many authors both ancient and modern, including myself, were reported as saying something like the opposite of what they had intended. That said, the young historian who was me could not be immune to the siren voices of Marxist history, nor to its non-identical twin, the 'Whig' history of inexorable and benign progress towards constitutional monarchy and liberal democracy. No more than my contemporaries could I, like a snake, change my skin and slough off those grand, overarching narratives. So, like everyone else, I took very seriously such a narrative as 'the rise of the gentry' and 'the crisis of the aristocracy' in seventeenth-century England, although a dose of better theory might have suggested that the categories were dubious, while the evidential bases for what historians like R. H. Tawney and Lawrence Stone were suggesting were very shaky. More to the point, Marxists, post-Marxists or anti-Marxists, we are all in debt to the emphasis placed on the materiality of the human condition, the economic infrastructure, which we owe in large part to Marx and those whom he taught and inspired.

Critics of the 'revisionism' which came next have accused its practitioners of reducing history to a meaningless chaos of illogical and unrelated events, one damned thing after another. Although the English Civil War had meaningful consequences, not least in the national determination to avoid another one, it had fewer meaningful causes, and, contrary to what was once believed, was not predicated by the state of the constitution and the condition of England fifty or a hundred years earlier. No one would now choose the title which Stone chose for one of his books: *The causes of the English Civil War*. It was now a matter of 'origins', not causes, and the origins were both circumstantial and short term. Oxford, from having been the home of lost causes, now became the home of lost causality.

Where did I stand in these debates? Was I a mere revisionist, a revisionist for the sake of it, or did I still aspire to make some overall sense of the past? My philosophically inclined students and colleagues in Australia were acute enough, and sufficiently sensitive to where I was coming from, to call me a butterfly collector. And it is true that no 'new' fact about the past, no tiny detail, did I ever mentally discard. One of the few academics with whom I have ever found a total lack of affinity was the Oxford anthropologist Rodney Needham, who took the view that we already had more than enough empirically derived knowlege: no more field work, thank you very much. Let's just think about what we've got. My capacity for thought, in the sense of philosophy, or simply the ability to follow a closely reasoned logical process: these things have always been as weak as my maths. But I do possess, and deploy, what I think are the most indispensable gifts for any historian: a good memory, and the faculty of loosely (rather than tightly logically) relating one thing to another. Let me offer a trivial example. In 1952, teaching myself sixteenth-century palaeography by reading in manuscript the primary sources for the history of my native town, Ipswich, I learned about certain great fishes which in 1563 had swum up the Orwell, and which had been carved up and sent off as smelly presents to the town's aristocratic patrons. (It's the thought that counts.) Thirty-two years later, in the Huntington Library in California, I found a printed broadsheet which recorded the same event and which included a fairly accurate picture of one of those great 'fishes'. Having been at Sea World in San Diego the day before I could readily identify the creature as a killer whale, or orca. Only connect! That capacity, which is not different from the ordinary intelligence of the man in the street, not rocket science, can transport you to that Ituri rain forest of the past, that other country where they did things differently.

L. P. Hartley's slogan is trite and has been quoted too often. But its implications, especially for the intellectual and social history of the societies, and individual minds, of the past could not be more important. They are at the root of a remarkable renaissance of history, the best kind of history, in our own time. Quentin Skinner has led the way in teaching us that we need to listen to past voices in their own tones, on their own terms, trusting those who were there to have believed, and to have meant, what they said, and then to place what was said in its context, a context of what it was possible and impossible to affirm, if not to believe, and of the materiality of local, human conditions, economic, social and political. Anthropologists of the generation of Clifford Geertz are advocating the same protocols. To observe every little gesture at a Balinese cockfight, the raised eyebrow, the little grimace, that is butterfly collecting. But it contributes to an understanding of that intricate web of meaning which is human culture, a web spun by those living within it. It is not for us to say what, on our terms, such things may have 'meant'. Functionalism is now dead.

What have I brought to this modern enterprise, this new history? Not much. I am not a Skinner, still less a Geertz. Introducing me to a sixth-form audience, a colleague and polymath, Ronald Hutton of Bristol, said that I was like one of those Japanese craftsmen who work endlessly and tirelessly on small pieces of ivory. In response I said that I recognized the characterization, and suggested that I was to history what Gerald Finzi was to music: a *petit maitre*. That's still true of me and my work, but grossly unfair to Finzi, whom I have since come to know better and to love more and more. But let that pass. My friends, and even my reviewers, credit me with writing history with a human face, with being a kind of resurrection man. My account of the Elizabethan Church of England was a story of men and women, not simply of ideologies. And I have been told that my very best work was in recreating such half-remembered, half-forgotten denizens of the sixteenth and seventeenth centuries as Sir Nicholas Bacon, father of Francis, two-faced Andrew Perne of Peterhouse and Archbishop William Sancroft, whose probably homosexual disposition led him to suspect and retire from the immense ecclesiastical power which he wielded; the consequence of that resignation the destruction of the Church of England which might have been. And how to do that? As often as possible to let people (and their critics and enemies) speak for themselves: no substitute for *ipsissima verba*.

Above all, I believe that we have to keep under very firm control the 'isms' which infest historical discourse: not only Marxism, but Feudalism, Capitalism, Fascism, Colonialism, Orientalism (the list is endless); and, yes, my own subject, Puritanism, a term invented for a malicious, polemical purpose, which has continually got in the way of our understanding of the religious history of early modern England, above all of its teeming plurality and diversity. We cannot hope to get rid of the isms altogether. They, like the no less pernicious 'periods' with which we all deal, are ways and means of carving and slicing up the past into manageable, intelligible and discussable pieces. But what is bad about a great deal of historical investigation and writing is that the isms, from being tools which have their uses, are reified, becoming the objects of study in themselves, which leads to the desiccated trivialities of a kind of scholasticism. I have been asked: 'what, in your opinion, is the future of puritan studies?' I devoutly hope that it has no future.

Something which was also in the genes, or at least in the nurture of my upbringing, was that I became, primarily, a historian of past religion, first of the Puritanism of

Elizabethan England and its legacy, and then of the Protestant Reformation more extensively; and even to venture thoughts on how the story of religion, more generally, might be told. When I started to study history, the history of religion, like religion itself, was a very marginal subject, almost confined to medievalists, who had little else to write about, and to the various churches which had a vested interest in their own histories, often to the detriment of historical truth. Now, fifty years on, religion is a subject hard to avoid, although recent events mean that it is more and more equated with Islam; while the polite and chattering, journalistic, classes go their own secularizing, deprecating way, writing the Christian Churches out of their map of the world. There is a curious contradiction here, indicative perhaps of the lack of much meaningful contact between what professional historians do and what others know and care about. For never before has the history of the Christian religion, especially in the sixteenth and seventeenth centuries, held centre stage in the way that it does today. But who out there knows, or wants to know?

Am I not only a historian of Protestantism but also a Protestant historian? When I started, there was no such thing. There were, of course, Catholic historians, who were suspect. My teacher J. E. Neale almost said that the only good Catholic historians were dead ones, except that the dead ones were especially bad. They inhabited a ghetto, and wrote for a ghetto. We non-Catholic historians were, well, just historians, as the French say *sans epithète*, telling it the way it was, without the bias and taint of religious bigotry. But more recently historians like Eamon Duffy have asked: if I am a Catholic historian, is not Patrick Collinson a Protestant historian? And while they ask that question, they, especially Duffy, who writes much more persuasively than I could ever hope to do, bring Catholic history back out of the cold. It is now, for sixteenth-century historians, in the mainstream of historical discourse. (That is not incompatible with discussing what, especially in Elizabethan England, we might mean by 'Catholic' and 'Protestant'. William Shakespeare, where do you belong?')

In these days of ecumenism and political correctness, one shrinks from the label of Protestant But I think that Duffy is right to ask the question. And the answer is, well, yes. It all has to do with God, and man. Catholics believe that man, by his own free will but assisted by grace, can reach the heavenly heights. That is what Catholic art and architecture, let alone the liturgy, is all about. Protestants, instructed by St Paul and reminded by Martin Luther, have a more immediately pessimistic take on human nature and capacity, and on human affairs. Their theology is a theology of the cross, not of triumph. It is pessimistic in respect of what Luther called this world, *Teufelsreich*, the kingdom of evil, only exercising hope in the life of the world to come, perceived and attained only through faith. Luther said that the only God that he knew was the helpless baby in the manger, the man on the cross, the bread become flesh in the sacrament: God invading human space, sharing in all its misery and mediocrity. Without that perspective I do not know how I could live with the knowledge of Auschwitz, Hiroshima, Rwanda. The alternative Catholic vision seems to me to be a theologized version of the Roman imperative which the popes have inherited. (It was Thomas Hobbes who wrote: 'The Papacy is not other than the Ghost of the deceased Roman Empire, sitting crowned upon the grave thereof.') We need social Catholicism, more than we need Socialism. The Vatican has an honourable record in speaking out in support of justice and human rights (and a dishonourable one when it comes to 'life' issues, faced with the Aids pandemic). But its voice is a religiously articulated version of the voice of this world.

Protestants intersect with current history more radically, or should. My kingdom is not of this world, but is from hence. I cannot repeat those words without hearing them through the medium of Bach's *St John Passion*: 'Mein Reich ist nicht von dieser Welt. Aber ist mein Reich nicht von dannen.' And soon, in the dramatic dialogue of the Passion, Pilate asks Christ: 'Was ist Wahrheit?' 'What is truth?' That is a question for historians. According to Francis Bacon, Pilate did not stay for an answer. But we must. In earlier days I understood *wie es eigentlich gewesen*, the famous slogan of the founding father of modern historiography, Leopold von Ranke, as meaning what actually, or really, was. The historian's task was to tell the truth about the past, the whole truth and nothing but the truth. And that was what historians had claimed to be doing, for 2,000 years. Following the classical writers, the first Elizabethan historian, William Camden, wrote that 'the love of Truth, as it hath been the only incitement to me to undertake this work, so hath it been my only scope and aim in it. Which Truth to take from History, is nothing else but, as it were, to pluck out the eyes of the beautifullest creature in the world.'

Sir Philip Sidney, Camden's contemporary, who believed that improving fiction was morally more useful than history, thought that this commitment to historical truth was the historian's burden, his shackle. 'The historian is so tied, not to what should be but to what is, to the particular truth of things and not to the general reason of things.' He was 'bound to tell things as things were', to stand upon 'that was'. History was Gradgrind's 'facts'.

But Sidney in his criticism went along with the traditional assumption that the historian was not only liable but able to tell true stories about the past. Until, that is, he remembered that to tell stories at all, and what is history but a story, it was necessary to employ another faculty than that of simple memory and fidelity to the record. 'Many times [the historian] must tell events whereof he can yield no cause; or, if he do, it must be poetical.' In other words, to make sense of the past, the kind of sense to be contained in a book of 500 pages, or an article of 8,000 words, the historian has to work with the past like a potter shaping his clay, giving it a beginning, a middle and an end. Without that poetic, imaginative input, history is indeed a tale told by an idiot, signifying nothing. And what comes out of this process is something different from reality. This means that I must at least half agree with Hayden White: that the historian's task is not absolutely alien to that of the writer of fiction. It is something else, in that the events dealt with actually happened, so far as the author knows. But what he does is to make out of them a shape and a pattern which has to be somewhat different from what simply was, which in its chaotic variety can make no sense at all. He is a teller of stories. History is made up, to the extent that yesterday's events are made up on the *Today* programme on Radio 4, by what is included in, and out. The editors of *Today* at least have access to most, even all, of what was happening and thought to be of some importance, world wide, in the previous twenty-four hours. (But not everything! How could anyone cope with that?) The historian of the sixteenth century is not so fortunate. His editors have now been dead for 400 years, and cannot be contacted by email. I now know that Ranke's famous slogan is better translated 'what evidently was'. The evidence is for us to select and interpret. We should always aspire to get it right, while knowing that for others, and above all for those who will come after us, it may not seem that we got it right. To that extent we are all postmodernists, or should be.

This anatomy of a historian, myself, has so far left out an account of for what, or rather for whom, we do and write our history. I have it on my conscience that all that

I have written (upwards of 300 books, essays, articles, reviews) I have written first and foremost for myself (that urge to get it right), and then for fellow specialists in my own field, to be counted on the fingers of a few hands, and perhaps, if I am lucky, for a few hundred students of the subject. I don't expect to be read and heard by the great public out there, nor, for most of the time, do I adopt the means and media to be so read and heard. That is true of the vast majority of academic historians, that is, those historians (no doubt a small minority of those who can claim the title) who are employed in universities. The exceptions to prove this rule, the David Starkeys and Simon Schamas of this world, we regard with a disdain which combines envy for their earnings with nitpicking criticism of the corners their slick presentations inevitably cut. But without these media dons, where would history be? And without some sense of history, where would we all be?

But History, as a serious commitment, lay some way ahead. So back to my 18-year-old self.

6

My Part in The Cold War

In 1947, history had to wait. First came something called National Service. Soon after leaving school I was called up and chose to serve in the Royal Air Force

> We are the Royal Air Force,
> No earthly use are we.
> The only time you see us is breakfast, dinner and tea.
> But when our country needs us, we call with all our might,
> Per ardua ad astra, blow you Jack I'm all right.

This was sung to the tune of 'Stand up stand up for Jesus', and it tells you most of what you need to know about my service to the crown. But the text has been sanitized ('earthly', 'blow you') and I regard the following lyric as more authentic, and as constituting four of the finest lines of English verse ever put down on paper (not, I suppose, that until this moment they ever were):

> Fuck all to do,
> Sitting on the grass,
> Bloody great spiders
> Crawling up your arse.

For me there was indeed fuck all to do. They tried to turn me into a radar mechanic, a trade for which I had no aptitude whatsoever. I never did a piece of radar equipment any good, but there were quite a few that I managed to wreck. My eighteen months of National Service, extended to two years with the crisis of the Berlin Blockade and Airlift, were in most respects a total waste of time. But not entirely. I met and lived with the working class for the first and only time. I shall never forget the Liverpool twins, each calling the other 'our kid', who assured me that in Wallasey, where one of my uncles lived, it was not a good idea to bend down and pick up your lunch box if you dropped it on the way to work. Better to kick it all the way there. (Get it?) For different reasons I remember the young Glaswegian in the next bed who when he came back from the pub vomited on the floor space between us. But it has to be said that I encountered none of the intolerance to which I had been subjected at school.

And then it was in the RAF that I discovered those hills and mountains which would be a part of me for the rest of my life.

After being introduced to the Air Force and kitted out at Padgate, near Warrington, there was square-bashing at West Kirby, in the Wirral. If my initiation as a boarder at Ely had been Purgatory, this was Hell. And the devils were the corporals, petty tyrants who ruled the billets in which we were housed, their weapons not pitchforks but foul, searing, excoriating language. We were a bloody shower (of shit), pregnant earwigs, creatures beneath contempt. The discipline, which I am sure was far more

15 In the RAF at West Kirby, October 1947: with me Richard Marks, a lover a Mozart, as miscast in the service as I was.

severe than anything to be found in any of Her Majesty's prisons, included folding
and building one's blankets into a perfectly regular cube, laying out one's webbing,
duly blancoed, in a prescribed pattern, the brassware shining, achieving an improbably high sheen on one's boots with the aid of a flame and the end of a toothbrush,
and cleaning one's rifle inside and out. If on the daily inspection six fag-ends were
discovered in or around the hut, that was six black marks. The RAF's idea of a
garden was a patch of soil with large stones painted white, and we did the painting.

Although our training included the firing of Stenguns, sticking bayonets into
hanging sacks of straw with bloodcurdling cries and struggling through the assault
course, the main activity was drill, marching and counter-marching on the square.
Sometimes we were taken into the camp cinema to see films about venereal disease,
but we were so exhausted that, sitting in the dark, we all fell asleep.

On the square I was a disgrace to the squad (something to do with my flat feet)
and liable to lose it points at the passing-out parade. So I was taken off square-
bashing and left to clean the billet. The way to produce a perfect finish on the
wooden tables and benches was by soaking the surface with water and then scraping
it with a razor blade. While I was supposed to be doing this I read *War and peace*,
which I hid under a cloth if I heard anyone coming.

At weekends we rode the electric train to Liverpool, which was visible from the
camp (at least the tower of the cathedral was). I became a regular at the Liverpool
Philharmonic, sitting on the cheap seats behind the brass section, which I found
consisted of breezy, beery chaps. It was a new experience to be called 'love' and
'darling' on the streets. I have only been back to Liverpool twice, but I shall never
forget it.

It was necessary to choose a trade. I opted for 'boatman', since the training
happened at RAF Bawdsey, at the mouth of the Deben, only ten miles from Ipswich.
But if you had your Higher School Certificate, you were more or less automatically
assigned to wireless and radar, and I was destined to become a radar mechanic, a
rather lowlier form of life than a radar fitter. The training took place at a large camp
called Yatesbury, a high and windswept place on the Wiltshire Downs. In the winter
of 1946–7 the station commander had been cashiered, or at least sacked, for failing
to close the camp down when everything froze up. But in summer it was a wonderful
place to be. Avebury and Silbury Hill were only a mile or two away, Windmill Hill
(of the Windmill Hill people) was actually within the bounds of the camp, with the
hill fort called Oldbury Castle overlooking it. There was a dew-pond up on the hill
which was full of goldfish, which I caught and took to London and sold. And down
the other side of the hill, where a stream came out of a little reservoir supplying the
nearby town of Calne, I caught trout, some of them big ones.

What about being a radar mechanic? First we were taught some basic things
about electricity by low-grade civilian instructors. ('A voltmeter is an appáratus
(accent on the second syllable) for measuring voltage. Everyone all right? Right-
ho.') This was easy, since the instructors, to save their jobs, told us the answers to
the examination questions in advance. But then I was put on to a course to become
a mechanic servicing ground radar gear. After a week or two on each piece of equipment, you were faced with what was called a phase test. I always failed the test
and had to repeat that part of the course. I was nearing the end when the training
of ground radar mechanics was phased out, so I was transferred to air radar, and
the whole process of testing, failing and repeating was gone through all over again.

The result was that I spent the best part of a year at Yatesbury, interrupted by some weeks at home after Christmas 1947, when I went down with Scarlet Fever. Many of the 'erks' (as we were called) at Yatesbury, their HSC's, like mine, in arts subjects, not science, never qualified as fitters or mechanics, and they became the Aircraftmen General Duties who manned the offices and ran the place. The result was a flourishing dramatic society, in which I acted as La Trémouille in *Saint Joan*, two music appreciation circles, an archaeological society and so on. I was much involved in the chaplaincy, and, being of indeterminate religious affiliation, and therefore classified as 'OD' ('Other Denominations'), had a great deal to do with a decent and interesting Baptist chaplain called Padré Raw.

I cannot leave Yatesbury without mentioning Warrant Officer Bancroft, an old sweat who had to deal with us cheeky chappies. Once, when Bancroft arrived late on parade, someone called out: 'They also serve who only stand and wait.' 'Who said that?' 'Milton, Sir.' 'Stand out in the front A C Milton!' Once Bancroft confronted three of us and said: 'You go and work in the NAAFI and you go and get your hair cut!' 'What shall I do Sir?' 'You keep your mouth shut when you speak to a Senior NCO!' We began to send these little stories to the *Daily Mirror* which printed them in its feature called 'Live Letters'.

From Yatesbury, having finally qualified as a radar mechanic, I was posted to RAF Little Rissington, in the Cotswolds – where there was no radar to be seen. So I spent my time engaged in the humble task of 'bedding brushes' for the wireless mechanics, who included David Gough, son of a history don at Merton, who with his sister (a gorgeous girl, admired from afar) was to read History in my year in Cambridge. Little Rissington was known as Number One Unit RAF, a cushy place where some aircraftmen even had separate rooms. Its *rôle* was to train those who in their turn would train pilots. It was always possible to go up in one of the little planes, to be involved in what were called 'circuits and bumps' at Moreton in Marsh (the original of the radio comedy 'Much Binding in the Marsh'), and even sometimes to take the controls. I caught (poached) plenty of trout in the Windrush, and shall never forget that delicious autumn of 1948, the rich colours against the mellow, golden Cotswold stone.

The most important thing that happened at that time was a holiday in Skye, which was an idea born when standing in a queue for a concert in Cheltenham and looking at someone's photos of the island. When you went on leave in the RAF, you were entitled to a railway warrant to wherever you wanted to go. So my warrant took me from Kingham Station, to which I walked, all the way to Portree, via Glasgow and Mallaig. It will never be possible to recapture the excitement of first seeing mountains, especially the mountains in view from the Sound of Sleat and running between Raasay and Skye on MacBrayne's ferry. I had never seen real hills before. This started off as a fishing holiday, but the hills soon took over. My very first climb was up the Storr, north of Portree in Trotternish, and down by the Old Man. I was terrified when I found myself on unstable scree. Later, I walked up the Sligachan river, gin clear and full of salmon, and went up Sgurr nan Gillean (did I really??) and Sgurr na h'Uamha, having no idea what the mountains were called and whether anyone had ever climbed them before.

In the winter of 1948–9 I was posted to a navigation school at Middleton St George, on the Tees between Darlington and Stockton, known locally as 'Goosepool'. Here they did have some air radar equipment, an advanced American version of the homing device called Rebecca. You had to pump these things up at the back of the plane, and I was quite good at that. A twenty-five-way cable communicated with

16 The hills: the Cuillins, October 1948

the cockpit. But it was insufficiently insulated and one by one the gears broke down. Spares could not be obtained, so soon there was, yet again, fuck all to do. I was assigned to night flying, but in the rotten summer of 1949 night flights were continually cancelled, which meant an excess of aviation fuel. We used it up, washing the floors of the hangars, and, when we went on thirty-six or forty-eight hour passes, planes would take us wherever we wanted to go. Once we crossed the Pennines to drop off one aircraftman in Shropshire before proceeding to Hatfield.

And now I really took to the hills, the Pennines around Swaledale and Teesdale. My father's lifelong friend, Ronald Hodgkin, had me to stay at Cotherston on the Tees, where we went to Quaker meeting in a little barn across the fields, furnished just as it was in the eighteenth century. I was excited when brown, peaty water came out of the bath taps. Because of my flat feet I was allowed to wear shoes, and was excused marching and parades. I walked to work, like a civilian. But on the weekends I put on boots and walked from youth hostel to youth hostel in the high Pennines. Cross Fell from Langdon Beck, via Cauldron Snout, was a good twenty-seven miles of very rough going. From Cauldron Snout you could also walk for miles over featureless bog in another direction, until suddenly the ground fell away from your feet at High Cup Nick, and there was the Vale of Appleby and the Lakes. Soon I got to the Lakeland hills, and on the hottest day of that summer walked from Ullswater up Helvellyn by Striding Edge, down to Thirlmere, and then over the St John Fells to Rosthwaite in Borrowdale. In May my friend Colin Ferrington and I went back to Skye, and now we knew more about the Cuillins, reaching many points on the ridge including the highest, Sgurr Alasdair, and walking around the coast from Glen Brittle to Loch Coruisk and back over the top via the Bealach na Bannachdich, a major expedition.

When I was demobbed from the RAF in September 1949 I was still a mere AC2, having never attempted to earn promotion to the dizzy heights of AC1. The kindly sergeant in charge of my section asked me what I was going to do next, what did life hold for someone as useless as me? He was surprised to learn that I was bound for Cambridge University. The wing commander, at a loss what to put on my final reference, wrote 'He has rowed for his school.' Even that was not true.

Between the RAF and Cambridge I was baptized by total immersion at Bethesda Baptist Church in Ipswich and became a member of that large and flourishing congregation. Then came a hostelling holiday in the Lake District with Hilda, her French boyfriend, Pascal Belanger, and her closest friend, Joy Laity. It is still almost too painful to look back on those days. Pascal was one of the boyfriends whom my father, in effect, forbade Hilda to marry, and, as we heard, he later made a rather unhappy marriage in France. And Joy, on the very night before she and Hilda were due to go on a skiing holiday in the Black Forest, died from an overdose.

There is one strange episode to recount before I get myself to Cambridge. My father had a friend, an old gentleman called Mr Till, on whom he often called as he walked up Bolton Lane from the town. Mr Till would pour him out a glass of (non-alcoholic) ginger wine. One day Mr Till had something to propose. If I would switch to Medicine, with a view to becoming a medical missionary, he would cover all my expenses. My father was greatly taken with the idea. But I had no interest in taking up Mr Till's offer. In the end he paid for the training of a doctor called John Tester. Tester was later in charge of the missionary hospital where Hilda worked in Nazareth.

7

Pembroke

Pembroke College Cambridge was the happy boarding school experience which I had never had. I was popular. At last I excelled in a sport, rowing. The Cambridge University Mountaineering Club became, not my spiritual home, since that was the Cambridge Intercollegiate Christian Union, or CICCU, but where I most belonged and where I found most of my friends. Having edited the *Elean*, I now became editor of *Cambridge Mountaineering*, and on the strength of that was elected to the prestigious, limited-membership Climbers Club; although by today's standards, and even by those which applied in the fifties, it was my climbing skills which were limited.

Pembroke, a middle-sized, civilized, all-male society, for all that it was founded by a lady, had just celebrated its sixth centenary (1348–1948). It was more noted for rugby and rowing than for academic prowess. Nor was I expected to make much difference in that respect. We were all, including many of the dons, on Christian name terms (whereas in the RAF we had addressed each other as 'Mister' this and that). So the Reverend Meredith Dewey, the perennial dean of the college, and immensely wealthy heir to the Prudential empire, immortalized in the memories of such luminaries of the college as Ted Hughes and Tom Sharp, was to all of us 'Meredith'.

But I am not sure that my History teacher, H. J. Habakkuk, was ever 'John' until about thirty years later, let alone 'Hrothgar', his real name. The college contained its due allotment of academic eccentrics: Wilfred Knox, brother of Monsignor Ronald and Evoe Knox of *Punch*, who died in my first year; Sir Ellis Minns, who had turned from conventional classical studies to Central Asia and the affairs of the Parthians, and who was never to be seen without a Pembroke scarf around his neck, even on his deathbed. The senior tutor, Tony Camps, another classicist, later to be master and yet to make himself unpopular by his stalwart resistance to the admission of women to the college ('there are simply not enough good women to go round' – slow handclaps), was very genial. And I think that we did call him Tony. One of his greatest moments was when he rescued a drunken Ted Hughes from imminent drowning in the little stream called the 'Pem' which flows past the college. 'The stars, the stars!' cried Hughes. Camps replied: 'It is interesting how you see things.' Without Tony Camps no laureateship, perhaps no Sylvia Plath? The master was Stephen Roberts of the Cambridge University Press. He told us on our first night that wherever we went in the world we would be Pembroke men and would identify with other Pembroke men, whether in Timbuctoo or Tunbridge Wells. He never failed to acknowledge you if you met him in the street. I was stirred by a kind of patriotism, for the first and only time in my life.

This was expressed, mainly, on the river. I joined the Boat Club in my first week and learned to row in the boat called a tub, when a man called John Hind was taught

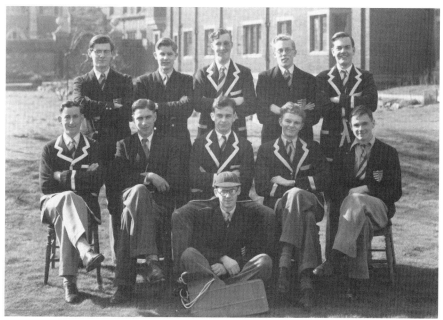

17 Pembroke fourth boat, 1950: Michael Apps (Father Bernard SSF) who died in 2007, is standing on the right; James Crowden, who as Lord Lieutenant of Cambridgeshire would invest me with the CBE, is seated one place from the left

18 Grassy Corner: PC is rowing at no. 6

19   Henley Royal Regatta, June 1950

to steer it. He went on to cox the blue boat, taking over from Tony Armstrong Jones, later Lord Snowdon ('Do you remember that stupid little cox we had last year?' I once heard a rowing blue ask), and who became a well-known rowing journalist, regularly reporting on the Boat Race for the BBC, along with John Snagge. Our captain of boats was a larger than life figure (who has grown larger with the years), James Crowden, later lord lieutenant of Cambridgeshire who, a lifetime later, would in that capacity confer on me the honour of Commander of the British Empire. The Pembroke fourth boat enjoyed great success in 1950, winning its oars in both the Lents and the Mays. The oars hung on the wall until I went to Australia in 1969, taking only the blades, which I burned before we came back to England. After all, I had burned my boats, both in going to Australia and in returning.

Towards the end of that first year, James invited me to row at Henley, explaining that most of the costs (which I certainly could not afford) would be taken care of. We did not cover ourselves with glory. But it was great to be there. We stayed at the Five Horseshoes on Remenham Hill, where I drank pints of shandy, almost the first alcohol I had ever tasted. The Korean War had just broken out, and my main anxiety was selfish: not to be recalled to the RAF. Harvard had won the Grand Challenge Cup in 1914 and 1939, and each time it had hung on to the trophy for five years. In 1950 Harvard won the Grand.

I rowed in the college first boat in the Lents of 1951, but not I think in the May boat. And instead of going back to Henley, I decided to walk across Lapland. It was there that I received a fat envelope from my parents, full of cuttings from the Daily Telegraph, which told me that Pembroke had won one third of all the then available trophies at Henley, including the Ladies Plate and the Visitors Cup. I sat on the tundra and told myself that, if I had been in the boat, the result might have been different. That was almost the end of my rowing career, as I began to take my work more seriously. But later, in London, I joined London Rowing Club and took part, year by year, in the Head of the River Race (a very exciting experience – a reverse Boat Race course – Mortlake to Putney), and in summer regattas up the river, beyond Teddington Lock.

The hills mattered more, and were not so easily abandoned. I can remember, again in my first week, going to St John's to meet the president of the Cambridge University Mountaineering, Club (CUMC), Chris Brasher, later the Olympic gold medallist and sporting journalist and entrepreneur. In the weeks before Christmas, the CUMC always went to North Wales and to Helyg, the hut of the Climbers Club in the Ogwen Valley, looking out to the east face of Tryfan. It was there that we learned the rudiments of rock-climbing, whatever the weather. We wore 'British nailed boots', which meant soft iron clinkers, not the harder-edged *tricounis* favoured in the Alps. The climbs on the Idwal Slabs were pretty severe in clinkers, especially the route called 'Hope', when ice-cold water was cascading into your neck and out at your boots. We went out with 120 feet of hemp rope, no other gear, and no helmets. It is a wonder that any of us survived, and some of us didn't. Helyg remains sacred in my memory and I can recall the very smell of the place.

Easter found us in the Lakes, at Brackenclose, a Fell and Rock Club hut at Wastdale Head. In the spring of 1951 we climbed on snow and ice on the north face of Great Gable and on the same day in gym shoes on the Napes Ridges, part of the same mountain. On an unforgettable night, two of us went up Scafell Pike by the light of the full moon, over crisp snow, and glissaded down into Hollow Stones from Mickledore. And then, with the start of the Long Vacation, it was back to Scotland. In June 1950 I was driven there by John Kay, a senior member of the CUMC and a distinguished chemical engineer, a pioneer, whether you like it or not (and I did not) of Sellafield/Windscale. I shall never forget sleeping, without a tent, on Stainmoor, and waking to the thrilling trills of curlews, followed by breakfast at the Station Hotel in Carlisle. The next day we were climbing the Crowberry Ridge on Buchaille Etive Mhor which guards the entrance to Glencoe. Then on to Skye. I am probably the only person in history to have abseiled off the Inaccessible Pinnacle on Sgurr Dearg, only to land on his head. I was not allowed to forget that. On 20 June, almost the longest day, George Jackson and I walked over the Cuillin ridge, down to Loch Coruisk, and back by the continuous 3,000 foot rock climb which is Sgurr Dubh: an eleven-hour day. I left for the Henley Royal Regatta the next morning.

On account of the war, I had never been overseas, and I was twenty-one. But in the Long Vacation of 1951 four of us formed the Cambridge Translapland Expedition and set off for the north of Norway. It was John West of Queens', a man with ideas above his station, who had thought of the expedition. He brought with him Mino Marker, a Parsee from Quetta in Baluchistan who was anxious to escape from his wealthy family, which had descended on Europe but would probably not make it north of the Arctic Circle. There were plans to marry him off, and rich Parsees not being all that numerous, he knew and disliked all the eligible girls who were on offer. Ernest Hemingway had had a powerful influence on Mino. 'Lapland, lovely land of the Lapps', he would intone, as we trudged over the tundra, 'you seen a mile you seen the lot.' And then there was myself, and George Jackson, an engineer whom I had met at Helyg and who has remained a friend for more than fifty years.

20   Mike Farnell on Lliwedd, December, 1950

It is impossible to recapture the excitement of first seeing a foreign place, and such a foreign place! Those who have travelled north from Bergen on the 'Hurti-grute' will know what I mean, although their palates will probably have been jaded by exposure to many other exotic locations. Huge slabs of rock descended into the dark fjords, waterfalls cascading down them. There were mountains with holes through them. The sun was low in the sky at midnight. Every rock and islet was covered with racks of drying cod, *torrfesk*. Pardon my Norwegian. We were armed with *Teach yourself Norwegian*, not a very good idea. When the ship berthed at Alesund or Bodo, I thought that I was asking when we would leave, but apparently what I said meant 'how many times will we march?'. George and I began with some climbing in the Lofoten Islands, a landscape of stunning beauty and awesome verticality. I think that you would have to go to the south of Chile to see anything else quite like it on this planet. The Germans had not long been gone, and we roped down from the pinnacle above Svolvaer called the Svolvaergaete (or Svolvaer goat) from German pitons. There are many Germans still here, the locals said, pointing to the floor. It was not clear whether the Huns in question were under the very floor boards of the room in which we were drinking coffee.

Our expedition had no point to it whatsoever. We were there because Lapland was there. We did nothing to it, but it did a lot to us, and perhaps for us. We each carried seventy pounds, which included food for six weeks: Gino Watkins's Green-land scale, consisting mostly of pemmican. Summer was late that year, and we had to cope with a lot of snow, and, the worst of conditions, breakable crust. Once below the snow line the mosquitoes rose from the bog in their millions. We had to cross a turbulent river, where George and I very nearly drowned. On the worst day we had to jump from tussock to tussock, but from each tussock grew horizontal branches of dwarf willow which might as well have been iron bars. It was pouring with rain, but that did nothing to discourage the mosquitoes.

At the end of that awful day we reached a little farm, Goatteluabal, the first inhabited place we had seen for a week. We knocked on the door but no one answered. We walked around the house several times, as the Children of Israel walked around Jericho, and in the end just went in, past furs and snowshoes and wolf traps. The people were surprised to see us, but they gave us coffee and we gave them chocolate. The calendars on the wall came from stores in three countries: Norway, Sweden and Finland. 'We har reissen fra Heligskogen in Skitbotendal pa fut.' 'Pa fut?' It was hard for the Sami of Goatteluabal to get their heads around that, as they spoke little more Norwegian than we did.

After another day, we reached a place on the river with a homestead on the other bank. We shouted and whistled, and the result was a scene from a Bergman film. There were two teenagers in the house, but I am not sure what the relationship between them may have been. The lad agreed to take us in his boat to Kautokeino, twenty or thirty miles downstream. All the way, with little current and a strong head wind, Sami pulling large salmon and trout out of the water in nets, he kept a little stub of a cigarette firmly gripped in his mouth. He left us on the beach at Kautokeino, got paid, and proceeded to row back.

At Kautokeino, we earned some money sawing the winter's supply of logs for the Sami school, digging graves and painting the cemetery fence. We were increasingly unpopular. The county council, or *Fylksparliament* was meeting in the town for the first time in its history. 'STORE DAG FUR KAUTOKEINO' proclaimed the local newspaper, *Nordkapp*. Mino Marker managed to sell a single wellington boot to Mrs Mortensen, the owner of the only store in the village, like all other shopkeepers in Lapland, Jewish. 'Hvor er andre?' ('where is the other?') George Jackson had lost it in that perilous river crossing. 'In jokka' ('in the river'). Still this shrewd Pakistani entrepreneur got two kroner fifty for the single boot. But then Mino was unwise enough to comment on Mrs Mortensen's bald head, which she concealed under a Lappish hat. Soon it was necessary to push on to Karasjok, and so up to Hammerfest, the most northerly town in the world, which the Nazis had destroyed in their retreat of 1945. Local postcards depicted 'Hammerfest bifor Tyskes behandling' and 'Hammerfest eftir Tyskes behandling'.

In Tromso we waited for an English trawler to take us home, hopefully for free. We had no money. While we waited, the generous Norwegians lent us a boat and some fishing tackle. We caught plenty of cod, which we sold in the fish market, and the odd halibut, which the man who lent us the boat insisted on paying for. When a whale was brought into the whaling station, we went round to collect free whale meat. In the end, a trawler came in and agreed to take us to Grimsby. It was a very rough voyage. 'Oos chaps joost call this a moderate breeze.' We taught the trawlermen to play Monopoly. It was not easy to make it to the dining room, which was over the stern. It was halibut every day, which sounds good, except that the cook suffered from a chronic nose bleed, which meant that from his nose a very long clot always depended. When we arrived in Grimsby, the men on the tug, looking at our ropes and ice axes, asked who we were. 'We've brought them across from Norway.' 'But they won't find mooch to climb here in Grimsby, will they?' 'No, they're English. You can talk to them. They'll oonderstand you.' We were home.

In post-war Cambridge, religion was much more popular than politics. I did join the Labour Club, and on 13 October 1950 went to hear a lecture by Herbert

21 CICCU Bible reading on a Saturday night: the reverend John Stott is expounding

Morrison. I was assigned, as part of a group studying colonialism, the Gambia. I read numerous blue books on that rather obscure subject.[1] But religion, the evangelical religion of the CICCU, was what dominated our lives, hundreds of us. I was the college representative for Pembroke.[2] There were daily prayer meetings at lunchtime; college Bible readings once a week, conducted by a librarian called Basil Atkinson, the pope of CICCU if truth were to be told; university Bible readings on Saturday evenings; the CICCU sermon in Holy Trinity on Sunday evenings, to which we were supposed to take non-Christian friends, with the intention that they should be converted. This must have eaten up all the time that could have been spent in going to the theatre or to concerts. CICCU was concerned to the exclusion of all else with personal salvation and sanctification. We never paid any attention to the social dimensions of Christianity, whereas the rival Student Christian Movement (SCM) talked about nothing else. The historic split between the SCM and the IVF (the Inter-Varsity Fellowship, with which the CICCU was affiliated) was a tragedy. For someone like my cricketing contemporary David Sheppard, a Cambridge convert, and later bishop of Liverpool, it was the journey of half a lifetime to reunite spirituality with an active social conscience. In the summer there were Christian camps and beach missions which had to be fitted around climbing in Skye and picking strawberries near Wisbech to make some money.

[1] Little did I know that more than forty years later I would have two sons for whose careers, medicine in one case, music in the other, the Gambia would be all important.
[2] When I went back to the college for a reunion in 2001, there were friends from that long lost world who thanked me for the spiritual leadership I had given, rather to my embarrassment.

So what about the subject that I was supposed to be at Cambridge to read? What about history? They tell me that I worked quite hard, especially in my final year, for Part Two of the Cambridge History Tripos. But there was less to read in those days. I took papers in Ancient History, Medieval History both European and English, English Economic History, Tudors and Stuarts: very little history from post-1800, apart from a paper on The Expansion of Europe. I became an enthusiastic student of African history, in the prehistory of that subject, when it still mostly consisted of the history of European colonization. I began to think that I might make African history my subject, even go to Africa.

It was already unfashionable to attend lectures, and when you went to Ralph Bennett on the middle ages, or to H. O. Evennett on Renaissance and Reformation (both admirable scholars, of course), you knew why. But we never willingly missed a lecture by the Russian-born economic historian M. M. Postan (husband until her untimely death of Eileen Power), although as often as not he was the one who failed to turn up. Brian Wormald of Peterhouse, author of a good book on Clarendon, and, much later, a very odd book on Francis Bacon, rubbed our noses in seventeenth-century English constitutional conflict; the only lecturer I have known to begin a lecture with 'Whereas'. Dom David Knowles returned from All Souls to tell us: 'Dr Rowse appears not to believe in the middle ages.' Someone who did was Walter Ullmann, whose rich Germanic pronunciation of the name 'Cardinal Humbert' was enough to convince you that the Investiture Contest really mattered. In the lectures given by the historian of the Hudson's Bay Company, Teddy Rich, master of St Catharine's, we were reduced to betting how many times he would use one of his overused words. A lifetime addiction to doodling caricatures came in useful. Oddly enough, I never attended a single lecture by G. R. Elton, whom I would succeed as Regius Professor a lifetime later. I cannot think why. In those days, Elton was still attracting big audiences. Instead I went to the lectures on the Tudors given by Christopher Morris of King's, who liked to use nursery rhymes as original sources: 'Goosey goosey gander, whither shall you wander?' This was Bishop Stephen Gardiner of course, and the old man who wouldn't say his prayers and got kicked downstairs was Archbishop Thomas Cranmer. Elton was meanwhile telling his audience that almost everything of consequence which happened in the sixteenth century was the work of Thomas Cromwell, but I am not sure that Morris ever had occasion to mention Cromwell's name.

I was not very well taught, which is sadly quite often the case in Cambridge, to this very day. But in my first year I read essays to the distinguished economic historian Habakkuk, who turned round from the window after the first sentence of my first effort: 'Well that's all dead wood isn't it?' Habakkuk had brought from South Wales a stern, residual puritanism. I also had as my medieval teacher a very fine historian of the Conciliar Movement, Brian Tierney. But then both Habakkuk and Tierney left Pembroke, Habakkuk for a chair at Oxford and, in due time, the presidency of Jesus College, and they were not immediately or appropriately replaced. A rather odd medievalist and cleric, John Dickinson, taught me English medieval history, after a fashion. He said that he liked an essay to read for forty minutes, and he was often in the bath while it was read. I went to supervisions in other colleges: to Betty Behrens in Newnham, one of the wives of E. H. Carr, who told me, after the first essay that I read to her, that it was 'a very considerable achievement'; and who was the first person to mention in my hearing the name of the Elizabethan historian J. E. Neale, who had just published *The Elizabethan House of Commons*.

22   Reading History at Pembroke

All that I remember of my supervisions in Ancient History was that Dr Woodhead of Corpus told us that the advantage of looking into that subject was that it had a beginning, a middle and an end. I doubt whether any early medievalist would have agreed about the end. Whether and when Antiquity gave way to something else (before or after Charlemagne?) is a good, and probably unanswerable, question. But I learned that Thucydides was one of the greatest historians of all time: his account of the unspeakable horrors of what happened in Corcyra in the Peloponnesian War has not been bettered in an age which has known worse things, in Bosnia, Kosovo, Rwanda, the Congo, Sudan.

In my third year the only tuition I got was from a research student at St John's, Roger Anstey. I enjoyed doing African History with Roger, whose subject it was. But his supervisions in Modern European History were an embarrassment for us both. (He had great difficulty in sorting out the various Fredericks and Ferdinands at the time of the Thirty Years War.) These experiences, in Roger's house up the Huntingdon Road, were shared with an Irish landowner called Mark Bence-Jones, who later published popular history on the Cavaliers and other such subjects. Twenty-five years later, Roger Anstey headhunted me for a job at the University of Kent at Canterbury, where he was Professor of Modern History and where I became Professor of History, in succession to the great Leland Lyons. We enjoyed our brief collegiality (Roger died in 1978), which was without any embarrassment.

I don't think that great things were ever expected of me. The stars in our little firmament were already clearly identified: John Elliott, later Regius Professor at

Oxford; Geoffrey Best, a powerful historian first of religion then of war and peace, and one of Churchill's many biographers; Alec Campbell, a promising Americanist. Towards the end of my second year my tutor, Bill Hutton, who ran the Boat Club, suggested that I might consider reading English for the second part of the Tripos. (Bill's advice was otherwise always the same: don't slack off, but on the other hand, don't overdo it.) To change triposes would give me two strings to my bow, which I was likely to bend as some kind of schoolteacher. I had already been in touch with people who might find me a teaching job in Africa: Gordon College, Khartoum; northern Nigeria; the Gold Coast; British Somaliland. All crop up in my diaries. But arrogantly, and I suppose ignorantly, I decided that I could read English literature for myself, without expert guidance, while I got on with studying history.

For Part Two of the Cambridge History Tripos you take a Special Subject, involving for the first time study of original sources, which in my case was a paper on the religion and politics of late seventeenth- and early eighteenth-century England, taught by Norman Sykes, Dixie Professor of Ecclesiastical History, who was soon to become dean of Winchester, in succession to my wife's uncle, Gordon Selwyn. I found that I loved it, especially reading many editions of Daniel Defoe's newspaper, with the front page full of fascinating small ads: stolen horses, rival eye surgeons slagging each other off ('he worked on my eye for the passage of an hour, and did no good'). We were a small but distinguished class, which included John Elliott and David Sheppard. Sheppard had already played test cricket in Australia and Sykes, who loved cricket, was thrilled to have him in his class; so thrilled that when we sat the examination, he came in and discussed the paper with David for some time, with his arm over his shoulder, which caused much amusement. It was, I suppose, quite a soft option. In June I received a telegram from a friend: 'YOURS WAS PEMBROKE'S ONLY HISTORY FIRST'. I won the college prize for History and spent the money on, God help us, abridged versions of Toynbee's *Study of history* and Frazer's *Golden bough*; as well as Neale's *The Elizabethan House of Commons* and Collingwood's *The idea of history*, which I found hard going.

So that was Cambridge. I had not been part of some golden generation. I went to debates at the Union, where the president, in my first year, was Norman St John Stevas, later kicked upstairs from real politics as Lord St John of Fawsley, who told jokes about his auntie, who was standing in for Margaret Thatcher in subsequent years. But I had few friends who were later to become famous, as I was probably at the wrong college for that. But someone who was so destined, Edward Braithwaite, later vice-chancellor of the University of the West Indies and a most distinguished Caribbean poet, came home to Ipswich to stay in April 1951, and was very properly critical of my playing of Bach's 48, as if the fugues had only one voice. And women had yet to make any impact on my consciousness. My diaries tell me that I very often entertained to tea, and saw on other occasions, a very nice girl called Annette Buckton, but the circumstances must have been chaste in the extreme, and if there were opportunities to be seized I was clearly not the person to have seized them.

Even before I heard about the First I had decided to go on with history, for want perhaps of any idea about what else to do. I talked Africa in Matthew's tea shop with the Africanist Robinson and the legendary Jack Gallagher, who was making Trinity a centre for Indian history; and I later presented myself in Oxford to Margery Perham, biographer of Lord Lugard. These were all great names at that time. Perham was at first enthusiastic. 'I'll get you to work on Bechuanaland Mr Collinson! I have a good friend there called Seretse Khama' (or was it Seretse's uncle, Tshekedi Khama?).

23   My father's last Christmas, 1951

But Perham was alarmed when she learned how little really modern history I had ever read. Soon I was told that I ought to go to London and attach myself to the famous Tudor school, headed by J. E. Neale. There I would get a thorough historical training, which I could later apply to the history of Africa, if I so chose.

So it was that I first met Neale, at the end of his first seminar of the October term, 1952. 'Come and see me! Hurstfield, you know where my room is, tell him where to find me!' 'Don't let him give you something awful', said an American student of Neale's, going down the stairs at the Institute of Historical Research. It was good advice, since I had no idea myself what subject I might research.

But before that, and into that new experience, came a time of emotional turmoil. I took a vacation job helping to run a Holiday Fellowship centre at Lynmouth, on the North Devon coast. My *rôle* was to lead walking parties over and around Exmoor (inventing episodes as I went from *Lorna Doone*, which I had never read). There I fell head over heels in love with a lovely Swiss girl, Elisabeth Egli. Not only had I never fallen in love before (and something quite like that never happens to you twice). With the exception of Annette, I had scarcely ever been on speaking terms with a female of my own generation, apart from my sister. In 1952, and coming from my background, I assumed that that ought to lead to a proposal, engagement, marriage. There were no such things as 'affairs'. All this must have been too much for Elisabeth to take. After weeks of passionate correspondence I returned to Lynmouth, only to be told on a bench, leading up to Countisbury Hill, the very bench where I had first kissed Elisabeth, that 'all this' could never be. Elisabeth uttered one word: 'Africa!' I can still taste the salt of my tears. So far as I know,

24 May 1952

25 Elisabeth Egli, Lynmouth, July 1952

Elisabeth worked for many years in a travel agency in her native St Gallen, but never married.

The next day I took another girl from Lynmouth Manor to the cinema in Barnstaple. As we came back in the bus it rained and rained. And soon the rain was something out of the ordinary. A cook at the Manor, who had grown up in India, ran around, celebrating the onset of the monsoon. By nightfall, nine inches of rain had fallen on Exmoor, and by the next morning thirty-six people were dead, half the village was washed away, and hundreds of cars had been carried out to sea. I remember, while it was still daylight, standing by the little green footbridge close to the pier as concave brown water, full of trees and God knows what else, rushed by at 80 miles per hour; the bridge snapped and disappeared. Later that night two of us stood at the bottom of the hill, by the bridge into the village. People were flashing torches from the hotel across the water; we thought to warn us that we were in danger, but in reality, of course, out of fear for their own lives. The next morning we queued for buses to take us away to Minehead, to London, and to the rest of our lives.

Two months later, my father died. Hilda, with my mother, held the fort in those last weeks. I should have been there, and it is for ever on my conscience that I was not, too busy sorting out what kind of person I was. And relations with my father had not been very good. He was a sick man, and could not understand why I should want to embark on another degree course. 'You know that I have four other children' – not that I was going to cost him anything. (Nor could my brother Bernard. He wrote: 'It seems that one degree is not enough.') On the early November Sunday that Daddy died, I was in Sussex, staying at another Holiday Fellowship house. Elisabeth was not there, but it was the closest that I could get. Walking in the rain that afternoon, I saw a single magpie. I have always been superstitious. Back at the Institute on Monday morning there was a telegram from Hilda: 'DADDY PASSED AWAY PEACEFULLY LAST EVENING. COME AT ONCE.' In spite of all, I really loved my father. At the funeral, I was too overcome with emotion to sing his favourite hymn: 'Through the night of doubt and sorrow / Onward goes the pilgrim band.'

8

Puritanism

And so back to London. I was twenty-three. For the past ten years I had lived in institutions, bad, indifferent and good, with some sort of meal on the table, three times a day. I had never known what it was to fend for myself. As an exhibitioner I had been allotted a room in college for all of my three years at Pembroke, for the last two in the old Master's Lodge, from where Monty Butler, Rab Butler's father, retired from the Punjab, had governed the college. Collegiate connexions in London were very different. I applied for a scholarship at Royal Holloway College, and was interviewed by the formidable Byzantinist Joan Hussey, who had once told a student: 'You probably won't want to read this text in the original Ethiopic, but fortunately there is an excellent Armenian translation.' One of the things she asked me was whether I played the French horn, since they lacked a horn player for the college orchestra. I didn't. Nevertheless, I got the scholarship, which paid very little, but the state made it up to enough to live on. But Holloway was twenty miles away in the Surrey countryside, across the Great Park from Windsor, and we postgraduates were invited to a cup of coffee, once a year, by the principal, Dame Edith Batho, who as a child had met Mr Gladstone. Only when I acquired a fiancée at Englefield Green did I have occasion to go there with any regularity.

My supervisor, J. E. Neale, was at University College, which is where I went for weekly meetings. ('I like this college, Collinson! I can remember when the Common Room was no larger than my office, and the chemists made the coffee.') But the Institute of Historical Research was where I soon came to belong. We ate our evening meals over the way at Birkbeck College. But where to live in the vastness of London? In late September my mother had come to sort me out. It must have been the very last time she was able to leave my father.

We found a place in Muswell Hill in a house owned by a Mrs Graham Goodes, and a large elkhound called Sacha, whose ascent of the stairs at night and descent the next morning was always noisy. ('Come along Sacha, Sacha will you come along? Woof, woof!') The attraction was that coffee and sandwiches in the evening were included in the rent, but it turned out that in order to get your refreshments you had to sit and watch television with Mrs Goodes. We were so close to the Alexandra Palace that there was no need for an aerial. Mrs Goodes thought that Bob Boothby was such a manly man, a view I gather she shared with the wife of Harold Macmillan. The only other lodger was a German shoe salesman called Eberhard. His English was not up to much, almost limited to 'It's good!', when he rose from the TV to go to bed; and 'It's not good!', when he complained about the regime under which we lived, as well he might. You were allowed one bath a week, provided you first spread sheets of brown paper on the floor and filled the bath to a depth of no more than four inches.

It was healthy exercise, cycling up Highgate Hill from Bloomsbury, sometimes racing against Miss Macdonald, one of the eccentrics who made the British Museum her home. Miss Macdonald was convinced that the Reading Room was infested with homosexuals, and indeed the novelist Angus Wilson was in charge in those days. Her response to this threat was to prowl around for half an hour before closing time, scrunching up any stray pieces of paper she could find. Miss Macdonald looked like one of those Whistler drawings, whichever way you held her up. She dressed in gym shorts and plimsolls and a double-breasted pink plastic mac. Like me she rode a bike with turned down handlebars. It was an evil day when Wilson gave way to an expert in Slavonic languages called Bancroft, who banished all those odd people who had nowhere else to go. Whatever happened to the man with a bulge in his head, which kept throbbing, and who filled many notebooks with an unintelligible scrawl; or to the man who looked like Karl Marx and who, as we understood, was compiling a vast bibliography of bibliographies? Until then they only had to decide what to do on Christmas Day. Now it was the rest of their lives. But Eric Partridge, the famous lexicograher of slang, whom we called Mr A1, since that was always where he sat, held his ground.

After three months of Muswell Hill my Quaker connexions found me a berth at the Friends' International Centre, no. 32 Tavistock Square. This was one of the luckiest breaks in a life which has been full of good luck. For one thing it was at the Centre that I made my friends of a lifetime, 'the Crowd' as we call them, most of them now living in Blackheath. The wardens, the Irvines, deserve a duplex place in that regular feature in *Reader's Digest:* The Most Remarkable Person I Ever Met. They had spent much of their lives in what was then the Gold Coast, at Achimota, where Fred Irvine, a biologist and agronomist, wrote the foundation texts on the plants, and fishes, of the region. His appetite for knowledge of the natural world could never be satisfied. When I knew him he was collecting information from all over the world about the consumption of snakes as human food. He went out in boats on the Thames Estuary to investigate the ecology, and he took me to Billingsgate at four o'clock in the morning, where the buskers, mistaking his grubby raincoated motives, presented him with a large codfish. Even then Fred knew that if Africa had a future it was in the villages and in rural development, not in the cities. He was a warm-hearted, liberal Quaker, a son of the Student Christian Movement, who spoke freely and naturally of 'my Master'. Dorothy, the hardheaded daughter of a Presbyterian manse in my native Ipswich, complemented Fred perfectly. The Irvines had a cottage at Stow Maries in Essex where we went for weekends of sublime informality.

How to describe the Centre in those days? Michael Scott, the pioneer campaigner for the rights of the inhabitants of what was then called South-West Africa, would often stay, and he and Fred Irvine would on the spur of the moment climb into a taxi on a Sunday afternoon to go to Downing Street to present a petition. The house was full of all sorts of nationalities, occupying the camp beds which had to be put up in the dayrooms every night. Down in the basement were the kitchen arrangements, ruled by Mrs Mockford. When an Indian guest politely declined the evening meal, she exclaimed: 'First time I met one of them continentals what don't eat beef!' A cleaner, coming into the library, exclaimed: 'My God! What a bloody waste of money! Oh, is this a religious house? I don't want you to think that I never read a book. My 'usband brought one back once called Inside Europe, which was all about two ladies in India. But I got fed up with it in the end and chucked it on the fire.' There were language problems. 'Which watch?' 'Such much!' 'Where is my parcel?' 'He is in his room, shaving.' 'I did not say Marcel, I said parcel.' 'Which is what?'

I shared a room at the top of the house with Hassan, from Pakistan, and Cedric Lazaro, a talented pianist from Burma, who remained a very special friend to the day of his death; Reg Jewkes, too, an Anglo-American medic who, with his future wife Doreen, would rise to considerable eminence in that profession. Later I squeezed into a little bedroom with Raoul van Caenegem, who would become the most distinguished of Belgian medievalists, and Dik van Arkel, later a professor at Leiden and an authority on anti-Semitism. We were all three engaged to be married, but Raoul was the only one to marry his fiancée. He would come back from evenings in her company at about midnight, and proceed to make his bed, loudly whistling Beethoven symphonies. In that room I learned that Dutch and Flemish are essentially the same language.

In the evenings things were laid on for the benefit, mostly, of elderly refugees from Germany and Central Europe. I remember one of the audience complaining in a thick German accent, after a term of lectures: 'Allow me to say, with the *utmost* tact, that the entire course has been an *utter* failure.' But not all evenings were failures. Sir Adrian Boult came once; and Benjamin Britten and Peter Pears, who fussed around the place wondering if Benjie was altogether happy. Once a week there was a Meeting for Worship, which had its fair share of eccentrics. After an occasion when a Friend had discoursed on the spiritual theme of feeding each other, a Hungarian count asked her: 'Speaking of feeding, friend, where can I find some prawns?' He was directed towards Billingsgate and was not seen again.

I have forgotten to mention what was the greatest advantage of living at the Centre. It was five minutes' walk from the Institute, where Raoul and I would compete to see whose name was first in the book at nine o'clock. Once I undertook to guide to the British Museum one of the Hutterite brethren from Shropshire who regularly used the Centre, a Dutchman with a red beard, their orchardist. I was carrying a shoe box, full of my notes. When we got there there was no entry. President Tito was inside. As we waited, no more than two or three policemen in attendance, people muttered quietly: 'Look at that man with the red beard.' And what about that box?

What was more to the point was that 32 Tavistock Square was a horizontal 300 yards from the UCL History Department in Gordon Square, and vertically about 100 feet below the room which I had been allotted at the top of that building. I was there until one o'clock in the morning, and within five minutes I could be in bed. Now I only needed my bike to cycle to Putney, and the London Rowing Club, and to Bermondsey, where I helped to run a youth club at the Cambridge University Mission and to teach Sunday School.

How come this unique privilege, a room of my own in the History Department (although I had to vacate it in the summers, when Wallace Notestein came over from Yale)? It goes back to my first, momentous, meeting with Neale, known to all and sundry as 'Jimmy' Neale, recalling the days when he had appeared in college concerts as 'Sunny Jim', a character on a breakfast cereal packet. (In fact his name was John. And when he got his knighthood he informed his colleagues that he did not wish to be addressed as 'Sir John', but only, as ever, as 'Professor Neale'.) It had to do with Puritanism, a commodity with which I have made my modest career. On that first encounter, Neale said that he would put me to work on the subject of Elizabethan Puritanism. I raised no objections. I had always been interested in religious history, which I suppose ran in my genes and my bloodstream. I was told that an American called Marshall Moon Knappen had written a book called *Tudor*

Puritanism, which turned out, on inspection, to be not particularly historical, by the standards which the University of London applied to the past. (Knappen regarded Puritanism as 'a chapter in the history of idealism'.) Apart from Knappen, not much had been written, outside the prejudiced pages of the denominational historians, not only of nonconformity but of Anglicanism, for whom it was a distasteful topic. In pointing me in the direction of Puritanism, Neale was not entirely disinterested. He rarely was. At the time he was embarked on a two-volume history of the Elizabethan parliaments. In the annals of that forum the people called Puritans often stole the front page, agitating for a further and complete reform of religion and in so doing challenging the prerogative will of the crown in the person of Queen Elizabeth I, who had made Neale's name as a historian in his biography of 1934. When Neale published the second volume of *Elizabeth I and her parliaments* in 1957, he thanked me for my invaluable assistance. As well he might. Supervisions with Neale consisted of unpacking my little parcel of trade goods and handing over what I had found since we last met. What did I get in return? Neale did almost nothing to guide me in my researches, which to be sure were lacking in direction; and he never read a word of what I wrote, until I submitted my doctoral thesis, which any competent supervisor would have pointed out was, at 500,000 words, about six times too long. And yet I never went out from Neale's presence without a spring in my step and the conviction that just around the corner I would come across something sensational: which sometimes happened. I have supervised a fair number of doctoral students myself. You need to do what Neale spectacularly failed to do. But if you don't do what he did do, you are not doing your job. It is all about encouragement, even inspiration.

The other reason why Neale put me on to Puritanism was that when I came to see him he had recently taken possession of several large boxes, which sat in his study even as we spoke. These had been sent by a shipping magnate in Liverpool called Bibby, whose daughter Edna had been one of Neale's research students back in the late 1920s. When I knew Neale, women were not allowed to do Ph.D.s. They could write MA theses, mostly on the subject of successive Elizabethan parliaments. One remembers, with affection and great respect, Norah Fuidge, whose parliament was 1563. She earned a footnote in the first volume of *Elizabeth I and her parliaments*. 'I owe these figures to Miss N. M. Fuidge. I have checked them.' But it must have been different in those earlier days. One of Neale's students, Elfreda Skelton, had written a doctoral thesis on the Court of Star Chamber, and Neale had married her. Another, Edna Bibby, had worked on Elizabethan Puritanism, but she had died in the year that I was born, 1929. It was her notes which were in those boxes, which Neale handed over to me on that October day of 1952. And, to house those boxes, I was given a room at the top of the UCL History Department.

In the fairy stories, good and bad fairies appear and present their gifts at baptismal ceremonies. I am not sure that my baptismal gift, the Bibby archive, was an altogether good gift. Ian Christie of the History Deparment was in no doubt that it was a bad gift. He chose to tell me so as we stood on the platform of a no. 77 bus, approaching Bush House, at the end of Kingsway. And of course he was right. It would never have occurred to me, in future years, to say to an incoming graduate student: 'Well, here is your subject. And, by the way, here is the better part of a thesis which someone else already wrote, and all the notes she collected.'

And yet Edna Bibby was invaluable. Putting it at its lowest, she secured for me that room. It was a room with secrets. There was a rolltop desk, and a drawer which

I could never open. At last, I succeeded. The drawer turned out to be full of the most compromising correspondence, letters written by Neale years before, and preserved in those purple mimeographed copies of yesteryear. Neale was head of the History Department at UCL for thirty-six years, and here was the evidence of what he had done to those of whom he chose to disapprove: E. R. Adair, a promising pupil of A. F. Pollard, Neale's own mentor, and in 1924 a fellow assistant in the UCL department; G. B. Harrison, a prolific Elizabethan historian sent off into outer darkness, or at least to North America. Shocked, and still innocent of such matters, I promptly closed the drawer. We are always being told of so and so that he (never she) is or was the last of the oldtime god professors. Whether or not he was the last, Neale was certainly archetypical in that respect. Once, standing in the urinals, where much serious business was transacted, he told the medievalist Frank Barlow that he would not be able to renew his appointment as an assistant lecturer. 'Nor Gash's, for that matter [Norman Gash, the historian of the life and times of Peel], although I can say to you what I could not say to Gash, that you are a good scholar.' Years later, when Professor Barlow presided over a committee to appoint a professor at the University of Exeter, I could not understand why I got such a frosty reception. I can understand why Neale was so detested by many in the profession, and not least by Sir Geoffrey Elton, who had been his pupil, and for whom hatred of Neale became an obsession, long after the old man was dead, shared with puzzled audiences not only in Cambridge but in New Zealand, where no one had ever heard of Neale. But I can only say that he was good to me, and that I was quite fond of him.

The Bibby legacy was more than that. She led me in directions which I would probably have found for myself, but quicker. And she had transcribed a huge Star Chamber case of 1591 which provided a large part of the evidence for my subject, and which would have taken many weeks to do on my own. She certainly did nothing to inhibit my own researches, which proceeded at a very rapid rate. I began to work as I had never worked before, or, perhaps, since. Mornings were spent in the old Public Record Office in Chancery Lane, with lunch at the LSE cafeteria; afternoons in the North Library at the British Museum, living with rare printed books of the sixteenth century, and in the Students' (which is to say Manuscript) Room. Those afternoons were very evocative, with a barrel organ playing in the fog outside, in Great Russell Street.

Early in this new life came the great killing smog of December 1952, when somehow or other I found my way from Muswell Hill to Liverpool Street Station and the train to Ipswich. That was the second of three man-assisted meteorological disasters to hit the British Isles in the six months from August 1952 to January 1953 (the first being Lynmouth); and each of them claimed more lives than any natural event since those few months. (Not everyone now remembers that.) The third came on Saturday 31 January, as the worst storm for centuries roared down from the north-west, overwhelming the ferry the *Princess Victoria* on her way across the North Channel, with the loss of 140 or so lives. I was at the London Zoo that afternoon with my girlfriend Maureen Bullen. It was certainly very windy, and on the way home we learned about the tragedy in the Irish Sea. That night the storm came down the east coast, drowning hundreds from Lincolnshire to Canvey Island, and 2,000 souls in Holland. By the Sunday afternoon, Cedric, Reg and I were in a house near Regents Park, helping the Women's Royal Voluntary Service to pack up parcels for the victims. The WRVS (unlike the Women's Institute) tended to be upper crust, and the ladies, ignoring us volunteers, talked about their bridge parties and 'my poor husband'. Walking back to Tavistock Square, Reg said: 'Quite honestly, some of those women were bitches.'

Back to the trivial round, the common task (which John Keble thought should furnish all we ought to ask). Teatime every day found me in the Institute, where the many students working on Tudor and Stuart topics converged to compare notes around the little tables, as they still do. On Mondays, Neale would come through the door, gleaming and beaming, and we would head for the five o'clock seminar. There was not much to be gained from those seminars unless you were working on Elizabethan parliaments, and even then half an hour could be spent on whether there were two or three MPs who shared the name Robert Johnson. Neale's lieutenant, Joel Hurstfield, sat beside him; S. T. Bindoff, who had recently left UCL for his chair at Queen Mary College, the author of that hardy best-seller, *Tudor England*, a little behind, but soon Bindoff absented himself altogether. And here is my chance to say that both Bindoff and Hurstfield were enormously helpful to me and to many others who had no formal claim on their time, far beyond the call of duty and of what the monetarist protocols of today's universities would permit.

Bindoff had his own seminar, which focused on economic and social matters, and where papers were read, as they were in R. H. Tawney's seminar, where I first read a paper of my own. It was necessary to attend the director's seminar, once a week. The director at that time was a kindly Welsh medievalist called Sir Goronwy Edwards. Once someone found himself in the director's native village and was told: 'Well yes, Goronwy has done very well for himself. But there is one thing for which the village will never forgive him. He left his old dad in the signal box.' At the director's seminar we learned that there are two kinds of historical evidence: written evidence and non-written, archaeological evidence. But I recall one piece of sound advice. 'Don't give your chapters fancy names, like "Bowing in the House of Rimmon."' We were taught palaeography by Francis Wormald, a great scholar. There was embarrassment at his first seminar, when a visiting, grey-headed American scholar was invited to read the first words of the Bible from a text in Carolingian minuscule. The words were as legible as if they had appeared in that day's newspaper. But, alas, the American knew no Latin.

After the seminar, I would do two or three hours in the England Room of the Institute, going through all the catalogues of the British Museum manuscript collections, and the reports of the Historical Manuscripts Commission, page by page. That way I missed almost nothing and to this day have a pretty comprehensive knowledge of the sources for Elizabethan religious history. Then, after a quick bite to eat, back to my room in UCL, where I would go over the day's findings until the wee hours.

This routine was only broken when I headed out of London to the Essex Record Office at Chelmsford, with its remarkable series of archdeaconry act books, or to Manchester, where the John Rylands Library housed Rylands English MS 874, the minutes and other papers of a conference of Puritan ministers meeting in and around Dedham in Essex in the 1580s, which, better late than never, three of us published in a very thorough scholarly edition in 2003. There were riches to be mined in Norwich, where the diocesan archives, recently returned from their wartime refuge in North Walsham, were all higgledy-piggledy in the chapel of the Bishop's Palace, looked after by Canon Williams. 'Yes', he would say, when you asked about the whereabouts of a rare act book of the Ecclesiastical Commission for the diocese. 'Yes, I do remember seeing it in one of these chests.' There was a good deal to do in my native Suffolk, especially in Woodbridge, where the three Redstone sisters kept house, and looked after the Seckford Library, which contained a treasure trove of transcripts by Lilian Redstone, a good Suffolk historian, and her father, the learned V. B. Redstone. There was an epiphany in the Record Office in Hertford, when I discovered an extensive correspondence between an obscure Puritan called Thomas Wood and Elizabeth's favourite of favourites, Robert Dudley, earl of Leicester, which revealed the extent and complexity of Leicester's dealings with the Puritans. This, more than anything else, made my name, and began to show me what my subject was really about, much more than a mere marginal irritant, an itchy spot, on the surface of the Elizabethan Church of England. I spent much time in that curious little time-warp, Dr Williams's Library, which is to be found along the pavement of Gordon Square, a few yards from the UCL History Department, and next door to the cathedral of the Catholic Apostolic, or Irvingite, Church, later the University of London Chaplaincy church of Christ the King. In Dr Williams's Library were the most important of all manuscript sources for the history of Elizabethan Puritanism, saved from oblivion by the late seventeenth-century dissenter Roger Morrice, whose interesting diary, more important in some respects than Pepys, is at last making him famous, three centuries after his death.

But there were holidays, which I began to spend in the big mountains. In 1953 it was the French Alps around St-Sorlin d'Arves, near St-Jean de Maurienne, where I led a party for the Ramblers Association (you got a free holiday that way), and nearly killed myself and the girl who was climbing with me on the Aiguilles d'Arves, which appeared to be made of rotten cheese, with boulders loosely embedded. A few days later, in the Aiguilles d'Argentière, above the Col du Croix de Fer (a notable stage in the Tour de France), a rock the size of a piano fell down the side of my leg and cracked the ankle bone. I was much criticized in the village. 'Il était blessé en la montagne. D'aller en la montagne sans guide, c'est pas sage.' 'Sans guide vous savez.' 'Pas sage! Et lui, le responsable!' (It has to be said that the guides of St-Sorlin d'Arves were by no means competent mountaineers.)

In the following summer, my friend Dick Marsh persuaded me to help him run a mountaineering holiday for boys of eighteen or nineteen, all graduates of the Outward Bound Mountain School in Eskdale, where Dick had been climbing instructor, some of them public school boys, others working class. There was a thinly concealed evangelical as well as social purpose, since Dick was on his way to becoming a clergyman. Around the camp fire at night he turned to evangelical advantage the story of how he and two friends called Thornley and Crace, with a team of sherpas led by one Tenzing, later of Everest fame, had tried to ascend Nanga Parbat in winter, where Thornley and Crace had died. I used Tenzing's ice axe. We started off in the Dauphiné and then, when the weather broke down, somehow got ourselves to Breuil (the boys all hitchhiked), on the Italian side of the Matterhorn, where we took parties up the Breithorn and then, literally the high point, Monte Rosa. In 1955 it was the Ramblers Association again, leading a group through those stupendous limestone mountains, the Julian Alps of Slovenia, where you can ascend or descend 2,000 feet, entirely on iron ladders and hanging on to wire ropes. Reg Jewkes and Dik van Arkel from the Centre came along for the ride. On the way home I stayed at St Gallen and saw Elisabeth Egli.

That was on a kind of rebound. In my early days at the Institute I dated a fellow student called Maureen Bullen, who was working on a topic in mid-nineteenth-century American history. Maureen was at Royal Holloway, as both an undergraduate and a postgraduate. My diary for early 1953 tells me how to find her: 7.24 from

26   Maureen Bullen (Lady Robson)

Waterloo, Egham at 8.0; bus from Egham Station arrives at the college at 8.9; Room West 302, far end of Corridor 2 and turn left. Most days we had lunch together, and I remember getting off the bus at Holborn tube to meet her and seeing the headlines announcing the death of Stalin. Soon we got engaged, which I assumed was what you did when a relationship began to develop in a promising way. I think that Maureen was always more sceptical about the whole thing than I was. 'When do you propose that this happy event should take place?', she once asked, reasonably enough, since neither of us had any immediate prospect of a job. I don't think that we were ready for that kind of commitment. But I went to the Antique Dealers' Fair and bought an exquisite late Georgian ring, set with slightly yellow diamonds. And there was a rather grisly little family party at 329 Norwich Road, to which my mother and Marjorie had moved after my father's death: the heavyweights of the family, Uncle Howard and Auntie Kathleen, in attendance. Many a Sunday afternoon was then spent at Elm Lodge, close to Maureen's college and, I suppose, mine, Royal Holloway. Maureen and her great friend, Rosemary Lund from Ulverston, as young women do, would be gassing on the rug in front of the gas fire in their twin-sets and pearls (Royal Holloway uniform in those days) while I – I'm afraid – worked, not far away.

On 21 August 1954 Maureen left to do her research in Washington and elsewhere in the States. Soon after Christmas, I went down to Southampton to meet her as she came off the *Queen Elizabeth*. We travelled back to London, and to the Centre. I am not sure quite what then happened, still less why it happened. On 27 December I had written a very ardent letter to Maureen c/o of the *Queen Elizabeth* at New York. I could not wait to see her. I still have the letter, which reached New York too late and was returned. But some time that night the engagement was broken off. We remained friends. Later Maureen married John Robson, another Cambridge contemporary, who had turned from late medieval history (a good book on John Wycliffe and Oxford philosophy) first to Spanish, or rather Catalan, history, and then to Latin American studies. John joined the Foreign Office, and had a career which included being in charge of the East Africa desk and ambassador in first Bogota and then Oslo. I am sure that Lady Robson is glad that that was how things worked out.

In the academic year 1954–5 I held one of the much-coveted research fellowships at the Institute of Historical Research, but spent most of the year in Ipswich, beginning to write my monstrous thesis. It was an interesting time for a quite different reason. The first migrants from the Caribbean were arriving in the town, the *Windrush* people. No one in Ipswich had ever seen black people before, except perhaps for the odd American serviceman during the war. Children in my sister Marjorie's Sunday School class told her that they were frightened. Two or three of us decided that something had to be done. We organized a dinner and persuaded various local ministers of religion, and even the mayor, to attend. And then we founded an Ipswich–Caribbean Friendship Association, the first function of which was to find the new arrivals accommodation. We made every mistake in the book, and were soon outwitted by a dodgy Jamaican called Fearon, who had his own, profitable, housing association. There was a death in mysterious circumstances. I believe that Fearon went to jail. We learned about the important difference between Jamaicans and small islanders.

The enterprise had its hilarious side. When we invited a man called Emmanuel Bradley to tea, with the intention of taking him on to Bethesda Church, my mother asked if he would first like to use the bathroom. He was gone for some time, and there was a noise of splashing. The water was stone cold, since my mother only put the immersion heater on once a week, for the statutory bath. Later Emmanuel got married, the first all-black wedding ever seen in Ipswich. He had another family in the West Indies, and people told us that while the marriage would be legal, they would not be coming. I acted as best man. Bethesda people were moved to tears by the spectacle. (Little did they know that the bride had interrupted her dressing to use the wash basin for an unusual purpose.) At the reception, laid out for forty guests, there were just six of us, but there were the usual speeches, and we finished up singing Sankey's *Sacred songs and solos* around an out-of-tune piano. Later I was photographed for the Shell house magazine, taking possession of some large steel drums which our club turned into an excellent steel band, which travelled around the country to village fetes and the like. The musicians were usually accompanied by a stout (in every sense) Quaker lady called Anne Porter, whom they would proudly introduce: 'This is our mistress.'

In October 1955 I became Sir John Neale's research assistant. The job mainly involved the slavish task of checking line by line the end-product of a lifetime's work on Elizabethan parliaments, the transcripts having been made by Helen Miller, who had preceded me. There was just one moment of excitement, when Neale sent me down to the British Museum to transcribe what turned out to be Queen Elizabeth's last speech to parliament, forgotten for 350 years. I was also given an essay class to teach, and soon realized that I knew very little about anything outside Elizabethan Puritanism. That is how you learn.

I acquired a motor cycle, found digs in Stoke Newington and began to help David Sheppard, the future bishop of Liverpool, in some of the pastoral work in that powerhouse of evangelical Anglicanism, St Mary's Islington, where he was serving as the curate. I took on a private pupil, Milo Bannerjee, who was progressing through the Higher School Certificate to, he hoped, a legal career, and whom I taught in a wretched room in Notting Hill which stank of joss sticks. Years later I heard his story. He had been forced into marriage with a cousin, a stranger who was in the last stages of TB, and who soon died. He wanted to become a lawyer only to get his revenge on the uncle who had done this to him. I remained in touch with Milo for some years, and he once told me that I was 'the only friend he ever had'.

And then I met Esther Moir, who was finishing her Cambridge doctoral thesis on local government in eighteenth-century Gloucestershire. Esther (as Esther de Waal) is best known these days for her writing on the monastic tradition, in particular the Rule of St Benedict, which has taken her to many parts of the world to conduct retreats for monastic communities. But she was and is passionately committed to local history. Indeed, it was a place and its buildings, Canterbury, which were responsible for her interest in Benedictine spirituality; and the landscape of the Welsh borders, where she grew up and now lives, which drew her to work on the Celtic past. After a fourth year at Cambridge, Esther became the first research student in the famous Department of English Local History at Leicester, under her mentor, H. P. R. Finberg. That introduction to non-verbal historical evidence has played a vital *rôle* in all that she has written since, from *The Discovery of Britain: the early English travellers 1540–1840* to her most recent book, which explores the art of seeing, of awareness. After twenty-five years of writing on spirituality (fifteen books) Esther is reverting to her name of Moir and to her earlier interests as a local historian. It was thanks to Esther that another name to conjure with in that field, Margaret Spufford, author of a little classic, *Contrasting communities*, found that she too had an unstoppable vocation in that same microcosmical direction. It happened on a rainy night in Cambridge when Margaret came into a room where Esther was lecturing.

I was Esther's contemporary in Cambridge and was one of many to have admired her fabled Pre-Raphaelite looks. But a chance encounter (was it in the British Museum Reading Room – my version of events – or in a lunch queue at the School of Oriental and African Studies – hers?) led to visits to her flat in Kensington (late night dashes across London on the motorbike, back to Stoke Newington) and then, presently, to Esther's home at Ross-on-Wye, where her father was a vicar, just outside the town. Later Esther would come to stay at 1a Kitchener Road, the little house which my mother had now built for herself in the garden of 329 Norwich Road. With a father coming from an evangelical tradition and used as a child to morning prayers at the table after breakfast, Esther enjoyed being part of the daily routine of readings from the Bible and *Daily Light*, with prayers for the Muslim world; visits with flowers to tbe cemetery where my father was buried; and singing hymns with gusto in Bethesda Chapel.

I was present when Esther took her Ph.D. in the Senate House at Cambridge in record time (exactly three years), and the next day I took her back to London on the back of the bike. Just after Christmas, Esther and her sister Meriel came with me to North Wales, staying at the climbing hut called Glan Dena, which sits below the north ridge of Tryfan. We climbed on the east face of Tryfan, and then I took Esther up a climb called Flying Buttress on Craig yr Isfa in the Carneddau, taxing in winter conditions, at least for us. What happened on those days sent me back to London in high excitement, which I shared with the Centre crowd when we celebrated New Year's Eve by going to the cinema to see *The lady killers*.

The year 1956 would prove to be an extraordinary one, I suppose the most memorable of any that I have lived through. In the early months, Esther and I went every Sunday evening to the Raphael Cartoon Room at the V & A. Rosalyn Tureck was playing Bach, following her triumph at Edinburgh in 1955, where for the first time she had performed the Goldberg Variations on the piano. At Easter Esther, Meriel and I went to the Climbers Club hut at Bosigran in West Penwith, climbing above the Atlantic rollers on good Cornish granite. On the way down to Cornwall the sun was hitting a red Devon field, and I said that that was the most beautiful sight since the creation of the world, which led to a conversation about existentialism. In June we crashed the motorbike at Nine Elms power station, coming back from the Battersea Pleasure Gardens. But neither of us was seriously hurt.

At first, Esther had not intended that our affair should last for ever. There had been a musical boyfriend, which meant that we got free tickets to the Tureck recitals. Then there was someone who had taught her to catch salmon in the Wye. I was the rockclimbing boyfriend. There was a walk beside the river at Ross when Esther tried, very gently, to bring things to an end, perhaps while there was still time. But I could not take no for an answer, and so it was for another three years of a far from casual relationship.

What was to happen next? Without any doubt, I was Sir John Neale's blue-eyed boy. When he came into the Institute tea room with me, he put his arm over my shoulder, with difficulty, since I was about eight inches taller than he was. But could I get a job? I was interviewed up and down the land for assistant lectureships, always with the same result. It took me some time to realize that it was not necessarily helpful to be Neale's blue-eyed boy. And I interviewed very, very badly. At Liverpool, the medievalist Geoffrey Barraclough, having explained how utterly hopeless his students were and how could I bear to teach them, asked what my research methods were. Coming from the severely empirical London school, I had no idea what method was; and simply answered that I had tried to look at everything which was remotely relevant to my subject, which was the truth.

Joel Hurstfield was offered a chair of Economic History at that same university and was in two minds what to do about it. He wrote two letters, one of acceptance, one of rejection, and walked twice around the block before posting the letter of rejection. So he stayed at University College, later holding Neale's chair, the Astor Chair of English History. If he had gone to Liverpool I think that there is little doubt but that I would have been given a job at UCL and, who knows, might have been there ever since.

I applied for an assistant lectureship at the University College of Rhodesia and Nyasaland (salary £950), and for the post of Assistant for Further Education in Ipswich (£710); and I thought about the Civil Service. The crunch came at Birmingham in June 1956. I was the favoured candidate. But when I was asked whether I would be prepared to transfer my research interests from England to continental Europe I answered no, and the job went to a friend called Bob Knecht, who had despaired of an academic career and had worked for a time for an outfit supplying pubs with historical decor. But Bob was to stay the course at Birmingham, becoming one of the leading historians of sixteenth-century France and the biographer of Francis I. At first, at least, I think that I came off best. A year later I returned from Khartoum, where I had had all sorts of adventures and, in between, had enjoyed a hectic social life. By then, Bob had been invited out for one cup of coffee.

Khartoum? Why Khartoum? There was nothing left but Khartoum, which is to say the infant University of Khartoum, once University College Khartoum (in 'special relationship' with the University of London, and, before that, Gordon College). I had a meeting with Dame Lilian Penson, a great power in the land in London, and in the emergent African universities. 'Go to Khartoum, Mr Collinson', she said. 'Take a risk. Look at Michael Grant, he's taking a risk.' Now Michael Grant had just been appointed the first vice-chancellor of the University of Khartoum. His risk had been to take a two-year secondment from the University of Edinburgh, where he was Professor of Ancient History. And after two years he would return to Edinburgh, only to become vice-chancellor of the Queen's University Belfast. As vice-chancellor of Khartoum (and I have served under a dozen vice-chancellors and principals) Grant was hopeless. He only visited the Faculty of Arts once, and he only gave one lecture, which was on the future of university education in the Sudan. We were never entertained at his residence, which was known as 'The Nineteenth Embassy', at a time when there were eighteen foreign legations in Khartoum. He seemed to be reliving his days at the embassy in Ankara, in the Second World War.

When the critical decision was about to be taken, Esther wrote a long letter at midnight. Her sister, Meriel, was begging me not to go to Khartoum. 'She says there will always be jobs in second-rate and dangerous spots, and you're not to rush at the first one which crops up.' Esther was of the same mind. 'Your work is good, it really is, so different from most of the stuff that's turned out of the academic mill. You've been given a good brain – it would be rather like betraying a trust not to use it to its fullest capacity, which I'm sure you wouldn't in Khartoum.' She said that I really ought to be a Tudor historian. 'Anyone has only to read a page or two of your work to see that you really have a grasp of the age.' And then, rather plaintively, knowing I was about to encounter the formidable Dame Lilian: 'If you do see the Dame could you tell her there's *me*.' My Cambridge teacher Norman Sykes offered the same advice: 'I should be inclined not to accept Khartoum if offered.'

However, Khartoum it was: Assistant Lecturer in History, salary £1,000. Given my family history, the things I had written about Egypt at seven years of age for 'The Prayer Club for Adults', and my more recently acquired interest in Africa, my disposition was far from negative. But Professor Neale concluded that this was indeed the end and said, in effect, that it had been nice knowing me. Expatriates teaching in Khartoum had a sense not so much of crossing the Rubicon as of having passed that bourn from which there is no return. There was an open-air night club called the Gordon Cabaret. And there we witnessed the spectacle of well-built Hungarian girls, kicking up enormous thighs, sheathed in black boots. It was clear that these women were at the end of the line, with nowhere else to go, and so, it appeared, were we. Gordon, after all, had gone to Khartoum on a one-way ticket.

But before Khartoum there was the visit to London of 'B. and K.', Bulganin and Khrushchev. I stood in the crowd outside No. 10 as the Russian leaders emerged

27 With Esther Moir at Fred and Dorothy's cottage at Stow Maries, summer 1956

with Anthony Eden. Someone called out three times in a loud voice: 'Tovarich!' I don't think Eden was the comrade addressed. And then Harold Macmillan came dashing up the road to No. 11 to pick up something he had forgotten. Eden was about to invade Egypt, and Khruschev to put down the Hungarian Revolution.

Then came the Alpine season of 1956. I started off with Dick Marsh and a broadcaster called John Earle. We began at Saas Fée with a stiff climb up the south ridge of the Lagginhorn: a difficult descent over ice, a fifteen-hour day! A letter from Esther told that David Sheppard had made 113 in the test, England 459 in the first innings, the Australians 84 and following on. (Those were the days!) Then came the Allalinhorn, and an attempt on the Rimpfischorn, frustrated by an uncrossable bergschrund. Back at the Britannia Hut I read Dostoevsky's *The idiot* 'and got very painfully burned doing so.' And so on to Zermatt, from which we made it to the summit of the Zinal Rothorn. Twice we broke off to drive some distance to take photos of the graves of climbing friends: Tom Bourdillon (one of the 1953 Everest party) and Dick Viney, secretary of the Climbers Club, killed in the Bernese Oberland; and a friend of Dick's, Andrew Cleland, who had fallen off a trivial little hill in Zinal.

Then Dick left and, on 9 August, Esther arrived, and we went up first the Breithorn ('the coldest I've been on a mountain') and then the Dufurspitze on Monte Rosa, my second visit to that second highest summit in the Alps. 'Esther did exceptionally well.' How fit we were in those days! In one day we went up the mountain from the Bétemps Hut, perhaps 6,000 feet, back to the Bétemps, and straight on down the Gornergletscher and Gornergrat to Zermatt, where we were not too late for a concert of Bach's violin partitas. I was home by 16 August, and preaching in a small Baptist church in Aldeburgh on 19 August. On 28 August Esther and I were at the Oval for

28   Esther on the Breithorn, August 1956

the final Test of 1956: Sheppard, Compton and Peter May, with whom I had shared supervisions at Pembroke. My diary tells me: 'May declared too late.'

Down in Zermatt, the English newspapers had told us that political storm clouds were gathering. Eden was not going to let Gemal Abdel Nasser get away with it. Esther wrote, on the eve of joining me in the Alps: 'I'll bring you out some news about Suez. You seem forced to live a life of imminent danger. Surely you won't be going out will you if they're evacuating British from Egypt?' Back in England, and driving up to North Wales for a last weekend in my favourite hills, the roads were full of military vehicles. But I was 'going out'.

9

First Taste of the Waters of the Nile

In September 1956 I was kitted out with the essentials for a life in Khartoum: a black tin trunk, some baggy shorts, long socks to the knee – and a black silk cummerbund. When I boarded the plane on 27 September it was the first time I had ever been on a commercial flight. It was a BOAC Superconstellation, on its way to Australia with many emigrating families and several athletes bound in their blazers for the Melbourne Olympics, including an English star of those years, Gordon Pirie, who gave me his autograph on the tarmac at Rome Airport. At Cairo, with a brief glimpse of the pyramids at Sakkarah, I transferred to a Sudan Airways Dakota and headed south. In mid-afternoon we stopped at Wadi Halfa, on the borders of Egypt and the Sudan. I shall never forget the first experience of that heat, coming at you with such solid mass that you could slice it, or what my diary calls 'oven-door gusts'. And then, there below, was Omdurman, its thousands of little dun-coloured houses, each with its courtyard and women's quarters, the 'hosh'. And there was the junction of the two Niles, the Blue and the White.

A senior colleague and old Sudan hand, Alan Theobald, met me at the airport, where you passed under a sign which said 'Welcome to the Sudan: Paradise for Hunters'. (We used to say that it depended what you were hunting.) Soon I was installed in the Grand Hotel, on the banks of the Nile, where the vendors of souvenirs would say, if they suspected that Germans were coming along the verandah: 'Bismarck good! Hitler, very very good!' I wrote to Esther, stretching my prosaic rather than poetic soul to its limits in describing those so important first impressions. 'The air is full of hundreds of wheeling kites, and storks and ibises fly across ceaselessly. Night comes suddenly and beautifully, with opal lights on the Nile and a sudden storm of insect life.'

Air travel, even then, was too fast, and I had only half arrived. I sat on the verandah, writing the next chapter of my thesis. Esther had urged my mother to make sure that I finished it. But I needed no prompting. I was determined to submit when I went back on leave in the summer of 1957, which I did, although it involved working through the stiflingly hot afternoons in that first year, when most people were asleep. But how strange to be sorting out the affairs of Puritan preachers in Elizabethan Suffolk when surrounded by so many exotic things: geckoes climbing up the walls in pursuit of praying mantises, camel spiders scuttling across the floor, the ceiling fan whirring, so that you had to put stones on all loose papers, genet cats in the roof and mongooses on the lawn, and outside abdin storks nesting in the palms; once a Nile monitor, first in my garden and then in the bath, scattering empty beer bottles with its tail; the people coming and going in their turbans and long white jellabeyas, walking or jogging up and down on the rumps of donkeys.

I was given a little house, one of a number of ex-army billets attached to a place called the Pink Palace, built by a religious leader of Indian origin on the bank of the

29 A carefully arranged group of students at the University of Khartoum: three women, one southerner, one Greek

Blue Nile close to the Power Station, at a suburban village called Burri, and occupied by the Emperor Haile Selassie on the eve of the invasion of Ethiopia in 1941. There was a squash court, where we played under lights at ten or eleven o'clock at night. The lights were full of dry debris, which used to catch fire. The smell of that would bring it all back. Early days were spent in expeditions to the furniture makers of Omdurman, where everything had to be made to order; and in acquiring a personal servant. I ordered a bed, two armchairs, a settee, a desk, a table, some occasional tables and verandah armchairs, to be delivered in ten days: total cost, £50. Mohi el Din, a Nubian from Dongola in the north, would do everything for me for the next five years. Everything included washing a good tweed suit in cold water and hanging it on the line inside out, to the consternation of a more experienced suffragi, whom I can still see running out of the house next door. But to this day I am gripped by guilt about Mohi. I paid him so little: £2 a week. I hardly knew where or how he and his wife and little son lived. The Sudan in 1956 had just become a republic, independent of both Britain and Egypt. Some of us took a Guardian-reading pride in the fact that we were not living and working in a colony. I made a point of not joining the Sudan Club, with its membership still restricted to Britishers.

But our way of life was still essentially colonial. I wrote to Esther: '*Nearly all* the English people here, *including* University staff, are not interested in the country or its people, and are living a closed, community, "club" life.' We had little enough to do with the Sudanese, even though half our colleagues were nationals. Those of us who tried to bridge the gap were called 'White Sudanese', and we were obviously currying favour in the hope of hanging on to our jobs. You were not expected to queue in the bank or the Post Office. I learned only a smattering of Arabic, enough to get by in the suq. (We lectured and taught in English.) There was a great deal of entertaining, hence the cummerbund, but it consisted of expatriates entertaining each other. I remember the wife of the Professor of Agriculture inviting me to dinner and explaining, to my relief, that the occasion would be informal: since, she said, it's not yet the Season. The university had a swimming pool, the property of the Students' Union, which the families of expatriates were allowed to use on one afternoon a week. Once we took it over for an evening party: a barbecue, some beer. Soon an angry crowd of the more conservative Muslim students gathered to protest. We explained that we had had permission to use the pool. 'Yes, but we didn't know that this would be an immoral party, with wine and women.' After that there were three kinds of parties: formal, informal and immoral.

The University of Khartoum, which shared its birthday with the Republic of the Sudan, had at that time some 1,200 students: all but forty or fifty of them northern Sudanese, Arabic-speaking Muslims. (More recently the university has contained 17,000 undergraduate students, 6,000 postgraduates, and has a staff of more than a 1,000.) The ablest students, certainly in tackling what we had to teach, were the minority of Christian, mission-educated southerners, whose English was excellent. Once a northern student in a class of five asked me for the loan of a book. I explained that I had already given it to one Hilary Nygilio Paul, later minister of labour in that rarity, a democratically elected civilian government. 'Who?' he said. 'Hilary Paul.' 'Oh', he said, 'you mean that *abd*.' Now *abd* means slave, and here was the tragic history of that country for the next fifty years in embryo. (I recall a Sudanese colleague, a man with a Ph.D., commenting on a photo of a southerner casting a net into the river. 'There you see what imperialism has done to my country. That man has no clothes to wear and he has to fish for fish.') Once, at the annual open day at the Students' Union, a southern law student called Abel Alier Kuai was due to make a speech but at the last moment pulled out, because he had little or no Arabic, to the derision of the student body. Later in the evening, Abel offered to fetch me a drink. By the time he came back with a coke I was chatting with a group of northern students. He sized up the situation and slipped away. Later Abel Alier would be vice-president of the Sudan, from 1971 to 1982. He was well named. Everyone who knows the country will acknowledge that he is one of the most able and distinguished Sudanese of his generation. In 2005 he played a part in the talks which brought peace to the Southern Sudan.

All but thirty of the students were men, with the few women housed in a special hostel, presided over by a firm-minded, middle-aged English woman, Nancy Moller, whom I helped to bury when, some years later, she died of the worst form of hepatitis. The girls dressed in the traditional tobe, which hid the face almost as effectively as the Afghan barka. When they took off their tobes in the science labs (they might, after all, catch fire from the bunsen burners), there was a student strike. We taught from seven in the morning until nine, and then, after breakfast, until two o'clock. Life resumed after five, with some early evening classes. We lectured rather slowly (or tried to – something I have never been able to achieve – 'you are lecturing too fast', I would be told) so that our words could be taken down and later served back to us in the examinations: rote learning, in a subject which we tried in vain to explain was one of selection, debate, emphasis, negotiation. Once, when I said that Marx had to be taken seriously, the students wrote 'marks'; and knew that to be true.

The male students, who wore a uniform of white shirts and grey trousers, changing into the more comfortable jellabeya when off campus, were on a conveyer belt which had brought them from their secondary schools to the university and would assure them a job in the administration of their country. They could not have been less entrepreneurial, or even ambitious, and certainly they were incurious. But they did constitute a fourth, perhaps a third estate. There was always a strike, towards the end of the second term (the academic year ran from July until March), which in my first year was directed at ridding the university of its remaining expatriate administrators – Michael Grant, the vice-chancellor, the registrar, the finance officer, 'imperialists' all three. These strikes were supported by 97 per cent of the students, with only a few medics, the elite of the campus, failing to comply. Once I entertained some students to tea. They left with fulsome thanks, saying that they had to get to a meeting at the Students' Union, but not telling me what the meeting was about. The next day I cycled in as usual to give my seven o'clock lecture, only to find the room empty. When faced with a student strike, the ultimate weapon in the hands of authority was to hand the students their railway warrants, since fathers would want to know what they were doing, coming home out of time, and would beat them to within an inch of their lives. But, a year or two after my time, student politics had its moment of glory when the army invaded the campus and there were some martyr deaths. That led to the capitulation of a military government, perhaps the only time in modern African politics when a ruling army has voluntarily gone back to its barracks.

I had been recruited to teach a course in English Economic History, which had been in the hands of Mr Wilsher, the principal of the University College, Wilsher having gone back to England to become a registrar somewhere. I was not an economic historian, so, still in London, I had gone to seek the advice of Professor Jack Fisher of the LSE, who was. Fisher told me to acquire the three volumes of Clapham's *Economic history of England*, which I did. But I tried to bring the subject alive with plenty of original documents, and pictures of bits and pieces of the industrial revolution, canals, railways, dark satanic mills. Once, when I had been explaining the open-field system of medieval agriculture, a student asked: 'Are you describing the system which is still to be seen at Laxton in Nottinghamshire?' Somewhat taken aback I said, yes, I was. Abd el Rahman, the son of a wealthy trader in trochas shells (from which shirt buttons are made), with whom I later stayed in Port Sudan, had done a year at the Regent Street Polytechnic and had been on a field trip to Laxton.

But such moments were rare. Mekki Shibeika, the Professor of History, explained that when I arrived the students would have reached 'The Decline of The Villeinage'. These words, including the definite articles, were written in letters of stone. Once I was supervising an examination in which the last question had to do with the decline of English agriculture after 1870. The students had been warned to ignore the last two or three questions on the paper, since the usual strike had prevented us getting that far. But one candidate beckoned me over and, pointing to that question, asked: 'Is this the decline of the villeinage?' I could only hiss '1870, not 1370'.

In that first year, no one paid much attention to my lectures, and I eventually discovered why. I was in the university store, collecting a new bed or something of the kind. And there were all Mr Wilsher's mimeographed lecture notes on English Economic History, perpetuating the hoary old myths which my lectures had been designed to dispel. They were still being handed out to students on demand. Clearly the lectures of this newly appointed and very junior member of staff were of less authority. Later, I taught Medieval European History and modern British Constitutional History, and even African History, with a little more success.

There was an exotic experience, early on in my time: the annual Mulid, the birthday of the Prophet. For several days a medan in Omdurman, ten times the size of Trafalgar Square, became a vast religious fair, with every variety of Sudanese Islam on display, entertaining all comers, There were sufis, squatting in a circle and working themselves into a kind of trance by endless repetition of 'Allah', groups of Ahmadiya whose dances were frenzied, poets extolling the virtues of the Prophet, while people closed their eyes and held their hands in the air. The two principal Sudanese *turuq* (singular *tariq* is often translated 'sect', but is much more than that), which were the Ansar, followers of the Mahdi, and the Khatmia, whose leader was the Sayedd Ali el Mirghani, held court in lavish carpeted pavilions, where we honoured foreign guests (the two of us were the only Europeans to be seen) were seated and served with refreshments. Sayedd Abdel Rahman el Mahdi, the son of the original Mahdi, had only just left. 'We are very honoured that you sit in our pavilion. Abdel Rahman el Mahdi shall be told that professors from the University, you who teach our country, have sat in his seat.' Outside there were a million electric light bulbs, flaring gas jets, dense clouds of dust, an enormous noise and pink sugar dolls for the children to buy. I wrote: 'Imagine the Arabian Nights, the Field of the Cloth of Gold, and Battersea Pleasure Gardens, all rolled into one.'

Later I became private tutor to the son and heir of el Mirghani, spiritual leader of five million people, the Sayedd Mohammed Osman el Mirghani. Nowadays Mohammed Osman is himself the leader of the *tariq*, and of its political expression, the Democratic Unionist Party. He enjoys an uneasy relationship with the current military regime of General Omar al-Bashir, the National Islamic Front; for a time in exile in Egypt, then leader of a widespread insurgency called the National Democratic Alliance, but later persuaded to change sides. I wrote to Esther about my distinguished pupil: 'This will be equivalent to teaching the pope's son, if there were two popes, and one of them had a son.' The family had bought a special house in the suburbs for his lessons, furnished Second Empire style, but otherwise austere, 'like the vestry of a very opulent nonconformist chapel, lacking only the portraits of former pastors on the walls'. Three times a week I was driven to the house in a Cadillac, and with the utmost formality taught the young man modern European History, in preparation for the Higher School Certificate. His somewhat outdated textbooks were ceremoniously carried in by a servant. I always felt sorry for Mohammed Osman, who was dressed in a traditional costume and never went anywhere; whereas his opposite numbers in the Mahdist family had gone to British universities and wore European dress.

Everyone knows what happened in November 1956: Suez. The day when we bombed the Egyptian airfields saw the formal opening of the Students' Union, with much of the government present. The fun consisted, for the students, in noting the errors made in the speeches delivered in classical Arabic, with which they all had difficulties. Professor Grant, who knew no Arabic, had to listen to a fiery denunciation in that language of Israel and Britain, and then respond. Several students asked me: 'Does Eden mean it? Will he do it?' I assured them that it was most unlikely. But, back at the Pink Palace, BBC World Service announced the first attacks. All through that night, I imagined that I could hear the mobs coming out to Burri to get me.

As it happened, we were in no danger and there was no need, as there was in

30   Khartoum University Students' Union, November 1956, hours before the RAF
bombed Egyptian airfields

other Arab countries, to take measures to ensure our safety. Our students were more
icily polite than usual, even while they were undergoing military training as volunteers. Only once did someone turn round from the saddle of his bike to shout abuse
at me. Down town there were demonstrations all day, schoolboys marching past the
fixed bayonets in front of the British embassy shouting 'Down Eden! Down Eden!
Down Eden!' Cycling home at whatever hour, one had to pass the armed sentries
now guarding the Burri Power Station, and often you heard the click as safety
catches were released. But the expatriate community in the university was bitterly
divided. If the Suez Canal divided the drawing room at No. 10 Downing Street it
also split the little office which I shared with a Welsh lecturer in English, who was
as bullish in his support of the venture as was his hero, Aneurin Bevan. Some of
us wrote a letter to the *Manchester Guardian*, in which we reported how mistaken
the whole thing seemed to be, from where we stood. Later we found that our names
were on a white list at the Egyptian embassy, and I got a visa to go to Egypt when
few other Britishers were so lucky. My diary for 9 January 1957 has, in capitals:
'EDEN RESIGNED'. It must have been a desperately worrying time for my mother,
since my sister Hilda was a missionary nurse in Nazareth and my brother Bernard
and his wife were missionaries in the mountains of Kabylia, in Algeria.

   At Christmas 1956 some of us went carol-singing from door to door, and we were
invited in to drinks by the British ambassador, whose name was Sir Edwin Chapman

Andrews. I found myself standing beside His Excellency, and remarked that he must have been having a difficult time. 'Yes', he said, 'but thank God we had a first class prime minister.' He did not mean Anthony Eden but Abdullah Khalil, prime minister of the Sudan. The local cinemas had shown films which purported to contain proof that hundreds of Allied aircraft had been shot down. A Sudanese colleague, a man with a Ph.D., asked me why we persisted when we had lost 700 planes and 30,000 men? The newsreels were from the Second World War, and Chapman Andrews got them withdrawn by threatening to put on a film show of his own. Abdullah Khalil's government successfully resisted moves in parliament by the pro-Egyptian opposition to have all British government employees (which meant us) expelled from the country, and we had been warned to be ready to leave at any time.

Early the following year, my own Ipswich MP, Dick Stokes, came to the Sudan. He was that specimen unknown in the politics of any other country: a Roman Catholic, the largest employer of labour in the town and a socialist. He was also a great friend of the Arab nations, where he did much business. But Stokes took the opportunity of his visit to tell an audience gathered at the Sudan Cultural Club that Egypt had lost very badly in the Suez War and must face facts. I admired his courage, especially when he was challenged, at excessive length, by one of our more militant students. Stokes bellowed: 'Shut up! You've had a jolly good innings. Now let me have a go.' He had a stentorian voice, which was just as well, since a few yards away the provost of the cathedral, George Martin, was ringing the cathedral bells for evensong, as he did every day, although only he would be present to say the office. Within a few months Stokes was dead, and we had a by-election in Ipswich, in which my mother reluctantly cast my absentee vote for the Labour candidate, Dingle Foot, who won.

Before Christmas I had had the first of many unforgettable adventures in the Sudan beyond Khartoum, so inaccessible unless you possessed the right kind of vehicle. Two or three of us attached ourselves to a medical expedition headed for the upper reaches of Blue Nile Province, the aim of which was to investigate that killer disease, kalaazar. The medical students were a tonic, so much more sophisticated and well read than our Arts students. As we bumped along, enveloped in dust, it was possible to have conversations about the novels of André Gide. But, outside our truck, was the real Sudan: villages of grass-roofed tukls with women fetching water, no longer veiled; flocks of carmine bee-eaters, catching insects in the smoke and flame of grass fires; on one occasion, a whole tribe of camel-breeders, who gave us warm camel milk to drink, freshly drawn. And then we came into a country where the economy consisted of picking wild gum from the acacia trees, a labour performed by a nomadic tribe whose whole life was cattle, the men dancing to the simulated noise of bulls, cows and calves, made with their hands. Now you would not come across such things in Birmingham. Europe's storks spend their winters in this region, and we saw a flock of many thousands. Often we were stuck in deep sand drifts. I hunted butterflies with a net, to the amusement of a delightful Sudanese dentist who for some reason was part of our expedition. He called me the great white hunter.

At last we reached our destination, not far from the Ethiopian border, which was the Ingessana Hills, a little lost world in the crater of an ancient volcano, inhabited by blue-black and thoroughly exotic Africans, dressed in little more than beads, some of them (then, perhaps no longer) riding white Abyssinian ponies, bare-back, armed with spears and swords (or throwing knives) of a distinctive and unique design.[1] They did not call themselves Ingessana, which was a corrupt form of an Arabic word meaning, more or less, 'absolute bastards'. They certainly had nothing good to say about their Arabic-speaking neighbours, the Fung, heirs of the once powerful Sultanate of Sennar. The Ingessana name for themselves is *jok gam*, people of the hills. The names of the two little settlements from which the area was administered, Wisko and Soda, were perhaps a joke of the colonialists. (Soda was a genuinely indigenous name, but 'Wisko' was more properly Bau.) But there was more to Wisko and Soda than administrative convenience. No one from Wisko would marry anyone from Soda. There were in fact four distinct districts, and peoples, in this country of 250 square miles and 40,000 inhabitants, divided by blood and dialect. Once, up a dried-up river bed, I caused more hilarity, this time to a courting couple of young Ingessana, as I still pursued my butterflies. For that matter all the Ingessana regarded us with tolerant amusement. Since we carried no weapons, we were obviously slaves.

We learned a little about the people: about the clubs for unmarried girls and boys, where everything goes except penetrative sex – much as in sixteenth-century France; how young men (like Jacob in the Bible) must serve their future fathers-in-law for two or more years before marrying, and how, after marriage, a complicated and extended set of rituals, involving at one point the blood of slaughtered pigs, the bridegroom's friends, or kin, have first access to the bride. (Both husband and wife shave their heads, and do not meet again until the hair renews.) We were told that the Ingessana are monotheists, believing that God inhabits a large hill in the centre of their region, although Wisko and Soda naturally had different gods, living in different hills. But the religion which impinged on their lives was centred on shrines or 'houses of god' erected within the circle of the homestead, a cult closely associated with dead ancestors.

The climax of our visit came with two or three nights of dancing. At the full moon the young women formed a circle around a musician, playing a five-stringed lyre. There were other instruments, including flutes, the kind of rhythm sticks played with the shoulder bones, and an enormous elephant tusk. The strong and infectious beat was produced, not with the hands, which were never clapped, but by feet stamping on the bare earth, which accompanied the singing. The hair was elaborately braided and decorated, and there was a strong smell of mutton fat, with which the girls' bodies were smeared. Stravinsky would have loved it, although there was no climactic sacrifice. I think that it was the first time that this scene had been photographed and the music recorded. I still have the photos, and the recordings. Through a policeman interpreter, our students were able to tell us what the songs were about: for the most part spiteful attacks on the reputations of many of those present, but including lyrics as inscrutable as these:

The women came walking.
They ran away and became shy.
Swarms of locusts appeared and fell like rain.
Shut, shut, shut, shut, she, sh. sh. sh.

---

[1]   This brief account of the Ingessana relies on my own experience and imperfect memories of fifty years ago. But I have compared and corrected these with the aid of a more authoritative anthropological study by M. C. Jedrej, *Ingessana: the religious institutions of a people of the Sudan-Ethiopia borderland* (Leiden, 1995).

Eva the werewolf, flew high, turning from side to side like a buffalo-hide shield.
And he became the wild eagle.
Shut, shut, shut, shut, sh, sh, sh.
Garret went to the field and he cut the *onkoleib* [a kind of millet] and he put it on
the ground. When Garret went back to the *onkoleib* the women found him and he
turned into the wolf of God.
The maiden went to the khor and she brought water and the maiden became old
and she walked on the swords.

I shall be glad to hear from any anthropologist who can decipher these arcane
texts, which had probably never been recorded before. I wrote about 'a cloud of dust
in the middle of an anonymous plain ringed with fantastic hills in a part of Africa
no-one has ever heard of'.

Throughout the epoch known as the 'Inglesiya' the Ingessana had been a closed
district, to both Christian missionaries and Muslim traders, a kind of anthropological game park. But now the traders were there in force, using the debts which the
local people inevitably incurred to gain access, under an abuse of tradition, to the
women. As we watched the dancing, they tapped the girls on the shoulder with their
canes and asked our students whether they wanted any of them. Already some of the
men had been persuaded to put on long white jellabeyas. I hope that the programme
of Islamization failed, and perhaps it did, since in recent years representatives from
the Ingessana people have walked for weeks to reach meetings of the National
Democratic Front, at war with the Sudanese government, in the strongholds of the
Liberation Army in the South. From the fastness of their hills, the Ingessana have
practised for generations what has been called 'a culture of resistance'. But there
can be no doubt that the National Islamic Front, which has dominated and complicated the politics of Sudan in the 1980s and 1990s, above all in Darfur, will have
oppressed the Ingessana no less severely than the non-Arabic peoples of the Nuba
Mountains, in Sudan's Mid West.

One of the advantages of working for the University of Khartoum was that you
were entitled to three months of leave in the Long Vacation, corresponding to the
holidays enjoyed by the old Sudan Civil Service, and you were given an air ticket
back to your home base. By paying a little more, you could divert your journey
through any part of the Mediterranean world which took your fancy. Arriving in
England in April, there was time for a couple of months of research and a holiday (in
my case, of course, a climbing holiday) before returning to Khartoum for the next
session in July: by which time you had forgotten the names of your students, who
were all called Ahmed Mohammed Ahmed, or Mohammed Ahmed Mohammed, or
Ahmed Ahmed Mohammed.

In early April 1957 I flew to Rome, and from Rome I took a train to Perugia
and was reunited with Esther, who had driven down to Italy in her faithful Hillman
Husky with her friend Jill Regan. We set off on a tour of Umbria and Tuscany:
from Perugia via Cortona to Arezzo, where we saw the great Piero della Francesca
frescoes, and on to Sansepolcro, Piero's birthplace, and later to Urbino. On Palm
Sunday we were in Assisi: banners and incense in the great basilica, mens' and boys'
voices singing Palestrina, setting off the Giottos; from there an excursion to Orvieto,
with its startling fresco of the Last Things, Fra Angelico and Signorelli. We were
always looking over the valley of the upper Tiber, which makes the backcloth to so
many of those paintings. Urbino was unforgettable; and there were more Pieros,

the Montefeltro portraits and the flagellation of Christ, the world of Castiglione's *Il Cortegiano*. We ended up in Florence, and the Uffizi, where the hordes of German tourists were no problem, since we were interested in the early rooms: Cimabue, Simone Martini and, above all, the Gentile de Fabriano Adoration of the Magi; in the afternoon, Sante Croce. Some people go back to Tuscany over and over again. This was almost my only visit, and I shall never forget it. I left Esther in Italy and flew to Paris and on to London. When we got to Mont Blanc, in what I suppose must have been perfect conditions, the pilot flew twice around the mountain, a little below the summit. That would not happen today.

In London I lodged with Cedric Lazaro in his basement flat in Gosfield Street, just behind the BBC and next door to the place to which Aneurin Bevan returned nightly from the House. Esther was now in a bijou flat across the road from Primrose Hill, very close to my beloved Zoo, 6 Albert Terrace. We saw *The cabinet of Dr Caligari* twice, at the Everyman at Hampstead. I put the finishing touches to a thesis of 1,200 pages, and struggled to compress its argument into the statutory 150 words of the abstract. My diary entry for 30 May reads: 'Terrible difficulty in writing abstract, and some mental agony in consequence.' It was finally written at 3 a.m. on 31 May. The title of the thesis was 'The Puritan classical movement in the reign of Elizabeth I'. 'Classical' had nothing to do with Greece and Rome but derived from the word 'classis', which meant a governing presbytery of the church within a Presbyterian economy: not a good title, nor as helpful as the title of the book of the thesis which followed in 1967, *The Elizabethan Puritan movement*. It was a thesis which cost my mother almost more than me, since she typed the whole thing and, later, for want of anything better to do, indexed it.

S. T. Bindoff, who had been appointed one of the examiners, took a somewhat mordant pleasure in my difficulty over the abstract. As the day of the viva examination approached, a Monday, 17 June, Bindoff sat out in the sun on the first hot weekend of that summer, perhaps trying to read the monstrous thing, and was so affected that he was absent from the examination. I suppose that what happened was barely legal. Neale, now retired, had had himself appointed external examiner, and the only other examiner present was Joel Hurstfield, who rarely found himself in opposition to Neale. So I got my Ph.D. Esther and I celebrated at the Lamb and Flag in Holborn, and the University of London brought in a new rule which absolutely prohibited doctoral theses of more than 80,000 words.

Then it was off to the Lake District and Brackenclose at Wastdale Head. We were a party of five, including Esther, George Jackson and a Polish colleague from Khartoum, an economist called Kim Kubinsky, with his very beautiful wife Cynthia. Kim had last climbed in the Tatra Mountains before the war. Such was his sense of humiliation when, halfway up Slingsby's Chimney on Scafell, he found he could no longer do it, that he collapsed in tears. We swam in Sprinkling Tarn in the altogether, something I suppose you would not do nowadays. Esther and I established what became an annual tradition: climbing a mountain on the shortest night of the year. On 20 June we set off for Lingmell at 11 p.m., and came down at 3 a.m. On the way back from the Lakes we found ourselves in Lichfield Cathedral on the feast of St John the Baptist, the choir singing 'Orlando Gibbons's 'This is the Record of John'.

I then took my mother off to Bruges. I remember that when we went to St John's Hospital to see the six priceless Memlings, my mother said, after ten minutes, well we've seen them now, what next? What was next was Ghent, and the great van Eyck altarpiece in the cathedral of St Bavo, where we spent more than ten minutes. A trip to Zeebruge, along the King Baudouin Canal, was, according to my diary, 'the Seine through the eyes of a Seurat'. Damme, a fenland village where, when it was still sea, the English won the naval battle of the Sluys in the fourteenth century, was even better.

On 11 July Esther and I went to Knightsbridge and bought each other watch bracelets: which I suppose was symbolic.

Soon after that, on 16 July, it was Blackbush Airport and the flight back to Khartoum with Sudan Airways. There was a stopover in Malta. Standing on the roof of the Phoenicia Hotel, I told a Sudanese colleague that I would use the couple of hours before dinner to explore the town. 'There is nothing to see here', he said.

Two days after getting back, there was the biggest swarm of locusts over Khartoum that I ever saw: trillions of insects making the sky black, kites and other birds in a feeding frenzy, and frightened people impotently banging saucepans.

10

The Sudan Years and Ethiopia

Life in the Khartoum years had several dimensions and was lived at as many levels. There was the public, political level, which continually washed over into the life of the university in a way which, except in 1968, has not often been seen in western democracies, and least of all in Britain. Then there was the academic round, not only the regular grind of lecturing, tutoring and examining in the History Department, but running the School Certificate examinations in History in the twenty-two secondary schools in the country ('Chief Examiner'), and also my little jobs on the side: tutoring my prince, Sayedd Mohammed Osman el Mirghani, teaching the girls in the church-based Unity High School, music as well as history, and discussing public affairs with the tiny handful of young women who could be persuaded to train as nurses (a hitherto despised occupation, close to prostitution) in a college funded by the World Health Organization and run by Canadian nuns. *Time Magazine* came into its own, but was continually corrected by Cairo Radio, a genuinely two-way traffic in information, disinformation and ideas.

In the university, I worked hard to make something of a little society of Christians, the so-called 'Christian and Cultural Association', rather more social than either cultural or Christian, and made up of a discordant crew of southerners, Greeks and Copts (the Catholics, naturally, having their own show). Once I went out to Wadi Seidna Secondary School, on the Nile north of Khartoum, and lectured on the subject of the existence of God to an audience of 1,000 students, all Muslims, assembled in a palm-fringed courtyard under a full moon. The question and answer time was lively. The headmaster said: if only you had read the Quran, you would have found the answers to all the questions you were asked. It is impossible to imagine such a thing happening in this twenty-first century. Even more improbable was a brains trust on personal relationships, in which the 'expert' panel consisted entirely of expatriate Europeans (myself included) and the audience of (mostly) Muslim Sudanese. One student asked: 'What's the point of marrying for love if the time you spend on love is less than the time you spend on shaving?' The Sudan had yet to wake up to the fact that it was no longer a colony.

I was still trying to research and write Elizabethan history, and to break into print. In May and June there were opportunities for that in London, and it was usually possible to prolong one's leave in order to attend the annual Anglo-American Conference of Historians before heading back to the Sudan. But always there was the question: what to do next? In Khartoum expatriate lecturers were on short-term contracts which could not be renewed indefinitely, and they were not always welcome or popular. In any case I doubted my capacity to be an academic historian and university teacher. For most of those years my thoughts and intentions were focused on ordination in the Church of England and an ordinary parish ministry, which I romantically supposed would be located in a deprived inner-city area of London or the North.

Without transport (or roads), and weekends consisting of only one day (Friday), Khartoum in term-time was a pleasant enough prison. But in the vacations, especially the December vacation, which was almost always prolonged by student strikes and the consequent closing down of the university, it was possible to break out in thrilling and exotic directions. In my case, Ethiopia became the country with which I fell utterly in love. Its landscape and ancient Christian civilization became an obsession. But there was also Egypt, and especially Upper Egypt: the Nile south of Aswan, Luxor, Karnak and the Valley of the Kings, when you rode there along a dirt track on donkeys; but also Cairo, at a time when it was still possible to climb to the top of the Great Pyramid of Gizah. April, between Khartoum and London, found me all over the Mediterranean: Jerusalem and Nazareth, Damascus and Beirut, Istanbul, Athens and the Orient Express, Venice and Algeria in the grip of its savage Seven Year War, which I experienced at close quarters while visiting my missionary brother. These were not things that happened to you if you were teaching in Birmingham.

But there was always the bitter-sweet personal, emotional dimension, which only appears in my letters to Esther, three or four a week for over two years. These letters, which Esther returned to me many years later, when we were married folks with four grown-up children each, are the diary of those Khartoum years. It was never clear where our relationship was going to go, if anywhere, and yet it was sustained and continued, with trust and fidelity on both sides, even when it was subject to conditionality and when we saw each other for only two or three months of the year. Incredible as it may now seem, it was a chaste, if far from Platonic, relationship. On leave in the summer of 1958, I spent thirty-eight days with Esther, twenty-five with my mother. Esther, too, could only see so far into the future. She had spent a year of intermittent theological study at King's College London, aware that her intellectual theological understanding fell far behind the standards she imposed on her history. But she remained a historian at heart, and in the spring of 1957 was elected to a research fellowship at Newnham College, which made her the youngest female don in Cambridge.

Religion, one might say her religion, was part of the bond between us, although it was also a point of difference, since Esther was moving from an evangelical background to a more sacramental, incarnational emphasis, reading Evelyn Underhill, discovering the mystics. It was mostly thanks to Esther that I became an Anglican (confirmed in Khartoum Cathedral on 9 January 1957), reading the books that Esther recommended. And so it was that I put myself forward for ordination. In May 1958 I was vetted at a conference at Farnham Castle and accepted for theological and pastoral training. It was a question whether this would happen at Wells Theological College or at Ridley Hall, Cambridge, where the bishop who took me in hand, the brother of the bishop of the Sudan who had confirmed me, had been principal. I accepted an offer to go to Ridley, and was due to start there in October 1960. But by that time I had decided to keep my collar the right way round and for the time being to stay in Khartoum. This was just as well, as things turned out.

Peeling this onion, we may start with politics, outside and inside the University of Khartoum. From independence on 1 January 1956 until 17 November 1958, the Sudan was supposed to be a parliamentary democracy. The politics were turbulent, and, or so we later learned, corrupt, but not corrupt by more recent African standards. The Sudan was not the Congo. Anybody who knows anything about the Sudan knows that this essentially artificial country, the largest in Africa (the size of Western Europe), divides between North and South, the North Arabic-speaking and largely Muslim, the South another world altogether, black African, ethnically diverse with on the one hand the Nilotic peoples, Dinka, Nuer and Shilluk, on the other several tribes of Bantu; already extensively Christianized through both Catholic and Protestant missions and schools. The Shilluk were not on good terms with the Dinka, or even with each other. The terrible civil war, which became a firestorm in the 1980s, was as much a war within the South as between the South and the North. But in the late fifties the war of the next forty years still lay just across the horizon. But there were plenty of warning signs. There had been an army mutiny in the South even before independence, and the southern secondary schools had been relocated to Khartoum. My cycling route to the university every day took me past that southern diaspora.

But this was very marginal to political life in the North. The northern Sudan was really a dual monarchy, not only its politics and religion but much of its economy dominated by the two great so-called 'sects' of Sudanese Islam: the Ansar, followers of the Mahdi, and the rival and somewhat less powerful and convincing Khatmia, led by the Sayedd el Mirghani, the father of my crown prince. When the current Mahdi (posthumous son of the original Mahdi of Gordon's time) died in 1957, on the night of a total eclipse of the moon, much of the country was plunged into deep mourning. On great occasions both movements could bring thousands of disciplined, uniformed faithful on to the streets and avenues. I went to the mother of all wedding parties when my prince got married: 4,000, who approached through an avenue of the Khatmia faithful, all in green and white uniforms. In 1960, Gemal Abdel Nasser arrived on a state visit, and again I was included in the Khatmia party, where bulls were slaughtered on the road as Nasser arrived. But the Khatmia lot were upstaged by the Ansar. When Nasser went to their stronghold in Omdurman, the whole route from the bridge over the White Nile to the Mahdi's tomb was lined by Ansar, making a kind of fence with canes. When Sadiq el Mahdi, with Nasser beside him, cried out 'Allah elul Akbar', thousands of throats replied 'Allah el Ham', and the president of Egypt was left in no doubt where real power in the country lay. But in more recent times, under the military and Islamic dictatorship of General Beshir, both movements are in mostly resentful opposition.

Back in 1957 and 1958, the political arm of the Ansar, the Umma Party, were in power, but there was chronic political instability. The rival party, which had been built up by the British in the later years of the Condominium to counter Mahdist nationalism, leaned towards Egypt and the objective of a united state of the Nile Valley. This was one reason why Abdullah Khalil, the Umma prime minister, was, in the estimation of the British ambassador, first class at the time of Suez. In February 1958 there was an international crisis involving disputed territory on the Egyptian border, an invasion, or at least incursion, and talk of war. The incident was choreographed to coincide with the first elections in the Sudan since independence. Anthony Mann, correspondent for the *Daily Telegraph*, who belonged to an era when correspondents stayed in one place and knew their way about, sat all night in the Foreign Ministry, advising a government inexperienced in such matters on what to do. The students tore down pictures of Nasser and marched through the streets shouting 'Sudanese land for Sudanese people!' It all came to nothing, of course.

There were other political players: the communists, and a vigorous and often effective trade union movement.

In the university there were, we used to say, three parties: the Muslim brotherhood, the communists and the Coca-Cola Party, roughly equal in strength. All could unite in denunciation of 'imperialism'. (I once invited my Unity High School girls to define imperialism, and the daughter of the foreign minister, Mutassin Mahgoub (later prime minister), said that it was one country being destroyed by another.) Later the National Islamic Front would dominate the politics of Khartoum University, where it was born and nurtured. Back in the late fifties, not only Suez but the war in Algeria was on everyone's minds, and when there were parties at the French embassy, on quatorze juillet for example, they were boycotted by most of the other (Arab) embassies, which meant that there was more excellent champagne to be drunk than was good for those of us who did attend. At the annual bean feast at the Students' Union in 1958, the president in his speech attacked, routinely, the departing expatriates in the government of the university (that 'corner-stone of British imperialism', Professor Grant, had just been replaced by a Sudanese), but also the imperialism represented by foreign professors and lecturers. In the Law Faculty, for example, the examinations had been devised with the sole purpose of failing as many students as possible. (There was an anti-Semitic dimension to this.) I got up (in the presence of the whole cabinet and sundry other bigwigs) and walked out. The president was one of my own students. The next day I wrote him a letter in which I said that if I heard any more of that kind of nonsense he would have the pleasure of saying farewell to another corner-stone of imperialist oppression. Such were the tensions. I was one of a minority of staff who had argued before it happened that we should attend this event.

On 17 November 1958 I set out as usual to cycle to the university from the house which I now shared with a colleague on the Hai el Matar, the Airport Estate. I knew that something was up when I passed a Bren-gun carrier, broken down and stuck on the railway level crossing. Soon tanks were cruising the streets, and we knew that there had been a military coup. It was not like the coups of later years, in the Sudan and elsewhere. The military hardware was antique. The new leaders were senior and quite elderly officers, headed by Ibrahim el Abboud, with a long mournful face, immortalized on the front page of the *Daily Mail* with the headline: MYSTERY OF THE EGG-HEAD GENERAL. Abboud lived, ironically, at no. 1 Parliament Street (Sharia el Barlaman), and, illegally, grazed goats on his front lawn. Egg-headed or not, our new leaders were close to the Umma Party, which had perhaps colluded in their seizure of power. The members of the former government were 'thanked for their services', which is not what would later happen in Liberia and in several other African countries.

But now we had one president, Abboud. Before, there had been a presidential commission of five who took it in turns to be head of state, including a Roman Catholic southerner with five wives. I used to cycle past his house every morning, observing that while this southern notable sat on the verandah, his wives laboured on traditional tasks out the back. The chancellor of the university was the head of state for the time being, and it so happened that this man was in office when we conferred our first degrees. By the following year our chancellor was, naturally, Abboud, who chose to wear his military uniform under his chancellor's robes, with the squashy velvet hat perched on top of his peaked army cap.

The new regime sought popularity by removing from the streets of Khartoum the

31   Graduation, University of Khartoum, 1959: the front seats are occupied by officers, with no one choosing to sit near them

statues of Gordon and Kitchener. Few, I think, regretted the deposition of Kitchener, who had sat on horseback, gesturing towards the battlefield of Omdurman where so many thousands of Sudanese had been slaughtered. But Gordon was another matter. He had perched on his camel on a roundabout outside what was now the Republican Palace, and what harm had he ever done to the country? I photographed both statues as they were taken down, and in the railway sidings at Khartoum North where they were boxed up for removal to England. Gordon and his camel are now to be seen on the corner of the cricket field at the Gordon School in Woking. Kitchener, I believe, has retired to Woolwich Barracks.

Any popularity secured by this symbolic act was short-lived. 17 November was a day for celebrating the glorious revolution, with a military parade through town. But the students were so hostile that it was felt necessary to change the university calendar so that they would not be around at the time. I got a bit of cheap popularity for regularly lecturing, with some irony, on the subject of 17 November 1558, the accession day of Queen Elizabeth I; for indeed the revolution had happened precisely on the four hundredth anniversary of that rather more notable event.

The military regime was no more stable than the civilian government which it had ousted. Soon rival commanders were vying for power. On one occasion, a column of tanks advancing up the railway towards Khartoum was met by a party who warned: 'The old man is fed up.' An attempted coup by junior officers led to some hangings, the first political violence since independence. After a few years, and beyond my time, concern about the developing war in the South, which Abboud had pursued with some fervency, led to widespread industrial strikes, led by the railway workers. When the students joined in with a debate on the issue, provoking the army to invade the campus, with tragic consequences, the regime capitulated.

But the civilian government which then came in (under Mahgoub) rivalled Europe's *ancien régime* monarchs in having learned nothing and forgotten nothing. So presently, in 1969, there was a new and altogether tougher and more ruthless military government under Colonel Jaafer Nimeiri, who used his own revolver to shoot a leading communist from behind his desk. This was not yet quite an Islamic republic, that was still to come. But Nimeiri introduced Islamic, *shari'a* law. And all the whisky in Khartoum (apart from what Nimeiri allegedly drank) was poured into the Nile, which, the wags said, led to a greater than usual interest in fishing, downstream. Nimeiri gained brownie points by negotiating a perhaps false peace in the South (before the discovery of oil, the North could no longer afford the war) under the terms of the Addis Ababa Accord. But the peace depended on the Islamization and Arabization of the South: Arabic in the schools, the harsh penalties incurred under *shari'a* for moral transgressions as well as crimes (a distinction denied by radical Islam), now imposed on non-Muslims. The war would resume.

Looking back reflectively and critically, the University of Khartoum was not a success, neither for its students nor for its staff. It appeared that no one had given much if any thought to how the two halves of the equation, Sudanese nationals and Egyptians, and European expatriates (mostly still Brits), were to live and work together successfully. There was a common room which was opened up once a year for the AGM to elect a new committee, but deserted for the other 364 days. Coffee and Pepsi Cola were drunk in our offices. And we tended to socialize with fellow expatriates, if only because if you went into a Sudanese colleague's room, perhaps just to ask the time, natural courtesy would require you to stay for at least a quarter of an hour. I was on the best of terms with one Sudanese colleague, but once, as I was cycling home, he leaned out of his Russian left-hand-steering-wheel car to clap me on the back, which might have caused a serious accident. I went round to his place, burst in, and probably called him a bloody idiot. He was entertaining some friends, and I believe that we hardly ever spoke to each other again. One of my students, Yusf Fadel Hassan, became a leading historian of the Sudan and vice-chancellor of the university. When he was forced into early retirement by the government, I realized that I now had an ex-VC as a former student, and I felt as you feel when policemen, or, as it may be, bishops, begin to look younger than yourself.

It turned out that my best friend in Khartoum was not any of my immediate British colleagues but the only German on the staff, Christoph Weiss, who taught Physiology. Every day we went swimming after work and before lunch, every day two lengths more than the day before, and I would stroll into Christoph's lab to observe his work on the toxicity of scorpion stings. (Now that is something else that you would not do in Birmingham.) Through Christoph I came to terms with Germany, which I had demonized in my heart throughout and after the war. He had been serving on the ground at Arnhem when my brother came through with the Somersets, and he told me that on the day of the drop he and others were coming away from lunch, wiping their mess-cans, when they saw the parachutes, and ran to get their rifles.

Al Kuhn was something else, an engineer, an American giant from Chicago, a national swimming and basketball champion. Al was about as American as you can get (he once asked me about Ethiopia – is it some kind of place?), but he loved the

Sudan and the Sudanese loved him. Al drove a little jeep and whenever we could we would pick up Elizabeth Kennedy, a teacher who lived with Nancy Moller in the girls' hostel, and headed north for the Sabbalouka Gorge (the sixth cataract) with a crate of beer on board. Elizabeth Kennedy was an important person in my Khartoum life, but she was not Esther. Before long she was safely married to Don Saville, a colleague in Physics.

The expatriate scene was diversified by the presence of Colonel Donald Portway, the first engineer to be a head of a Cambridge house, who had retired from St Catharine's to become Professor of Engineering at Khartoum. Portway was given to remarks like: 'I suppose I'm the only person here to have taught the late king the differential calculus', or 'I suppose no one else here was ever bowled out by the late W.G. Grace.' He called his students 'the young men', and clearly regarded them as rather darker versions of Cambridge undergraduates. But they were very fond of him. The university flew out the children of its expatriate employees for Christmas, and Donald took advantage of the scheme to get a free ticket for his daughter Daphne, who was in her forties and a senior officer in the Women's Army. When the registrar complained, Portway said: 'Well if that's their attitude I'll leave. I only came here to avoid surtax.' Apparently he had had to decide whether to go to Khartoum or become lord lieutenant of Cambridgeshire.

Educationally, there were policy issues, which mostly had to do with that thorny question of failure in examinations, and therefore 'standards'. In the second ('Intermediate') year, students took two courses: Medieval European History with me, and the History of the Arabs with Dr Fawzi Gedalla, a Coptic Egyptian, whose company was very agreeable. The highest mark I ever found myself able to award was 60 per cent; the lowest Dr Gedalla could manage 65 per cent. Students passed the year or not, and of course they all did, by averaging the marks and conflating two graphs which had originally looked like two mountain peaks which did not overlap at all. I spent much time on the Faculty Board, vainly trying to obtain a ruling that students must in future pass *both* papers.

Similar battles were fought, and lost, at the secondary school level. The scope of the syllabus, and consequently to all intents and purposes the content of the examination papers, were matters overseen by a board on which the chief examiner had one vote, as did each of the twenty or so teachers of the subject. That enabled the teachers, many of whom it must be said were British, to dish out specimen answers to the questions they knew would be coming up, which were memorized and reproduced under examination conditions. So it was that all fifty candidates from a school at Wad Medani were aware of 'certain ambiguities' in the British attitude to the Manchurian question around 1930. But there were rewards for the chief examiner, particularly in a lifetime's supply of howlers. 'A certain honest iron broker, von Bismarck.' 'The German police was having big navels to protect their colonies.' 'Hitler was a painter and then he joined a beer factory. He found a group of men discussing the political situation and became their leader.' (What more do you need to know?) 'Kaiser Wilhelm II was thought to be a nephew of Queen Victoria.' 'The League of Nations contained many other useful bodies, such as the Trade, Industry and Prostitution Communications bodies.' 'An end was put to prostitution at that time.' And, on a famous episode in nineteenth-century Sudanese history, when the son of the Egyptian Khedive Ismail was murdered at a banquet: 'The sheikh planned a dark revenge, which was to give a cocktail party in his honour.' That is something which has happened to all of us.

My best memories of the Sudan belong to prolonged visits to some of my students in their home towns and villages. I can almost forgive the boredom of long hours spent sitting with the men, drinking coffee and lemonade, while shrieks of laughter from over the wall, in the women's quarters, suggested that that was where some fun might be had. There were fishing trips on the Red Sea with the wealthy family of my student Abdel Rahman, among the dhows of pearl fishers, when all that you pulled up to the surface were brightly coloured heads, the sharks having eaten the rest on the way up; and when we were nearly capsized by a 40-foot long whale shark. And what about that time at Berber in the far north when we were drinking illicit cheap sherry in a palm grove by the Nile at night, when the original Russian sputnik came into view, and the students, all self-declared communists, shook their fists in mock anger at this invasion of their airspace?

The expatriates in the History Department were a bright lot, and in the event none of them finished up on the academic scrap heap. G. N. Sanderson, 'Sandy', who succeeded Professor Mekki Shibeika as head of department, was a good Balliol man, who had turned from Christopher Hill's kind of history to the Sudan ('whoring after false gods', he used to say). He got his London Ph.D. on the Fashoda Crisis of 1897 in the same year that I got mine, and both theses were grossly over-length. Sandy would go on to a chair at Royal Holloway. Richard Gray, a contemporary from Cambridge, was brought in to teach African History, which many northern students thought was meant to insult them. Richard, an expert on the Southern Sudan, would be a professor at the School of Oriental and African Studies for the rest of his career. Sadly, Sandy and Richard are no longer with us. Peter Bietenholz, a fine cultural historian from Basle, who, as a member of Switzerland's thirty-strong Quaker community, had come to Khartoum to avoid military service, has spent the rest of his time in Saskatoon in Canada, becoming a world authority on Erasmus of Rotterdam and his contemporaries. Peter had the bright idea of teaching an innovatory course on the interaction of Islam and Christendom in the middle ages: partly to establish that there was more to those dealings than the crusades; partly so that the students would discover that the West was always more interested in Islam than Islam had been in it. No, the University of Khartoum was not intellectually dead.

Those two months in London each early summer were almost enough to keep one's hand in as a serious player in Tudor history. There was a kind of validation when, in 1957, Joel Hurstfield, as one of the three editors of the *Festschrift* intended for Sir John Neale, invited me to join the party. I was a good deal younger than any of the other contributors. I chose to contribute to *Elizabethan Government and Society* an essay on an Elizabethan preacher called John Field, whom I represented as a kind of Lenin figure in the history of Puritanism, a religious bolshevik. Later, when the book was published, the review by Hugh Trevor-Roper would make my day, and perhaps rather more than that, by singling my essay out for particular praise.

Khartoum, with its ferocious heat and stifling social exclusivity, was a place to escape from. Fishing, as always, was my main relaxation, in both the Blue Nile and the White: perch-like bulti, green mud fish (easy to catch and excellent eating), 15 pound Nile perch, and khasm el banat (girls' mouths), just as you see them carved on the walls of Rameses III's temple at Luxor, Medinat Habu.

But it was good to escape altogether. Each September some of us would travel by Sudan Railways at a stately pace (you could have kept up with the train by running alongside) to Erkowit in the Red Sea Hills, an old government rest camp, now partially Sudanized. Here ploughshares were being beaten into swords, for when the local Hadendowa people (Kipling's 'fuzzy-wuzzies') sold you a spear, you might find that it had been made from one of the old flags on the governor general's golf course. Golf courses were wasted on Erkowit. The hills were on about the same scale as Snowdonia, but, of course, dry as dust, the main vegetation giant cactuses (the trees called euphorbia candelabra) and dragon trees. I collected lizards and snakes for the museum in Khartoum and had the local population running over the hills catching what I wanted. I soon had twelve species of lizards and eight of snakes. As you scrambled down little ravines with a few pools of water, baboons ran barking up the rocks, with their babies hanging on like grim death. Once there was an unforgettable sight: a pack of up to 150 baboons either attacking or being attacked by five or six Handendowa boys, who were hurling rocks at them from a pinnacle on the ridge. I did some silly things. Once I slipped down the scree and finished up halfway over a sheer cliff. I had no water, nobody knew where I was and the temperature was 96 degrees in the (non-existent) shade.

There was a big mountain to the south, called Jebel Erbab (the door mountain), shaped much like the Snowdon Horseshoe. If you went up it in the daytime (and I once or twice did) it was impossibly hot by the time you got to the bottom of the hill, which was five or six miles away. So I decided that the thing to do was to climb the Jebel at night. There was a full moon, so everything was visible, including the leopard which simply walked past me on the white sand between dark ribs of rock. I skirted the Hadendowa villages to avoid their dogs, and what the people would have made of it if they had come across me I don't know. On the top, at midnight, I saw the lights of the distant rest camp go out and then heard hyenas in the valley. I picked an olive branch from the summit to prove that I had got there. (I believe that the olive originated in such places, which makes that part of the story of Noah's Ark very credible.) On the Red Sea coast, 4,000 feet below, was Suakin, a beautiful Turkish port two or three centuries old, deserted except for thousands of cats and crumbling back into the sea from which the coral had come to build it.

I went to Egypt once or twice, most memorably one Christmas with Peter Bietenholz, when we took the steamer from Wadi Halfa to Aswan, past all those temples, including Abu Simbel still standing where it belonged, before the High Dam was built; and so on to Luxor, where on Christmas Day we walked deep into the desert hills behind the Valley of the Kings. I wrote at the time:

> Egypt is so different from the Sudan – more than halfway to Europe in some ways – swarms of European tourists of all kinds – Italian teddy boys, French boy scouts with a beret-and-soutane priest, Dominicans from some institute in Beirut, swarms of girls under the care of nuns, and heavily armed troops all being sick out of the train window. And in the hotels endless, identical parties of Americans, all consisting of thirty-seven unmarried women between twenty-five and forty – terrifying to allow oneself to think of the aggregate of circumstances which brings them all to Egypt – a forcedly cheerful courier. And the dirt, the wonderful smells, the sprawling villages under the date palms, with swarms of children in all colours. The Sudan is uniform white gowns, dignity, order. Egypt is smells and dirt and life and colour and complete and utter roguery and it's quite a relief if you don't have to live there (as the Egyptians do).

But Ethiopia was so much more. For whatever reason, no one from Khartoum had ever thought of going there. But a colleague at University College, the medievalist Ralph Davis, had told me that I must get to Ethiopia, and he had very generously given me a volume of *Archaeologia* containing an article on Ethiopian rock churches by the late David Buxton. In early December 1957 I set off with John Ingledew, a colleague from the English Department. The journey itself was an adventure: the huge bulk of Jebel Khatmia at Kassala, sacred to the Mirghani family, as you approached the frontier between the Sudan and Eritrea; Kassala itself, with its dom palms, trains of camels, wild Hadendowa and Beni-Amer tribesmen, the civilized touch of a party of prisoners escorted through the town and going into every café to greet their friends. Then we crossed to Tessenei in Eritrea, a little town I came to know well but which was wiped off the map in the wars to come between the Eritreans and the Ethiopians. The journey up to the highlands and Asmara through the night in the cab of a truck lives in one's memory for ever: a jungly world of cold moonlight, the line of solid, dark blue hills, the driver taking savage pleasure in running down two duiker antelopes on the road, one under each wheel; and then the high plateau just as the sun rose, round white-washed churches on every hilltop, each in its grove of eucalyptus trees, Christian Eritreans in their white cotton shammas. It was a Sunday. Asmara was still an Italian city, a place of handsome streets, excellent restaurants and innumerable beggars: 'Hello Johnny, me very hungry.' (The town was full of GIs.)

When all the paper work was complete (no trivial process) we left for Axum by bus, descending to the Mareb river which was the frontier with Ethiopia proper, with views across to the mountains of Adowa, where the Ethiopians had trounced the Italians in 1896. The driver stopped to load his pistol with bullets. In Adowa we were followed by a crowd of 200 children. One boy said: 'It is against the law of our country to take photos.' We learned that the locals got rid of the children by throwing handfuls of stones at them.

Axum was once the capital of an ancient empire which has left behind monuments which are only now, long after our visit, properly understood: great obelisks or stelae, the tallest stones ever erected in antiquity; the Ethiopian equivalent of the Stone of Scone; and, from the Christian epoch, the famous church of St Mary of Sion, not the original church, which was destroyed by the Muslim invader Mohammed Gran in the sixteenth century, but its replacement, built in semi-Portuguese style in the 1630s. Ethiopians believe that this church contains the original Ark of the Covenant, brought to Ethiopia by Menelik I, the son of Solomon and the Queen of Sheba, and accompanied by Zadok the priest. Every Ethiopian church contains, in its Holy of Holies (*qedus qedusan*), a replica of this ark, a shrine for the two tablets of the Mosaic law, which are the altar stones, the *tabot*. Only priests are permitted to enter this sacred precinct, although the *tabot* is ceremoniously carried out of the church once a year at the spring festival of Maskal, celebrating the invention of the True Cross by the Empress Helena; whereupon everyone repeats their baptism by plunging into any available water. You will gather how thoroughly hooked on all this I became. Once, in a little deserted church, I broke the rules, entered the darkened *qedus qedusan*, and pointing my camera in the right direction, secured with the aid of a flash a photograph of the *tabot*: a simple piece of country furniture.

We were fortunate to be in Axum long before the days of organized tourism. When we went to get our permits to visit the sites from the religious governor, the Nebrut Mokair, the courtyard was thronged with petitioners and litigants, much as it would have been in medieval Europe (we had to ask ourselves all the time, are we seeing the middle ages?), and when the Nebrut led the way to his office we were followed by a huge struggling crowd. As others approached they bowed deeply at fifty yards' range, not to us, of course, but to the Nebrut. We gave the Nebrut some medicine for his numerous ailments, and he served us strong tej, Ethiopian mead, drunk by the notables. We were given a schoolboy guide, Takla Haimanot, cheerful and courteous, who answered every question with 'Why not?' I shall never forget Takla Haimanot and his friends. At night, they did their homework on the ground under the lights outside our hotel: the only electric light in Axum.

At the church we were met by the priests and bent and kissed their hands and the crosses always carried in the right hand before being escorted inside. It was the twelfth of the month, always dedicated to St Michael, and there was a service which lasted eight hours: the steady ground bass of drums, the rattling of sistras, an intoxicating chant, bearded monks dancing with their praying sticks. We photographed the paintings (not frescoes but painted on cloth), were taken to the treasury and shown illuminated manuscripts, crosses and three crowns: one of Menelik II, the founder of modern Ethiopia; another of his predecessor, the Emperor Yohannes, killed in battle by the Mahdists; one given by Haile Selassie.[1] Meanwhile scripture students (*debtera*) were intoning the Scriptures in the ancient ecclesiastical language, Ge'ez, reading from a great manuscript Bible under a gaily coloured golfing umbrella. We went into the ancient church of St Takla Haimanot with many more paintings, and we descended into some of the royal tombs, still with their stone coffins and bones. Always we were surrounded by crowds of impoverished children, cripples, rags, faces crawling with flies. Waiting for transport out of Axum, we invited our schoolboy interpreters to sing. 'The scoundrels will laugh at us', said Takla Haimanot. 'But aren't you scoundrels?' 'No we are student-ees.' Eventually they were persuaded to sing 'One man wen toomoo', and 'Jesus lovez aller cheeldren / Aller cheeldren ovver world, / Reddanyellowblackenwhite / All are pleshus innis sight, / Jesus loveez aller cheeldren ovver world.' Even the scoundrels joined in. Those children would now be over sixty. But I doubt whether the scoundrels ever made it.

The bus which should have taken us to the ancient capital of Gondar crashed on its way from Adowa, killing two people and seriously injuring twenty-eight. We travelled instead on the back of a truck, through the night, over the Takazee river, and then up the endless hairpin bends of the astounding Wolkofit Pass, almost to the top of the Simien Mountains, home to Simien ibex, Ethiopian wolves and spectacularly handsome geladas, which apparently are not quite baboons, all making a living on those sparse grasslands. The climb takes you up 6,000 feet to 12,000 feet. There is nothing like it in the Alps, unless you pile one pass on top of another. At first light, a party of geladas leapt from the side of a culvert and sprang up the rocks, chattering at us. The scenery was some of the most dramatic on earth. I wrote: 'a fantastic country of dark depths, jagged ridges and a great tangle of gorges and ridges'. But at the top you enter upon a fair imitation of Salisbury Plain, dotted with Italian farmsteads every few hundred yards, now abandoned, which the road had served. An Italian shopkeeper in Khartoum said: 'That was Mussolini's mistake. He built roads like that in Africa and did nothing for the Italian mezzogiorno.' At our first stop a beautiful woman got on the truck and proceeded, under an umbrella, to do with an Ethiopian fellow passenger what the Ethiopians seemed to do all the time,

---

[1] The rest of Ethiopia's regalia, and many priceless manuscripts, are in the British Museum where they ought not to be, part of the loot filched by General Napier's expedition mounted in 1867 against the Emperor Tawdros ('Theodore'), its mission to rescue western hostages. These are Ethiopia's Elgin Marbles.

while John and I found more interest than ever in the scenery. We were passing through the country of the Falasha Jews, many of whom would later be airlifted to Israel in what I believe to have been a deeply misguided operation.

Gondar, the Ethiopian capital in the days of Robert Bruce's journeys in the eighteenth century, like Norwich, is a city of forty-four churches, and of a palace complex dating from the seventeenth century – a curious imitation of Versailles in remotest Africa: castles, a library, a chancery, a place for the lions. It is essentially a traditional ghibbi, or tented camp, but the first attempt at a fixed capital for the Negus of Ethiopia, a Portuguese idea and probably, for Ethiopia, not a good idea: including a long banqueting hall where up to 1,000 could sit down to the feasts of raw meat described by Bruce. Outside the town is another royal residence, Cusquam, with a tall tower rising from a grove of juniper trees and a famous eighteenth-century manuscript of the Miracles of Mary. We fell, as anyone would, for the country church of Debre Behran Selassie (the hill of the Light of the Trinity), built in about 1690 by Yassus the Great; an exquisite roof studded with angel heads, and vultures roosting in the junipers outside, a view of what could have been the Golden Valley in Herefordshire. In Gondar we were looked after by a German couple, the Jaegers, doctors, but above all interested in Ethiopian religious art, on which they were expert, and were publishing.

Then came Lake Tana, perhaps the most beautiful lake in the world, which we crossed in a boat commanded by Gunther Deininger, an ex-U-boat captain with an Ethiopian mistress: a seventeenth-century palace built by the Portuguese for the Negus Susenyos, above a bay full of hippopotamus; the magical monastic island of Dag Istafanos, a mausoleum in dense jungle for the kings who had followed Susenyos, where the monks gave us honey in the comb. At Bahar Dar, at the southern end of the lake, where the Blue Nile, or Abbai, begins its marathon course to the Sudan and on to Egypt, we navigated tankwas, the local canoes made from papyrus, crossing to the point where the Nile leaves the lake. On the banks of the river were four old men in a row, all playing single-stringed fiddles, which they continued to play as they crossed on a tankwa ferry: a subdued noise like a swarm of bees. And then we went to Tiss Abbai, or Tissisat ('smoke of Abbai', or 'smoke of fire'), one of the most stupendous waterfalls in the world. At this point two English school-teachers from Khartoum joined our party, by prior arrangement, one of them Lillian Passmore, head of a girls' secondary school in Omdurman, who would later marry Sandy, my head of department. Lillian also became a tireless campaigner against female genital mutilation. An Ethiopian Airlines Dakota took us from Bahar Dar to Addis Ababa, and from there on Christmas Day we began a four-day journey by bus north to Asmara, travelling along and up and down the vast precipitous escarp-ment which makes the eastern side of the great Ethiopian plateau. And so back to Khartoum on New Year's Day.

Esther was supposed to have come on this expedition, but for reasons mostly financial didn't.[2] But in December 1958 I went back to Eritrea and Ethiopia with my mother, who spent a couple of winters with me in Khartoum. On Christmas Day I preached the sermon at a service for British expatriates in Asmara. We travelled to missionary outposts manned (but usually womanned) by old colleagues from the

---

2   Half a lifetime later, Esther's son, Alex de Waal, became a leading expert on Darfur, the Sudan more generally, and with a particular association with Ethiopia.

Egypt General Mission, now, since Suez, relocated in Eritrea as the Middle East General Mission. We stayed at the village of Makboola, south of Tessenei, where, in the war which was about to break out, the entire population would be marched into a nearby wadi and shot. I took my mother to Axum. The Nebrut was absent, but his wife was there and able to issue the permits we needed to inspect the antiquities. She offered us drinks, and while she was looking the other way, I explained to Takla Haimanot that my mother never drank alcohol. The Nebrut's wife said that she quite understood, and when the drinks arrived, poured only half a tumbler of the governor's very potent tej, topping it up with soda water. And that my mother drank, to my knowledge the only alcohol she ever tasted. On Sunday my mother set off for what she was told was the women's church, with hat and handbag, much to the delight of the women sitting in the market. She found that it was not possible to enter the church (no Ethiopians do – they are all technically excommunicate since their often short-lived marriages are customary and not blessed by the church). But the priest appeared and asked my mother to mend his broken alarm clock. (We *ferangi* ('Franks') were known to be technically proficient despite our deficiencies in other respects.). My mother came back to the hotel and asked me to help, but I am afraid that I too could do the clock no good.

For most of those years I thought that I was going to be ordained in the Church of England. This was partly under the influence of Esther, who had brought a new and more Catholic strand into my complex religious persona, reinforcing the influence of the Anglican Society of St Francis, which I had encountered at Sunday afternoon tea parties in Cambridge, and in Cable Street Stepney, where we used to go from the Friends' International Centre to teach English to stranded Somali seamen. (The elderly Franciscan who looked after us, Father Algie, was once asked, by Fred Irvine, what book he was reading. 'I'm reading *Tracts for the Times*. We go up and down the country and people ask us about the church, and the answers are all here. This copy comes from the Stepney Public Library. It was first borrowed in 1911 which is also the last time it was borrowed.') I now called myself an evangelical Catholic, and embarked on reading authors like George Hebert, Michael Ramsey and Dom Gregory Dix.

To be sure the answers to those questions about the church were not to be found in Khartoum, where the Christian scene was depressing to anyone with a conscience and a vision. We worshipped in the Anglican Cathedral, a handsome building in African Byzantine style, which stood hard by the gates of the Republican Palace. The cathedral was run by the provost, George Martin, the kind of cleric whom the old Sudan hands liked to call 'padre', and who excused his other *rôle* as archdeacon of that whole vast region (I think it took in Aden) by calling himself 'archdemon'. George was a wise and good counsellor, but for all that he was practically anti-Sudanese. The bishop, who confirmed me, Oliver Allison, was a robust, indomitable figure, a missionary from the South. But breakfasts in Clergy House after communion on Fridays live in a painful memory. Sometimes there was an assistant bishop, a Dinka called Deng. But he never spoke and seemed to be treated with condescension and even contempt. He was later defrocked for some moral transgression. In the decades to come the church in the Sudan would be reborn, Phoenix-like, in the fires of civil war and exile, many authentic Sudanese bishops sharing the suffering of their people, as they still do.

But back in the fifties, we knew little of the indigenous congregation which met in the cathedral on Sunday mornings for their own vernacular worship. Our services, in the evening, were all-white affairs, entirely expatriate. We knew nothing of the needs of our Sudanese fellow Christians, many of whom were probably starving. But we spent a lot of money on a state of the art electronic organ, on which the British Council representative played Bach most beautifully. John le Carré has best captured the way it was, if for another African country many years later, in *The constant gardener*.

It was not always that bad. In February 1958 I was an observer at the first ever diocesan synod, meeting in Khartoum, with Sudanese pastors and missionaries from the South, chaplains from Aden and Port Sudan, and the aged and distinguished Canon Matthew from Addis Ababa, who had been ordained in 1907. Sunday night that week was different. Two deacons from the Nuba Mountains were ordained before a congregation which included hundreds of Southern servant boys, row upon row of portly Sudanese women in their tobes, everything said and sung in Arabic as well as English: a brief vision of what Christianity in the Sudan might have become. (But that was before the outbreak of the Forty Years War.)

All the time there was that inner life which I have called bitter-sweet. Sometimes, especially in that first year, I was depressed, writing to Esther on one occasion: 'I am extremely unhappy in Khartoum.' But a few weeks later: 'This is an intensely interesting country and one is lucky to be here. I'm a completely different person from the bored, fretful and dull man who wrote you the last two or three letters.' Again and again I told Esther that, desperately though I missed her, missing her was the most precious thing in my life. 'To miss you is a sweet treasure I wouldn't be without.' When, in October 1957, it became clear that she would not be coming to Ethiopia, I wrote: 'Oh *darling* Esther, I can't bear to wait seven months before I see you next. I love you so terribly.' But the complicated nature of our relationship runs through these letters like small earth tremors before an eruption.

> I feel and have always felt that when I came here to the Sudan particularly, and indeed before that, I could have no claim on you whatsoever, and that looking at it from every rational point of view I could do nothing but mess up your life. Often when I examine it in my mind there seems to be an inexorable determinism which makes it impossible that anything should come of our relationship. Me out here, you at home, the impossibility of marrying for years, your career, our difference in religion, all that you have a right to expect, all that I can't give you.

> I'm not thinking in terms of marriage in the near future, as you know well. Meanwhile you are the most precious friend I possess and I value your affection more than I can ever express. As for marriage, I could never be a second best to anyone as you must appreciate – I would never marry anyone on those terms. So perhaps we had better exclude that from our minds altogether? I don't know. I can say that and yet I can love you with all my being while I say so.

It is a pity, from the point of view of the historian, and perhaps not only from that point of view, that only one half of this correspondence survives. When I returned to the Sudan for the third time, in July 1958, I wrote: 'I have come to one conclusion in these days – that I would not come back to the Sudan next year without you – whatever becomes of *us*, and I think that I mean that.' But I did go back to Khartoum in July 1959 without Esther, and when I returned for the last time, in July 1960, I was already engaged to marry someone else.

11

The Most Beautiful Place on Earth

Neale always told me not to put too much into one chapter. The reader would feel a sense of achievement and reward if he or she (but Neale would never have said 'or she') reached the end of a chapter. So in his *Elizabeth I and her parliaments, 1559–1581* we find chapter headings: 'The succession question renewed' and 'The succession question continued'; and 'Religion' and 'Religion continued'. So I think that what happened outside Khartoum in the springs and summers of 1958 and 1959 should make a separate chapter.

On 8 April 1958 at 2.15 in the morning I took off from Khartoum for a Middle Eastern journey which would bring me to London on 25 April. Dawn came up as we approached the Pyramids and the Suez Canal. I arrived at Beirut, with two colleagues from the university, at breakfast time, and we booked into the Hotel Normandie on the seafront, which did not yet know that it would be caught up in the civil war of the eighties. On the same day I went to Byblos, where the idea and the physicality of 'books' began, an amazing hodgepodge of the successive presence of Neolithic, Phoenician, Byzantine, Frankish and Islamic humanity. On the way you pass the narrow entrance to a gorge, the Nasr el Kelk, which every invading army for millennia was obliged to pass, leaving many inscriptions in various characters on the rocks. The next day we went to Baalbek in the Bekaa Valley and wondered at those famous ruins, especially the six graceful columns which survive from the Temple of Jupiter. Again neither we nor Baalbek knew that this would be a fortress and a school for terrorists in the violent years which were to come, a place the Israeli Army is more likely to visit than tourists.

On then to Jerusalem, which is to say East Jerusalem, still (before 1967) under Jordanian control, which I reached on Maundy Thursday, according to the Orthodox Calendar. I stayed at St George's Cathedral and set out almost at once with a small Anglican party to witness two foot-washing ceremonies, Armenian and Orthodox Syrian. We were headed in procession by a dragoman with an ornate and heavy staff. The churches were very different. The Armenian community in Jerusalem is rich, the church interior all expensive carpets and chandeliers. The patriarch, who resembled Peter Ustinov, officiated, and the twelve apostles were all represented by bishops in full regalia seated in golden thrones, one of whom fell asleep and set his beard on fire with the candle he was holding. The Syrian community was poor, with plain deal benches and a simple altar. The officiating bishop looked like a brigand, and apparently once was one. He was the old rogue who at one time had had the Dead Sea Scrolls in his possession. He continually turned from the altar to shake his fist at the noisy women and children in the gallery, and at once you realized what St Paul meant when he said 'let your women keep silence in the churches' (1 Corinthians 14.34). On this occasion the disciples were played by poor peasant priests, with St Peter, as tradition required, played by a young boy. The bishop washed their feet energetically (and they needed it) with a large bar of green soap. The air was full of the mingled scent of soap, sweat and incense. And then they all clustered to wash the episcopal feet, pulling up the bishop's robes to reveal that his purple socks were secured by elastic suspenders which had cut deep furrows into his ever so white legs.

Good Friday was spent in appropriate devotions and a rapid round of the holy sites in and around Jerusalem and Bethlehem. Wherever we went there were hundreds of aged Greek women in black, many of them Cypriots, who come to Jerusalem in the hope of dying there. Then came Holy Saturday and the ceremony of the Holy Fire in the Church of the Holy Sepulchre. The church was crammed to bursting hours before things began, the crowds chanting anti-Israeli slogans. The event was being recorded by an Italian film company. When the Orthodox patriarch prepared to enter the Holy Sepulchre itself he was accompanied by the military governor of Jerusalem and other dignitaries. (An American priest crammed up against me said: 'All the notables being filmed in front of the tomb of Our Lord!') Miraculous fire, a lighted torch, soon emerged out of the tomb, the patriarch having not forgotten his matches. At once the flame was taken all over the church. A young and athletic priest leaned out from the dome, far above, waving a lighted candle, everyone was shouting and ululating, and everyone lit the thirty-three tapers they had brought (one for each year of Our Lord's life) only to extinguish them at once with a damp cloth (to avoid the many fearful accidents which have happened in the past). The place filled with smoke and at that moment the choirs of many churches, Orthodox, Armenian, Syrian Jacobite, Coptic, began to process around the tomb, all singing their own liturgies, while the bells rang out. The Ethiopians in Jerusalem are confined to some makeshift structures on the roof of the Holy Sepulchre, but in the early evening of Holy Saturday everyone turns out to witness their traditional procession in search of the body of Christ: nostalgic for me, with drums, sistras and Ethiopian chant. Then, as midnight approached, we went to the Russian church in the Garden of Gethsemane, and to an Easter service which went on for ever. Christ is Risen! He is Risen Indeed! The Russian nuns and their priests (old-fashioned Tsarists, but the abbess was English) left us in no doubt about that.

The next day I set out with two passports, one in each pocket, for the crossing point between Jordanian Jerusalem and Israel known as the Mandelbaum Gate – not so much a gate as a ruined suburban street. And there was my sister Hilda, who had gone to serve in a missionary hospital in Nazareth in the same week of 1956 that I had arrived in Khartoum. It was a dramatic and joyful reunion. This was my only experience of Israel, still in the energetic and almost ascetic stage of its history: all battered briefcases and shabby shorts. After another day of sightseeing we took a train to Haifa (it was hard to imagine Elijah slaughtering the priests of Baal on Mount Carmel since it looks so much like Bournemouth); and so by bus up to Nazareth, which I described in my diary as 'a soft-stoned yellow town, lying in a bowl of hills, with steep, chalky hill paths, churches and monasteries, country very like that around Assisi'. But already, in 1958, there was the threat, as it seemed, of the new Israeli Nazareth on the crest of the hill, with its white apartments and a chocolate factory. I found that Hilda, now fluent in both Arabic and Hebrew, was greatly loved in and around her hospital. Together we went to Tiberius and Capernaum and swam in the Sea of Galilee, which was full of the sorts of fish which, I suppose, we read about in the Gospels. There was an evangelistic visit to a remote village inhabited mostly by Druze, who entertained us with coffee and sweets and listened politely to the Christian Gospel, which is their way. Back on the coast, I stayed with another of the Allison brothers, Roger, a missionary with the Church Mission to the Jews. At the evening service in Jaffa there were many strangely disordered people wandering aimlessly about: exiles from both the Holocaust and Judaism.

After a week in Israel, I left via Tel Aviv for Nicosia and Athens. On Monday 21 April, at eight o'clock in the evening, I boarded the Orient Express for Paris, where we arrived on Thursday morning. The carriage was full of young Greeks going back to school in Lausanne, who at first resented my presence, but then became very friendly, with guitars and songs. The spring was delicious in its beauty as the train trundled across Greek and Yugoslav Macedonia and Bosnia, trees in bud, thin minarets across the ever so green fields: another war zone in gestation. At Belgrade the train stopped for three and a half hours, so that it was possible to go up into the town, where the communist secretariat was hung with the hammer and sickle to celebrate the congress meeting in Ljubljana. So it was with the little country stations across Croatia and Slovenia: red flags, loud speakers broadcasting Tito's speech and little hairy pigs rooting around. And so through the karst country to Trieste and Venice, where there was time to walk out of the station and look up and down the Grand Canal. Then the north Italian plain, with a superior restaurant car, the Simplon, and the departure of the Greek students at Lausanne at 3 a.m. A French couple who boarded the train at Dijon remarked on the filthy state of the carriage and were surprised to learn that I had come all the way from Athens. Thursday in Paris, and then, the next day, on to Calais, Folkestone and Victoria, where Esther met me with the faithful Husky. That evening we went to Romani Santa's in Greek Street for dinner, and talked and talked.

The next few weeks were divided between home visits to Ipswich, research days in London (my essay for the Neale *Festschrift*), and as much time as possible with Esther in Cambridge, usually staying at Pembroke. I had a session with Neale, who was excited to learn about my essay on John Field, and that I was working on the remarkable life of an Elizabethan woman known to history as Anne Locke, the closest friend of the Scottish reformer John Knox, whom she had joined in Geneva, leaving her wealthy city husband behind, and who was briefly married to the exemplary Puritan preacher Edward Dering. Neale said: 'Write it with a volume of collected essays in mind in the future', and I thought 'long future at my rate of writing!'[1]

On 12 and 13 May I had my selection conference for ordination at Farnham, and then I took my mother down to Kent for a missionary conference, which included a series of masterly addresses by Professor Sir Norman Anderson, the leading authority on Islamic Law. Late in May I had an interview at Wells Theological College, and that was an excuse to take the Husky through the Cotswolds, and up through Bath to Hereford and Esther's parents and sister Meriel. We went to Brecon and over all the Beacons, and on another day explored the Black Mountains. Back in Cambridge, I showed my Ethiopian slides to a distinguished audience at Newnham, which included two authorities on early Christian history and culture, Norah Chadwick and Kathleen Hughes. When I put on the same show at the Centre, my old Swiss girl friend Elisabeth Egli turned up with her cousin Renée and fiancée. Soon after that I took my mother to Scotland for a week, to see Auntie Rita and other relations. Cousin Dave Dowie got me to address his local Rotary Club on 'The

---

[1] But that volume, *Godly people*, complete with the redoubtable Mrs Locke, was duly published, twenty-five years later.

problems of North-East Africa'. Although it was early June, there was a persistent and bitterly cold easterly haar on the Fife coast, and I felt sorry for the fellow guests at the hotel whose main holiday this was. Because Esther and I were about to do something very different.

The Professor of Philosophy in Khartoum was a gentle Swede, with an even gentler Swedish wife: Hakon and Siv Tornebohm. Hakon's publications were all called *Physik og Philosophie*, or *Philosophie og Physik*, and his lecture to the Philosophical Society of the Sudan was on 'The concepts of space, time and causality in the history of relativity'. In spite of all that, I was very fond of the Tornebohms and saw a good deal of them. In their house, early in 1958, I had met Malte Nyberg-Tolf (which is to say, Malte Nyberg the Twelfth), a former Swedish weightlifting champion, who had broken one leg ski-jumping and the other in an accident as a circus performer. He was one of the best-known avant-garde artists in Sweden. This was a momentous meeting. Esther and I had planned to spend part of the summer in Skye, perhaps even in Rhum, an arrangement which would have involved Dick Marsh. But Dick was unavailable, and before I knew it our plans were changed. We would visit Malte Nyberg at his home at Naske, near Ornskoldsvik in northern Sweden, and then make a return visit (for me) to the Lofoten Islands. It would involve travelling the entire distance on the longest electrified railway in the world, from Stockholm to Narvik.

And that was what happened, in June 1958. On Saturday 14 June we sailed from Tilbury to Goteborg, spent Monday with the Tornebohms, who lived there, and then went on overnight via Stockholm to Ornskoldsvik, which is a paper-manufacturing town high up on the Gulf of Bothnia. Malte Nyberg took us to the paper mill, where he said that all the men were looking at him with hostile envy: why had he escaped from the kind of life that they led? While he painted he had a wife who designed textiles (whom we didn't meet), and they spent their winters in Spain. He lived on the edge of a fjord in a large eighteenth-century wooden house, red and white, with deep blue stairs and a little white cat. Malte was not wholly divorced from the paper industry. Indeed, his main source of income was collecting logs which had broken free from their rafts as they were being taken to the mill and which were stranded in their thousands on the shores of the many little islands on the edge of the Baltic. He got a krone for each log. And so we spent the next few days on his boat, the *Sonia*, rowing ashore in a dinghy to manhandle the logs and get them on board. Nights (but no darkness) were spent at anchor in little wooded bays where the song of the redwings was almost a nuisance. It mostly rained. Once we landed on an island where there was a hotel to buy some matches. The dining room was full of people who seemed to be on the verge of Munch's 'Scream'. Strindberg had exaggerated nothing. But then we found that they were inmates of the Ornsoldsvik Mental Hospital, on their annual outing.

At the end of that week we went on to Narvik through Swedish Lapland, and so to the Lofotens. The plan was to reach Moskensoy, last but one of the islands (Vaeroy, a famous place for birders, is the very last), jumping from island to island by the small ferries which at that time were the only form of transport. Reine in Moskensoy has been voted the most beautiful place in Norway, which must mean on earth. Mountains of the most astonishing verticality rise straight out of the fjords, the red and white village with its fishing boats nestles beneath, every available piece of land, or rock, covered with the racks which dry the torrfesk. Far across the blue Vestfjorden were the mainland mountains, behind Bodo; to the left a view along the Lofoten wall to the great mountain of Vagakallen above Henningsvaer and the peaks beyond Svolvaer. We camped on a ridge above the town, beside a little black lake (lochan one would say, in Scotland, or tarn in the Lake District) with tongues of snow coming down into it from the forbidding cliffs above. We kept up the tradition of climbing on the shortest night of the year, and indeed on every night that we were there. Night? At midnight, on the top of one of those mountains, the sun, low in the sky between Spisstinden and Helvestinden, turned Kjerk Fjorden to pure gold. It was difficult, and dangerous, and especially unnerving to look down into the sunlit but deserted streets below, knowing that if anything happened to us, nobody would know, or care.

What came next was the result of some careful homework with timetables before we left England. We sailed up through the Raftsund to Sortland, where we caught the daily coastal steamer, or 'Hurtigrute', travelling south towards Bergen. But at Trondheim we left our stuff on board, caught a train up into the interior to Dombas, and then another train down to Romsdal, where we camped in the shadow of the great Romsdalshorn. The next morning we sat on the edge of the pier at Andelsnes, waiting for a local ferry to take us to Alesund, where we rejoined the Hurtigrute. It was a Sunday morning, and we read the office together. The collect was for the fourth Sunday after Trinity: 'that, thou being our ruler and guide, we may so pass through things temporal that we lose not our hold on things eternal'. Our old theological differences resurfaced. My Protestant and Puritan inheritance made me read 'pass through' as meaning that we should have as little to do with those 'things temporal' as possible. Esther had, or would progressively acquire, a better understanding of what through, 'per', meant: through, totally and entirely, whatever might come, whether for good or for not so good.

Later we were eating in a restaurant in Bergen before catching the boat back to Newcastle. It was raining, as it always is in Bergen. The rather stupid conversation brought into the open the tensions which underlay our relationship, and this was probably the beginning of the end. A week later, I was back in Khartoum.

In mid-October 1958 I wrote Esther a letter which was meant to be decisive, and was.

> As you know, this is the week when we pray the great collect that 'thy Holy Spirit may in all things direct and rule our hearts.' With that prayer in my mind, I want to do what (to the best of my knowledge) I haven't done before, for all our marching and counter-marching around and over the issue – to ask you: Will you marry me early next summer? Can you pray that prayer and then bring yourself to say yes or no? I love you, I believe that our lives should be one, I want to marry you, and I want to marry you in May 1959.

The reply was not the one that I had longed for. Esther explained to my mother that our vocations simply did not lie together. I told my mother that that was something which I had to accept and to learn to live with, 'however sadly (and still rather rebelliously) at the moment'. 'It may well be that God wants me to serve Him in a celibate ministry. Don't necessarily look for grandchildren through your son!' (My elder daughter was born less than four years later!) A week later I reported that Esther and I now both felt that the break in our relations was for the best, and that, though sad, we were more sure of our vocations and less uncertain in our lives. 'We shall probably not be writing to each other again, but Esther would be glad to hear any major news through you from time to time.' In November, Esther wrote to my

Plate 1 My Khartoum servant, Mohi el Din, with his family

Plate 2 Central Khartoum, 1958

Plate 3 Kitchener. About to be removed, following a 'traditional' ceremony

Plate 4 The Ingessena dance

Plate 5 Pop idol, Ingessena style

Plate 6   Coup d'état, November 1958

Plate 7   Celebrating the first anniversary of the Great Revolution, November 1959

Plate 8 Suakin

Plate 9 Ethiopia

Plate 10 Eritrea: the prickly pear has been eaten by the baboons

Plate 11 Axum

Plate 12 Ethiopia, people of the book

Plate 13 Emperor Haile Selassie visiting the University of Khartoum: President Abboud and the vice-chancellor head the procession

Plate 14   Esther Moir in the Lofotens between Narvik and Svolvaer, June 1958

Plate 15   Lofoten reflections

Plate 16   Midnight above Reine in Moskensoy

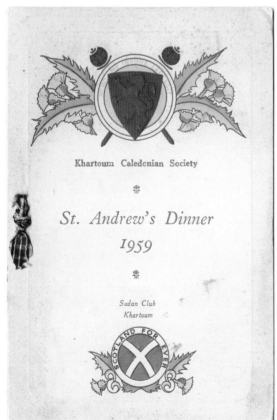

Plate 17   The Khartoun
Caledonian Society St
Andrews Dinner, 1959

Plate 18 Liz and our beloved dog Adonis

Plate 19 Honeymoon: Liz navigating a tankwa on Lake Tana, Ethiopia

Plate 20 Christmas Day in the morning, 1960

Plate 21   Tissisat, Tis'Abbai: Tissisat means 'Smoke of Fire', Tis'Abbai means 'Smoke of the Abbai'; today the flow of water is much reduced by a hydro-electric scheme

Plate 22   Tissisat, 'Tis Abbai'

Plate 23 The children in Australia, May 1970: Helen and Andrew on the log, Sarah getting there, Stephen out of reach

Plate 24 Patonga Creek

Plate 25   Senate House Cambridge with Caroline Litzenberger after she had taken her Ph.D.

Plate 26 The Council of the Royal Historical Society, late 1980s: the late Professor Gerald Aylmer is presiding, and a future president, Professor Peter Marshall, sits on his left; lower down the table the late and much lamented Colin Matthew, founding father of the *Oxford dictionary of national biography*, is close to the camera, with leather patches on his elbows

Plate 27 Honorary Doctor of the University of Kent at Canterbury: Jo Grimmond, the chancellor, is third from the right; David Ingram, vice-chancellor, is on the right.

Plate 28 The coming generations, at Steve and Nicky's wedding, August 2004 – *back row*: Helen, Helen's partner Julian, Sarah's husband Jeff, Nicky, Steve, holding Sarah and Jeff's Matt, Sarah, Andrew's wife Debs, Andrew; *front row*: Andrew and Deb's Isabel, Helen and Julian's Maya, Helen and Julian's Zoe, Andrew and Debs's Tom, Sarah and Jeff's Will, Andrew and Debs's Jack is not visible, although at this time *in utero*; Steve and Nicky's offspring Andrew and Debs's Elsa; Sarah and Jeff's Jack is not visible, although at this time *in utero*; Steve and Nicky's offspring due to appear in April 2010. Compare this with Illustration 1, a family group photographed 100 years earlier.

mother as she was about to set out for Khartoum: 'Please give my love to Patrick. I miss him very much indeed, but I think that this was the right decision, for this moment at any rate, though perhaps ultimately things will change.' As we shall see, that was not quite the end, only the beginning of the end, and the beginning of other things.

When I next left Khartoum on leave in April 1959, I first went to Cairo and down to Luxor. At the Luxor Hotel, an Edwardian fossil, I was the only English guest and felt that I ought to apologize to all those Germans, Americans and Swedes for the English cuisine and a hotel library which consisted mainly of the novels of Marie Corelli. I made the usual tour (Luxor Temple, Karnak Temple, the Valley of the Kings, Deir el Bahri, Medinet Habu, the tombs of the nobles) in the company of a Coptic guide, Tawdos Boutros, who told me: 'St Anthony when he come to Egypt find no difficulty make Egyptian people Christian. He find them believe in Amun, Mut and Khons. He tell them believe in Father, Son and Holy Ghost' (here crossing himself).

I then plane-hopped along the North African coast, with stopovers at Tripoli and Tunis, and so to Algeria, where my brother Bernard and his wife Joyce were missionaries. Bernard met me at Algiers Airport and drove me up to their village, Djemaa Sahridj, near Mekla and Tizi-Ouzou in the mountains of Kabylia, where I settled in to stay with Bernard, Joyce and the children, five-year-old Yvonne, three-year-old John and baby Evelyn.

It was not a conventional holiday or family visit. The savage Seven Years War was in its later stages, and there was military activity all around the village, twenty-four hours a day. At night the howitzers bombarded the FLN in their bases in the mountains. In the daytime machine guns chattered much of the time (the children were told that it was only *les cigognes*), and towards teatime the tracks around the village were routinely mortared. What scared the children most was the noise made by the jackals, which could no longer be controlled and came into the village at night to scavenge. The premises opposite my brother's house had been commandeered by the French army after a wealthy baker, who had refused to pay his dues to the FLN, had been disappeared. The day we arrived, some kind of explosive device was thrown across the road from behind my brother's hedge. Bernard was a consummate diplomat. We went down to Mekla and met the officer in command. Bernard said that he would probably like him to cut down that hedge. 'Oh, I don't think that that will be necessary.'

As anyone who has been there knows, war always has its comic, absurd side. One morning, as the French troops were preparing to mount a local offensive, helicopter gunships overhead, a local farmer appeared with a white cow with a livid red shrapnel wound on its flank. Everything stopped while a medic examined the wound. On the day that I left Algeria there was one of the many elections and referenda of those years. (De Gaulle had been in power for a year.) At Djemaa the polling took place in the school, next door. In the days before the referendum, the French toured the village with loudspeakers, exhorting the population: 'Il faut votez!' At night the FLN told people that all who participated would have their throats cut. In Kabyle villages, everyone must do the same thing, which is no doubt why my brother's mission had made only a handful of converts in seventy years. The boy who helped in the garden asked me whether we had to vote in my country. When I told him no, he said: 'Ah, vous avez de la bonne chance!' On the Sunday morning troops surrounded the school, and the people were brought up to vote. On the way to

Algiers, we passed lorry loads of women escorted by soldiers, all excitedly ululating on their way to the polls. On Monday, in London, the *Times* thought it interesting that participation had been higher in the rural areas than in the cities.

I got home to find my mother laid up with a mysterious illness, which it took the doctors months to get to the bottom of, although by the time she came back to Khartoum in the autumn she had recovered.

In that summer of 1959 I was seeing Leonora Freeman, a nursing sister who had recently left Khartoum. We used to meet under the statue of the duke of Bedford in Russell Square. We went to *West Side Story*. We ate at Italian restaurants in Soho. We went to Lewes and the South Downs, punted on the Thames at Egham, and took in the Henley Royal Regatta, where Pembroke won the Visitors' Cup. But it was a rather half-hearted affair, on both sides I think.

In late June, a last-minute arrangement, I met Esther and her friend Jill Regan at Kyle of Lochalsh where you caught the ferry for Skye, and we proceeded to Glen Brittle, where the girls stayed in a guest house and I camped beside Loch Brittle. What followed was obviously a mistake, given my feelings towards Esther, which were unchanged, but it was one of the more memorable mistakes in my life. (When she came to hear of it, my mother was worried, but Esther wrote: 'Tell her we are now each other's oldest and very best friend' – not exactly how I saw it.) We began with a hot sunny day on the Cuillins: Sgurr na Bannachdich, Sgurr Dearg, the Inaccessible Pinnacle, followed by beer at the Sligachan Hotel. The following day we set out in Ronald Macdonald's boat for Rhum, where one is not allowed to stay the night except by special arrangement. It was a blue, blue day, the sea covered with rafts of razorbills. With two old climbing friends from CUMC days we went up one of the two big hills on Rhum, Hallival. When we set out for Skye that evening, Ronald's boat broke down again and again, and there was nothing for it but to spend the night on Rhum. Most people found somewhere to sleep in a shed, but Esther and I took the chance to go up a hill on something like the shortest night of the year, the last year we would ever do it. It was 24 June. So we climbed Askival, the more challenging of the two peaks. It was an unforgettable experience. Thousands of Manx shearwaters nest in the burrows on the lower slopes, the parent birds were flying in, and out of the very ground on which we were treading came that unearthly, evocative noise which shearwaters make. Soon the going was too difficult to attempt in the dark, and we sat on a ledge, waiting for some daylight, and (my diary says) 'discussing L.', I suppose Leonora. As the sun came up, the noise of the shearwaters subsided, and there was a blackbird singing in the valley. As we descended, many deer were silhouetted against the rising sun, pure Hollywood. The rest of the party were crawling out of their shed as we reached Kinloch Castle, where the warden served us plenty of good porridge.

Two days later we were involved in a tragedy. An eighteen-year-old student called David Fulton, who was about to start Medicine at Liverpool, was missing in the Cuillins. Soon we heard that a body had been found at the foot of King's Chimney on Sgurr Mhic Choinnich, and we set out with a stretcher. If only David had read his guidebook he would have known that he could have avoided King's Chimney by taking a route called Collie's Ledge. We found the lad at midday, the only time in my life that I have had to deal with a corpse. There was little sign of injury; only the change scattered from his pockets, and his broken spectacles. It took us three hours to get him down a gully and on to the Great Stone Shoot coming down from Sgurr Alasdair. At the foot, in Coire Lagan, we were met by the Police Mountain Rescue

Team from Portree, who relieved us of the burden. Dead bodies are very heavy. That evening, Esther and I went back up to Sron na Ciche, the great cliff which runs out from Sgurr Alasdair. We sat on the top until nearly midnight, as the sun went down over the Western Isles, having another of those rather unsatisfactory conversations. Later I would write about the 'mental and spiritual anguish of that strange evening'. I served supper to Esther and Jill at my camp at 1.30 a.m., and the next morning had my usual swim in the loch, left in the Husky, parted from Esther at Kyleakin, and went on by train to Inverness and London. (More than forty years later Liz and I drove down Glen Brittle, the first time I had been there since that strange evening. We overtook an elderly couple on bicycles, and as we got out of the car and they off their bikes, the man said, not good morning, but 'are you reliving old memories?' You could say that again.) On 30 June, Esther wrote: 'Perhaps we might write once or twice a year? I should love to hear what you are doing. It would make me very happy if Leonora works out.' In fact she wrote rather more often than that, but mostly about the things I was supposed to be writing for the *Cambridge Review*, of which she was (the first woman) editor.

Back in Khartoum life was busy rather than sad, and soon my mother came out for a second winter in the sun. But in November I wrote to Esther: 'I am confused (I have *very little* light on the future I'm afraid), and still rather desperately in love with you.' Leonora and I corresponded regularly, but that was going nowhere, as we both knew. To Esther, and at first only to Esther, I confessed that I was by now 'extremely uncertain about ordination', and soon that feeling was replaced by certainty that I would *not* be ordained. I suppose that that was a consequence of the new situation. But 10 August had been my thirtieth birthday. The tumultuous twenties were over.[2]

---

[2] Esther married Victor de Waal, a Pembroke man and a priest who was to become chancellor of Lincoln and, in 1976, dean of Canterbury. By a strange twist of fate I and my wife, Liz, arrived in Canterbury in the same year. Victor and I were both fifty in 1979, and we celebrated a hundredth birthday party in the Deanery, with our eight children doing all the work. Esther and Victor have four sons, all remarkable men: John, a barrister and Buddhist; Alex, founder of *Justice Africa* and a great authority on all things African, from Darfur to the Horn; Edmund, an internationally celebrated ceramicist; and Tom, Russian and Caucasus expert, author of books on the war in Chechnya, and on Azerbjhan. It stretches the imagination to think that those four men, all with families, would not have had the same incarnation if Esther and I had come to a different conclusion, that rainy night in Bergen. And where would my four children and eight grandchildren have been? Nowadays Esther continues to write, travel, lecture and takes retreats. She spends January and February each year in Washington DC, where she is a Senior Fellow of the Cathedral College, but finds her stability in the cottage in the Welsh Borders, given to the family by her father, forty years ago.

12

It was all down to the Khartoum Caledonian Society

Socially, Khartoum consisted of a variety of hermetically sealed ethnic cells. It was possible to gain entry to any of these as an outsider (my friend Richard Gray became very thick with the Armenians, to his financial advantage), but not to belong. The twelve Germans in the town found that they had no choice but to form their own little club. There was no civic life. This was a legacy of the Ottoman and Egyptian past as much as of British colonialism. Most Brits belonged to the Sudan Club, although I was one of those who did not. (In 1988 the Club, a symbol of colonialism, would be raked with gunfire in the first episode of 'terrorism' in Khartoum, when the Acropole Hotel was blown up.) University staff had little to do with the commercial expatriate community, whose bosses had assumed the leadership *rôles* previously played by the members of the Sudan Political Service: president of the Sudan Club, church warden in the cathedral, and so on.

One exception to this rule was my friendship with Jock Morrison. Jock was a considerable character, a raw Scot from Lanark. He had secured a position with the Sudan Mercantile Company, partly by assuring those who interviewed him that he had been to a public school, not knowing what the question meant. The Sudan Mercantile was owned by a family called Keymer, and Ronald Keymer was the stoutest lay pillar of the cathedral. Consequently Jock found himself landed with the job of treasurer to the (Christian) Unity High School, where I was honorary secretary to the governing committee. (It was at that same Unity School, in 2007, that an English teacher found herself in serious trouble for naming a teddy bear Mohammed.) So it was that Jock and I became friends, which otherwise would not have happened.

On St Andrew's Day (30 November) 1959, Jock rang me up and asked me to come to his rescue. He had formed a little party to go to the annual dinner of the Khartoum Caledonian Society, someone had dropped out, and he needed a man to help him escort two nursing sisters from the Civil Hospital. Although the dinner was at the Sudan Club I accepted his invitation, and great fun it was. After the Haggis, Roastit Bubblyjock and Craigrownie Puddin', and all the mandatory toasts, there was Scottish dancing. I enjoyed the dancing so much that I began to go to the Club for Scottish dancing on Monday evenings. And it was there that I met Elizabeth Selwyn on 22 February 1960, 'properly', as my diary records. (I don't think that we had previously met improperly.) Elizabeth had just arrived as a nursing sister at the Civil Hospital and one of the other sisters, Lily, had given me her name and phone number. My wallet contains, to this day, the crumbling card of an Asmara taxi firm on the back of which I have written: '3818 Elizabeth Selwyn 1.30–2.15.' It turned out that Elizabeth was living in the same room which Leonora had inhabited, a year before. Our relationship was destined to last rather longer than three-quarters of an hour.

Elizabeth was tiny, beautiful and vivacious, with shining eyes. I fell head over heels, and fortunately she liked my blue eyes too. It was a lightning courtship: had to be, since less than six weeks after 22 February I was due to go on leave, and would be gone for three months. I was my father's son, the son of the father who had come home on a Saturday in August 1940 with a carful of unexpected chickens, the father who had proposed to my mother almost before he knew her.

I was now the proud owner of a red Ford, dating from about 1930, with no roof and no handbrake (there were no hills in Khartoum, except for the railway bridge, and I always kept two bricks in the car in case of breaking down). So it was possible to take Elizabeth (who, I find from her letters, became 'Liz' halfway through my leave) fishing up the Blue Nile, to a good spot called Norah's Hole, where we caught plenty of tasty green mudfish. Before distributing them to our friends, I took Elizabeth home to meet my mother. When I got back from returning her to the Sisters' Mess, my mother said: 'Well that's the nicest girl you've produced so far. But I just wish that she wouldn't drink so much whisky!' Elizabeth had been living in Hong Kong, where the standard tipple was whisky and dry ginger. Every day I picked Elizabeth up when she came off duty, and we would go off to Gordon's Tree on the White Nile, or to the Five Palm Trees on the Blue Nile: more fishing than either of us has ever done since.

Louis Armstrong came to the Sudan, and we went to hear him in Omdurman. (His concerts did not go down well with the locals. 'Khartoum!', he told me, 'hot days and cool nights!') On the way back from the concert, we did a little snogging among the trees of the Sunt Forest. But the Forest was full of sheep and goats which were being imported from the Ansar HQ at Aba Island on the White Nile. We were surrounded in the dark by a threatening crowd. 'Mamnour!' ('It is forbidden!') I proposed, in the car, outside the Burri Power Station, and was accepted. I had never known that life could be that simple. For too long I had refused to accept no. Now it was only yes. With Jock Morrison we made up an inseparable threesome, regularly frequenting a little club on the river where they played again and again the only record they had, a Frank Sinatra rendering of what Jock insisted was 'Bewitched, buggered, and bewildered'. Jock thought that Elizabeth was a thoroughly good thing, but believed that he could detect a touch of temperament. He thought me a bit mean and had grave doubts about the marriage which was soon arranged; to such an extent that, although he was my best man, it was I who had to reassure him on the night before the wedding.

On 1 April, Elizabeth took me with Peter Bietenholz to the station and we caught a train for Wadi Halfa, Aswan and Cairo. I must have been full of trust, to leave my fiancée behind in that country which, as we were reminded at the airport, was 'a paradise for hunters'. And there were plenty of hunters. I needn't have worried. Liz wrote: 'I feel so incredibly free where the odd bachelors are concerned, as if I was already married'. And Jock, the oddest bachelor of all, took good care of her. He wrote to me to say that much of their conversation was 'about that fascinating character Jock Morrison'.

To my mother Liz wrote of 'the deep and growing affection I have for Pat. I love him dearly and hope that I may always be worthy of him and the love that he so abundantly bestows upon me.' She even went on about my 'sweetness of character', which suggests that she did not yet know me all that well. She was more at risk

32   Liz Selwyn

when she went horse riding in the desert. Once a spirited Arab with a hard mouth and a strong homing instinct bolted for a dense thicket of acacia trees, and Liz had no choice but to abandon ship, doing terrible things to her back.

I wrote to Liz from Cairo: 'I am almost continually aware of a very strong invisible anchor, giving me steadiness and direction. I just praise God for you and for bringing us together.' Later, from London: 'I love you deeply and completely and with the most glorious abandon, and I have a constant feeling of security, stability and just sheer happiness which I don't think I have ever felt before.' In May I saw Esther in Cambridge (to discuss my article in the *Cambridge Review*), and was able to tell Liz that she was very glad about our engagement, and that 'we are just old friends now'. In late June I passed on to Liz the news that Esther was marrying Victor de Waal in September. 'She wanted you and me to know especially, and to say how happily it seems to have worked out for us all, and how terribly pleased she is about us, as well as about her own forthcoming marriage.'

Elizabeth Selwyn was the younger of the two daughters of Major Geoffrey Selwyn and his wife Helen, born two months after me, in October 1929. Geoffrey was one of the six sons of Edward Carus Selwyn (and there were two daughters), successively dean of King's College Cambridge, principal of Liverpool College and Headmaster of Uppingham, which he left under something of a cloud in 1907. Geoffrey's elder brother Gordon was a distinguished Anglican theologian and dean of Winchester, who died in 1959, so I never knew him, although before I met Liz I had bought some books from his library, thanks to Blackwell. Two other brothers were killed in the First World War, and Edward Carus Selwyn died in the great influenza epidemic of 1918. Geoffrey had an interesting, but hardly a good war. He wangled his way out of the trenches and got to East Africa, where he had many adventures and some bloody encounters, mostly in Portuguese East, where that war, thanks to the best general on either side of the 1914–18 conflict (a German) went on for ever, indeed for two weeks after the eleventh hour of the eleventh day. As a result of malaria and other complications, Geoffrey was left almost paralysed down one side, unable to use one arm and dragging a useless leg after him. It was in hospital that he met his wife, Helen Worrall, a masseuse who was the daughter of an unsuccessful artist and his wife, Marijama, who ran a boarding house for other painters at Leigh-on-Sea, and who saw that her five daughters all had the means to earn their own living.

In 1920 the Selwyns became beneficiaries (if that is the right word) of the Soldier Settlement Scheme, and found themselves trying to make a go of it on a farm outside Kitale in the far west of Kenya, the Trans-Nzoia, which they called Friston Estate. (Friston was the ancestral estate in Sussex.) Liz was born in London but lived in Kenya in the early thirties, while her sister, seven years older, was boarded in a convent at East Grinstead in Sussex. On 8 June 1934 a terrible tragedy began to unravel at Friston. The Selwyns were almost paranoid with anxiety about the petty thieving, and even cattle-rustling, which went on all the time and which involved the Pokot tribe (known at that time to Europeans as 'Suk') whose reserve lay only a few miles away. When the cow bells were found to have been stolen from around the necks of the cattle, no doubt preparatory to stealing the cows themselves, the Selwyns took the law into their own hands, made a citizens' arrest of six Suk, and took them back to the farm, where they were beaten on the orders and under the watchful eye of Helen. Seventeen days later, one of the six died in hospital, as the (fairly remote) consequence of the beating. The colonial government seems to have decided to make a test case of the matter (to prove its judicial even-handedness), and Geoffrey and Helen were jointly charged with the man's murder. But Geoffrey, who was in prison in Eldoret, died of blackwater fever before the trial came on. Helen, under guard in the Kitale Nursing Home, had been unconscious herself for two days, but was put in the car and taken to Eldoret, not knowing quite what was happening to her, where she arrived just before the end. She wrote: 'And now I shall never see him again on this earth, never that dear voice, never that poor halting step, none of the thousand little things I had to do for him; never hear him making fun of Elizabeth, and hear them laughing together.'

The trial continued in Geoffrey's absence. Helen, who was a very sick woman, was found guilty of manslaughter and sentenced to a year's imprisonment, which she served in the old Portuguese fort at Mombasa, with some remission. During that year, Liz lived with a family of neighbours, who had children of about her own age. When Helen came back it was clear that she could not carry on with the farm.

She brought Liz home to England to join her sister Barbara at East Grinstead. She then went back to Kenya to settle her affairs, came home again in 1939, but found that there was no room for her in the new profession of physiotherapist. She had no choice but to return to Kenya in a wartime convoy. She died there in 1948, of stomach cancer. In 1997, the BBC took Liz to Kenya, and she traced her parents' graves at Kitale and arranged to have a memorial stone erected. Barbara died from Alzheimer's disease in the early eighties, and her faithful husband Peter passed away in January 2007.

St Margaret's East Grinstead was a place where repressive religion amounted to barbarity. Six-year-old Liz was always ill, with malaria and the consequences of malaria. Although Barbara did her best to protect her, the sisters interpreted all this as so much wickedness. But Liz had a godmother who proved to be a fairy godmother. This was a woman in her fifties, Christina Stubington, who lived with two unmarried sisters in a house with spacious gardens and grounds and a large staff, at Rowlands Castle in Hampshire. There were in all five daughters of Colonel Stubington, a local brewer who was a caricature of a patriarch and succeeded in preventing all but one of his daughters from marrying. (When the colonel died, his widow was quite unable to write a cheque.) Liz came to stay with her godmother in the holidays, and the local GP pronounced that if she went back to East Grinstead she would not last for very long. Thereupon 'Aunt Chris' decided, to the alarm of her sisters, to adopt Liz (not, I think, a legal adoption as such). So Liz grew up in this remarkable household, with blessed relief from the (very kind) aunts to be found below stairs and behind the green baize door. She was poorly educated (as indeed, in their generation, were the aunts themselves, for all that Aunt Grace was chairman of the Education Committee of Hampshire County Council – this England!), but after leaving school made a success of nursing, qualifying as a State Registered Nurse with a medal to boot. After going on to train as a midwife, wanderlust and the Overseas Nursing Council took her, in 1955, to Hong Kong and the Queen Mary Hospital, a place where you worked hard and played hard. When Aunt Chris died in 1959, Liz felt bound to come home, but after a few months went back to the Overseas Nursing Council, which gave her a choice of Khartoum or the Bahamas. Luckily for me, she chose Khartoum.

Because Liz had been effectively orphaned, it was many years before we began to piece together her ancestry. The Selwyns are an ancient family, mentioned in Domesday Book, with branches settled for many centuries at Friston in Sussex and at Matson in Gloucestershire. There was an Elizabethan John Selwyn who performed the feat of jumping from his horse on to the back of a stag and slaying it in the presence of the queen, an incident engraved on the Ascot Gold Cup. Liz's second name is 'Albinia', a name confined to relatively few families (including the Hobarts and Townshends) from the date, 1604, when it was conferred on a daughter of Edward Cecil, Viscount Wimbledon, a grandson of William Cecil, Lord Burghley. The genealogical annals of three centuries are reconstructed in a bibliographical curiosity *The Albinia book*, published in 1929 by Albinia Lucy Cust. Albinia Cecil married Sir Christopher Wray and no less than seventeen peers could trace their descent from that marriage. Their daughter Albinia Wray had a daughter Albinia who married General William Selwyn of Matson, who was governor of Jamaica. Their grandson was the famous eighteenth-century wit and gambler George Augustus Selwyn, friend of Horace Walpole, whose hobby was spectating at executions, the grislier the better. There have been Albinias in every generation of Selwyns. George Augustus, who liked women, and little girls, but remained a bachelor, entailed Matson to the heirs of his niece Albinia, daughter of his brother-in-law Thomas Townshend, third son of the second Viscount Townshend. Their only son, Thomas Townshend, was the first Viscount Sydney, and it was after him, as William Pitt the Elder's secretary of state, that Sydney in Australia was named. I used to assume that Liz must be a great granddaughter of that later George Augustus, the bishop of New Zealand, after whom Selwyn College is named. But you have to go back to the mid-eighteenth century and to a governor of Montserrat to find a common ancestor.

Rather more interesting are Liz's relations on the side of her paternal grand-mother, Edward Carus Selwyn's wife Lucy. Lucy was the granddaughter of Thomas Arnold of Rugby, one of the daughters of Thomas Arnold the younger, that Victorian wanderer, in religion and much else, a very learned man (classics, foreign languages, Anglo-Saxon studies, English literature) but forever checked and frustrated in his career; and of the spirited and difficult wife he had married in Tasmania, Julia Sorrel. Thomas's brother Matthew Arnold dropped dead in the streets of Toxteth, Liverpool, on 15 April 1888, only a few yards away from the Selwyn home where Liz's father Geoffrey was born at about the same time, perhaps on the very same day. But Edward Carus Selwyn could not have been there at the time since he was at the Arnold family home of Fox How, conducting the funeral of his mother-in-law, Liz's great grandmother, Julia Arnold, who had died in Oxford eight days before. Six years later he lost his own wife, when Liz's grandmother died suddenly, aged only thirty-six and leaving seven children, including Geoffrey, who was six at the time. Lucy Arnold's elder sister Mary is known to history, and to literature, as Mrs Humphry Ward, the novelist, founder of the Mary Ward Settlement and a militant opponent of women's suffrage, who was therefore Liz's great aunt. Lewis Carroll was a close friend of the Arnold family, and we have his photograph of Mary's wedding, with Liz's grandmother as a bridesmaid. In her last years we saw quite a lot of Mrs Humph's daughter Dorothy (the sister of Janet, wife of the historian G. M. Trevelyan), who in the early 1900s used to support her mother in her anti-suffragette rallies. Another sister, another Julia, married Leonard Huxley, son and biographer of Thomas Huxley, so that Aldous and Julian Huxley were Geoffrey Selwyn's first cousins. Julian was among those who contributed to the fighting fund raised by Liz's Uncle Gordon when her mother went on trial.

In 1960, Liz and I had very different summers. She worked in the Khartoum Civil Hospital right through the intolerable heat of those months, which I never experienced. Conditions took her back into a pre-Florence Nightingale world. She found herself in charge of a surgical ward without a single pair of surgical scissors to be seen. Patients were visited by extended families which scattered food over the floors. Cat traps had to be set under the beds, but the cats bred more rapidly than the traps could be emptied. Liz wrote: 'Never in my life have I experienced such frustrations.'

Meanwhile I had gone on from Cairo to Jerusalem. This time Hilda came through the Mandelbaum Gate to the Old City and we had some days together, one of them at Jerash, the great Roman city north of Amman. When Hilda went back to Israel, I travelled by shared taxi to Damascus. I spent a whole day in and around the Umayyad Mosque and another in the wonderful Damascus Museum with its mock-ups of the Douros Europos synagogue and Queen Zenobia's Palmyra. I was arrested for taking photographs in the old fortress. The short-lived United Arab Republic, a union of Egypt and Syria, had just been formed, and I was forced by the soldiers to say how much I admired Colonel Nasser. Then on to Beirut and Cyprus, where I had only twenty-four hours, but hired a car and saw St Hilarion Castle, Kyrenia and Famagusta, touring much of the north of a still united island. I flew to Ankara, spent a day or two there, and went on to Istanbul. The weather was miserable, the tops of the minarets disappeared into the low cloud, and the Golden Horn looked like the Mersey. In Beirut I had changed a great deal of money into Turkish dinars at a very favourable exchange rate, intending to buy my rail ticket back to Europe with the proceeds, only to find that the ticket had to be purchased with dollars. I used up the useless money on presents for Liz, and in nightclubs (very decorous establishments where you drank 'votka' (the local araki) while fully dressed women bawled into the microphone). Soon after I got back to London the military overthrew the government of Menderes, and their first act was to close all the nightclubs.

From Istanbul I caught the Orient Express and travelled up through Thrace to Bulgaria, where, even on the avenue running up from the railway station in Sofia, I saw no cars. Once again the train took me through the delicious springtime scenery of Bosnia, Croatia and Slovenia. But this time I spent several days in Venice, with a good camera and no one to hurry me along. The original horses (not the copies one sees these days), the quadrivium stolen from Constantinople in 1204, were still on their platform on the facade of St Mark's and one could photograph them with a zoom lens from the top of the campanile and in every detail, close up. I fell in love with the Ca d'Oro. I got to England, via Paris, at the end of the month.

On Monday 9 May I had lunch with Professors Neale and Hurstfield in University College. I told them that I had decided not to go into the ordained ministry, and Neale said that he was very anxious to get me back into English academic life. They then told me about an Assistant Lectureship in Ecclesiastical History at King's College in the Strand. Neale seemed to think that the job was mine for the taking, and urged me to put in a late application. This was perhaps the only chance I had of getting back under the wire. Until that moment I had been thinking of some other overseas posting. Three or four years later, when all those new universities opened their doors, York, East Anglia, Kent, Warwick, Lancaster, Essex, Sussex, it would have been easy to get a job, but that would have been too late for me. Moreover the King's job entailed, mainly, the teaching of church history in the Reformation period, right up my street. So I applied, and waited. Four people were seen on Tuesday 17 May and at the Institute there were rumours and counter-rumours. The job was all but offered to my friend Gareth Owen, another pupil of Neale's who, like me, was working on Elizabethan religious history. But on Friday 26 May the committee reconvened and I was interviewed and offered the job. I accepted, after a certain amount of haggling, in an effort to raise the salary above £900 to £950 (with the London allowance that would make £1,010), much less than I had been earning in Khartoum, and an exchange of cables with Liz. After a distinctly false start, this was where my career as an academic historian was about to begin.

This was not like earlier summers. I commuted on a weekly basis between the Institute in London and Ipswich. And I worked very hard indeed, mainly on a monograph which would contain an edition of the important and revealing letters I had found in the Hertfordshire Record Office: *The letters of Thomas Wood, Puritan, 1566–1577*, a Special Supplement of the *Bulletin of the Institute of Historical Research*. This, and my essay on John Field in the Neale *Festschrift*, appeared at about the time that I started at King's and helped to make my name. Both Christopher Hill and Hugh Trevor-Roper reacted enthusiastically, Trevor-Roper in the *Sunday Times*, where he suggested, unkindly, that I had written all the stuff about Puritanism in the second of Neale's volumes on the Elizabethan parliaments. And the Clarendon Press wrote to express interest in publishing the big book which it was hoped I had in hand. But apart from one article, that was the sum total of all that I had published, or would publish until 1964, and the big book did not appear until 1967. Nowadays, in this age of Research Assessment Exercises, I would not be in the running for the most precarious and menial of academic posts.

But it was not all work. I bought an engagement ring and a wedding ring and made the wrong choice in both cases. It was not a good idea to be 2,000 miles away from my fiancée. I drove down to Hampshire to meet Liz's aunts, Aunt Win and Aunt Grace, in Rowlands Castle, and their sister Aunt Edie, and Uncle Gordon's widow, Aunt Barbara, in Winchester; and later Aunt Dot, the fourth of the surviving Stubington sisters, in Cobham. I can still remember drawing up outside the more modest house, Beechwood, to which the two aunts had moved after Aunt Chris's death, and hearing, for the first time, Aunt Grace's rather forbidding voice: 'He's here, Win, he's here!' They told me: 'We're so glad that you have turned up because, you know, we couldn't go on looking after Elizabeth for ever.' Now wasn't that remarkable? You would imagine that if two or three women in late middle age were to adopt someone like Liz they would have regarded that as an insurance policy, someone to look after them in their declining years. But not a bit of it. The aunts were remarkable women, forthright, even on occasion intimidating, but so warm-hearted. A few weeks later I met Liz's sister Barbara and her husband Peter and two children, Gillian and Christopher, in north London. Christopher was about to be sent off to a very bad boarding school where he was miserable, and if only I had known Peter better I would have tried to stop that happening. Pete and Bar were scratching a living in a part of London which they regarded as infra dig (but you would need more than half a million these days to buy their Crouch End house), and they were hanging on desperately to their family connexions and credentials, to the detriment of the children.

Just before leaving for Khartoum I had two or three days in North Wales, staying, for most of the time alone, in my beloved Helyg. What energy one had in those days! On the day I arrived, at 6 p.m., I walked across the Carneddau, and swam in the dark little lake of Dullyn (the Black Lake, and it is – half an hour swimming across and half an hour back again) before walking back over the mountains, getting to Helyg at 10.45. The next day I walked over the Glyders, did the Snowdon Horseshoe, and back over the Glyders, a total of 8,000 feet of ascent and descent. It was not very sensible to tell Liz that I was doing several (easy) rock climbs, solo. But a week later I was safely back in Khartoum.

The wedding was set for 6 December, and in spite of the treadmill of the academic year, beginning all over again, the five or six months which led up to it were some of the happiest of my life. We had a little dog, a mongrel rescued from a garage fore-court, which we called Adonis. After lunch I would be at my desk (back in a Pink Palace house) behind closed shutters, with Adonis on my lap. Cars would come and go. But when Liz turned up the drive in her little Fiat Topelino, Adonis would leap off and run for the door. We took her for walks in the desert just before sunset. Once we left it too late to get back to the car and lost it, among the acacia trees. Instead of finding it for us, which is what happens in sentimental animal films, Adonis's body language imitated the catch phrase in another kind of movie. 'This is another

33 Our wedding, 6 December 1960 – from left to right: Marion Charlton, my mother, PC, Liz, Jock Morrison, Aunt Grace, Frank Charlton, Aunt Dot, the page boys, Greg and Geoffrey Woods

34 Wedding photo

fine mess you've got me into.' We had to hitch a lift back to Khartoum in a lorry and to apologize to our dinner guests, who were being looked after by Mohi el Din. Later that night we drove back in someone else's car, and there was our little red Ford, forlorn among the trees.

At first Liz was intimidated by the prospect of having to mingle with academics, fondly imagining, as people do, that conversation would be conducted only at the most elevated of philosophical levels. On 14 July I had to work hard to persuade her to go to the French embassy, where there was all that free champagne. And on leave, I had had to reassure her. 'If I had thought that you were not mentally stimulating I don't suppose that I should ever have fallen for you in the first place – and believe me you *are* mentally stimulating. I certainly don't want another historian, or I would have hung on for one. Jock is probably right to say that you are at least as intelligent as me, darling, if not more so.' Erkowit broke some ice. We went up there in September, Liz was the life and soul, I corrected the proofs of *Thomas Wood* and did the index, and we all got to the top of Jebel Erbab. Soon after that Liz and her colleagues threw a party at the Sisters' Mess which ended disastrously, and it was all my fault. I devised a treasure hunt by car, and one of the clues was concealed on a telegraph pole outside the Egyptian embassy. Half the party were arrested and interrogated for half the night by the commissioner of police.

My mother was there for the wedding, and so were Aunt Grace and Aunt Dot, who brought out the wedding cake and a cheque to pay for the reception. This was otherwise looked after by a lovely couple, Frank and Marion Charlton, who, without children of their own, had virtually adopted Liz, and the reception happened in their garden. The guest list threatened to get out of hand, since people were invited whom we didn't even know, but who were known to have a good cook. But all of our colleagues were there, academic and medical, and such distinguished guests as Sayedd Mohammed Osman el Mirghani. When it came to cutting the cake, this was no token cut by the happy couple. No one came forward to help us and we had to slice the whole thing up ourselves. The service, in the cathedral, could not have been more lovely. Well, we devised it ourselves. The university librarian, Michael Joliffe, a Roman Catholic, said how good the Church of England was at weddings. Jock was a very competent best man. And we had two little page boys, Gregory and Geoffrey, sons of a neighbour and colleague, who somewhat tactlessly came banging on our doors and windows soon after we got back from the party.

But two weeks before all that we had had a civil wedding in the British embassy. This was the only legal ceremony and we had it well in advance (to the disgust of a rather suspicious Provost Martin) because Liz needed a passport in her married name before leaving for Ethiopia on our honeymoon. What happened in the window of an office in the embassy was almost more memorable than the real wedding. Three things happened at once. We signed the register. Jock had a mild epileptic fit (he suffered from petit mal). And, down below, Gemal Abdel Nasser, on a state visit, emerged from the gates of the Republican Palace in an open car.

Soon after the wedding the aunts travelled north to Luxor, where they engaged my faithful Coptic guide of a year before, and my mother went to Cairo, on to Jerusalem, and crossed the frontier to stay with Hilda over Christmas. By then we had begun a rather unusual honeymoon. We travelled by train to Kassala and were taken across to Tessenei in a car provided by Sayedd Mohammed Osman. As we came into town, the driver waved towards a large army camp and said 'military troops!' In the coming days we were to see more of those military troops. The bus journey up to

35 Wedding photo: Mohi el Din can be seen through the windscreen

36 Sayedd Mohammed Osman el Mirghani arrives at our party

Asmara, in daylight, was the most thrilling and beautiful that Liz had ever undertaken. There were ground hornbills, as well as the usual colourful bee-eaters. While we were in Asmara the first attempt to get rid of the Emperor Haile Selassie was made in Addis Ababa, in the name of his son, the crown prince. Winds of change were blowing, even in Ethiopia.

Haile Selassie had been in Brazil, but he flew back to Asmara, arriving on a day when I was out of town, visiting a famous monastery. Liz was frustrated that she was not able to climb up the mountain to Bizen: no female thing is. She wanted to see not so much the monks as the hyraxes, which abound on the rocks around the monastery, breeding in defiance of the rules of the place. Richard Gray and I argued for hours to get to see the sacred books. (Ethiopians, whose precious books often finish up in western libraries, are rightfully suspicious.) At last a great Bible was brought out, under an umbrella, and placed on a carpet. When the Prophet Mohammed called Christians 'the People of the Book', he meant that books were treated like totems, talismanic, mystical objects. The book was opened. Marginal devices indicated that this or that passage was open to debate and exegesis. St Paul's Epistles were innocent of any such marks. The passages addressing the subject of prohibited meats in Leviticus were heavily annotated. How to apply those rules to the fauna of Ethiopia?

Back in Asmara, Haile Selassie had processed through crowded streets, before boarding a plane for Addis, where order was being restored. We were advised by the British consul not to proceed any further, but we ignored the advice, and went down, as planned, to Axum. As usual, it was a question how to get to the next point on our journey, Gondar. But there in the market was an Ethiopian Airways pilot whom we had met in Asmara. Hearing that we were headed for Gondar he said, get your stuff together and I'll take you there. He had just flown into Axum with the body of the provincial governor, the Ras Seyyum, son of the Emperor Johannes, an elderly man who had been killed by the rebels in Addis. We raced back to the hotel, to which the one taxi in the place was ferrying the aristocratic mourners, mostly women. As we got to the airfield, it was surrounded by troops with machine guns, since there was a report that the leader of the insurgency was at large in a plane. Nevertheless, we took off, the only passengers. The ropes were still there in the central aisle which had held the coffin of the Ras in place. 'Would you like to see some ibex?' the pilot asked, and flew the plane on its side along the vertiginous cliffs of Simien. We saw no ibex and arrived at Gondar airfield, which had no lights, when it was almost dark. That kind of experience is one reason why we have no particular desire to return to Ethiopia, nearly fifty years on, as tourists.

Gondar was under curfew, which meant that we played a lot of poker (for the first and last time in our lives) with the motley expatriate community. At this time there were many bodies hanging in the public square in Addis, but Gondar was quiet. We sat among the giant sorrel under the juniper trees at Debra Behran Selassie, which could have been somewhere in Umbria, until the vultures came flapping back to roost at sunset. Soon we flew down to the little hotel on Lake Tana at Bahar Dar, which was our honeymoon destination. After exploring the headwaters of the Abbai (the Blue Nile) on a tankwa, we set off for the great falls of Tiss Abbai in the old-fashioned way, with a military escort, on mule back. We remember losing our way and approaching a country church where there was a funeral, hundreds of people, a buzz like a swarm of bees. We stood respectfully, hats off, until someone told Lieutenant Feleke Mengistu[1] where to go. As we sheltered in a little booth in a harvest field, the farmers asked the soldiers to shoot some baboons which were eating their crops, and Feleke Mengistu pulled out an Addis paper and read the news. I knew enough Amharic to recognize that they were talking about Haile Selassie, and whether he was or was not of the true Solomonic royal line. (In Gojjam, where we were, the Shoan dynasty of Ras Tafari (Haile Selassie) with its jumped up capital at Addis Ababa, was despised.)

We stayed the night in a tukl, among a large family of all ages. It was, according to our calendar, Christmas Eve. A beautiful young girl washed our feet, raising each big toe as she finished to give it an almost sacramental kiss. Her legs were hugely swollen with elephantiasis, which is a death sentence. The next morning we met a party of men coming from the milking and drank from their gourds: not a very sensible thing to do. Then there were some cows in a stream, a scene which Constable could have painted. But beyond the trees it was all white mist and there was a roar. And there were the falls, one of the most stupendous sights in Africa. Nowadays there is a hotel, and a decent road, and no doubt hordes of tourists. And much of the water is now diverted to make electricity. But on Christmas Day 1960 it was just us, the lieutenant and his two soldiers. Later, back at Bahar Dar, I caught some huge catfish in the lake, we entertained our friend Feleke Mengistu to supper, and Liz did a stint behind the bar of a tej house, which I am afraid in Ethiopia is the same thing as a brothel. The rest of the honeymoon was fun too, but more ordinary.

We were due to leave the Sudan in April 1961, and in the meantime we enjoyed our first months of married life. Liz had resigned from the Civil Hospital, but kept her hand in at the private nursing home which looked after the expatriates. We were allocated a good house on the Airport Estate where we lived with Adonis and a cat, and, of course, still with Mohi. We often went water-skiing on the Blue Nile with the Charltons and their commercial friends. Liz did quite well, but suddenly began to falter. The reason was that she was pregnant. We acted in *Murder in the cathedral* in (where else?) the cathedral. Then came the ritual for all departing expatriates of a Friday morning auction of most of our effects, a man ringing a bell, the dealers outside with their flat carts and miserable, mangy horses. Our car failed to make its reserve price of £110, the highest bid being £42. (It later went to a dealer for £60.) I have my father's shopkeeping instincts and estimated that the sale would make £243. In fact it came to £225. And then, on 29 March, after a flurry of farewell dos, including a dinner party laid on by Sayedd Mohammed Osman el Mirghani, we took off from Khartoum for Cairo and the rest of our lives.

The Sudan: looking back in anger and regret

There is no especial reason why, but we have never been back to the Sudan (now simply called 'Sudan'). To follow from a distance its unutterably tragic history over the ensuing decades is to be constantly reminded that our years there were years of falsity, futility and self-delusion. Neither we, nor above all the Sudanese, of so many ethnic and linguistic identities (175, with 325 smaller groups), had yet come to

---

[1] I have no reason to suppose that 'our' Lieutenant Mengistu was the same man as Mengistu Haile Mariam, who took power as the Marxist dictator of Ethiopia after the overthrow of Haile Selassie. There is a certain resemblance. But the name Mengistu is common enough, and the Internet even reveals many Feleke Mengistus.

terms with how, and even whether, such a state, if it was a state (rather, the anomalous outcome of colonial history), could be made to work; although those in power at any time knew what the answer to that question was – for themselves.

It was never a simple matter of North and South, Arabs and black Africans, Islam versus Christianity, as the western media have represented it, on the rare occasions when they have taken any notice of that part of the world, and of an almost endless conflict which has caused more deaths (in excess of two million) than any other since the Second World War. A better informed analysis would point to an asymmetrical relationship between the centre of power, Khartoum and the riverain groups along the Nile (who have formed all governments since 1956), and the rest of the country. As in much of sub-Saharan Africa, a narrowly based colonial administration handed power to an equally narrow centrist elite, excluding a periphery amounting to most of the territory of Sudan. Consequently there have been and are insurgencies not just in the South but among the Beja (Hadendowa and Beni Amer) of the Red Sea Hills to the north-east, the Fung and Ingessana of southern Blue Nile Province to the south-east, the Nubians of the far north (victims of the construction of a huge dam at Merowe), the polyglot blue-black peoples of the Nuba Mountains in southern Kordofan, and, most notoriously, Darfur.

The military regimes of Abboud, Nimeiri and, under Bashir, the National Islamic Front (now the National Congress Party), with a measure of connivance from the civilian parties of the Umma (the Mahdists) and the Democratic Unionists (my friend Mohammed Osman's Khatmia) have held the country together (as they would claim) by pursuing a policy of Islamization and Arabization (in Darfur Arabization is more to the point than Islamization, since all Darfurians are Muslims) directed with ruthless military force against subordinate subjects, rather than co-citizens of what is supposed to be a republic. Those in power insist that Sudan is an Arab, Arabic-speaking polity, although many, perhaps most, Sudanese are not Arabs. Their strategy has always involved exploitation of pre-existent ethnic differences to provoke proxy wars, a cynical policy of divide and rule.

This is something now familiar to all of us from Darfur, where Arab pastoralists have been unleashed as the so-called Janjaweed against non-Arab dirt farmers. (Both ethnic groups can be fairly represented as victims, victims of land and water shortage, as desertification creeps south.) But this was not where it started. When, in an earlier episode, the Arabic-speaking Baggara of Kordofan and Darfur raided and enslaved their Nilotic neighbours to the south, in Bahr el-Ghazal, and they were all cattle people, these were things which had always happened, long before the *Inglesiya*. And when, in 1992, the Nuer followers of the warlord Riek Machar (who had an English wife, Emma McCune) massacred 2,000 Dinka at Bor, on the White Nile, the situation on paper may have been that Riek was fighting for an independent Southern Sudan, against John Garang, leader of the Sudan Peoples' Liberation Army, an African tyrant in the making, who ostensibly sought a 'democratic' constitution for the whole of the Sudan. The reality was more traditional and tribal. The SPLA was Dinka-led, and such mileage as Riek had was fuelled by Nuer resentment of the Dinka. That was not new. But what was new was modern weaponry and the willingness of Khartoum to add more fuel to the fire by arming Riek.

The analogy is apt, since there is oil under those cattle pastures. The *Inglesiya* is now to be followed by a Chinese chapter, for China is buying much of that oil. (There are also Malaysian and Canadian interests.) Only China can now stop the genocide in the far west, Darfur; but of course China will do no such thing.

According to the terms of the peace accord which ended the war in the South in January 2005, the South has the right of self-determination and will vote, in 2111, either for unity with the North or for separation. But with or without secession (and would Khartoum ever allow it?) the (contested) frontier between North and South runs through those oil fields. And, as of now, every drop of oil is being pumped north, to Port Sudan. One does not have to be a pessimist to foresee that the outcome may be a regional rather than local conflict more calamitous than anything seen in Darfur. Many things have never changed; but what has is not only the oil but that people are now armed to the teeth with deadly modern weapons; and the terrifying power of a state machine, financed by oil revenues. Britain should never forget, but of course it has never known, let alone forgotten (for what is 'Britain' and what did 'Britain' have to do with it?), that it was largely responsible for this cataclysmic mess, if only by defining as it did the borders of this vast non-country.

The verdict of Julie Flint and Alex de Waal on Sudan in the early twenty-first century is chilling:

> The serial war criminals at the heart of Sudan's present government once sought absolute power in pursuit of an Islamic state. Now they seek power for its own sake. Today, as yesterday, the people they perceive to be challenging that power count for nothing. They can be subjugated, shot or starved without compunction. If local allies have different axes to grind, they are free to grind them, no matter how much blood they shed. Mass killing has become so routine that it no longer needs conspiracy or deliberation. It is simply how the security elite do business. It is ingrained intent, atrocity by force of habit.[2]

It is no less chilling to reflect on the fact that for five years Patrick Collinson was cheerfully working in the delivery room where this appalling future was gestating.

Back to ourselves, leaving the Sudan behind us. From Cairo we flew to Jerusalem. It was the Catholic Easter weekend and on Maundy Thursday we got trapped in the Holy Sepulchre by an interminable footwashing ceremony, and only escaped by walking right through the icons and clergy officiating at the altar in the Greek portion of the church, which seemed to bother nobody. Hilda came through from the other side on Good Friday and met Liz for the first time. We went to Jericho and the Dead Sea, and saw Qumran. It was a bitterly cold, wet spring, but the wild flowers, cyclamens, poppies, anchusas, tulips, loved it and never looked more beautiful. The desert all the way down the Jericho road to the Dead Sea was green. The storks were strutting in the fields, and we knew that they were the very same storks which we had seen in Eritrea in December, and circling high up in the thermals above the Blue Nile in March, like a big ball of wool unravelling as the birds began to head north. After Hilda went back through the Mandelbaum Gate we went up to Nablus and Samaria, saw Jacob's Well where Jesus had that remarkable conversation with a disreputable woman, and met the Samaritans who duly showed us 'the oldest book in the world'.

And then, again, that journey around three sides of a square, across the Jordan to Amman, up to Damascus, and over the mountains and the Bekaa to Beirut. That evening some of us decided to go twenty miles up the coast to the Casino de Liban

---

[2]   Julie Flint and Alex de Waal, *Darfur: a short history of a long war* (London, 2005), p. 134. These paragraphs are also indebted to Jok Madut Jok, *Sudan: race, religion, and violence* (Oxford, 2007).

and forced a hard bargain on a taxi driver. His driving seemed erratic and when we got to the night club we discovered why. He had only one leg. And that was our only means of getting back again.

From Beirut we went on to Athens, where the Orthodox Easter was getting under way. We went on a little tour to the Temple of Poseidon at Sounion, got bored with the guide's exposition, went down to the sea and had a swim in the altogether: fine, until we swam out from under the overhanging cliff, to find all the tourists looking down at us in the crystal clear sea. It was Good Friday, and when we got back to Athens the city was closed down for the burial procession of Christ: the whole cabinet, the army, the fire brigade, bands playing the Dead March in *Saul*, all neon signs turned off and every window full of people holding candles. A moment's reflection on whether such a thing could ever happen in Oxford Street made one understand that this was a different kind of Christian civilization. The next day we went to Delphi, scrambled among the temples and theatres, saw that bronze chari-oteer who perhaps belongs with the quadrivium in Venice, and looked out over an endless sea of olive orchards while the griffon vultures and lammergeyers soared overhead. Easter morning woke us early with fireworks as well as bells. We made a quick visit to the cathedral and then caught a plane for Vienna, and on to London. The first plane was a Sabena flight, full of other people leaving Africa: Belgian refugees from the Congo, where Patrice Lumumba had been murdered in February. In London I reported at King's on the morning after our arrival. We first put up at the Friends' International Centre and then found a rather unsatisfactory couple of furnished rooms in Lewisham. We began to house-hunt and I started on my new job. It had been a strenuous time, what with all that travel and the humping around of boxes and cases. On a weekend visit to the aunts at Rowlands Castle, Liz had a miscarriage. But there were better things to come.

37   Delphi, April 1961

13

King's College London and Honor Oak, 1961–1969

From June 1951 until April 1961, from twenty-one to thirty-one, I had never stopped travelling: Arctic Norway, the Alps, the Sudan, Ethiopia, the Mediterranean. But from 9 April 1961 until 15 August 1969, when we took ship for Australia, I never once left Britain (and only got to the Scottish part of the island once or twice). We had the statutory two-week holiday once a year, first in Pembrokeshire and then in Cumbria. On a rare trip to North Wales to meet up with my old climbing friends and their families, one of our children was taken to buy boots in a shop in Nant Peris where everyone was talking Welsh. Envious of what her friends at school boasted about, she asked in hushed tones: 'Are we abroad?'

But I had four children to show for those years, and a substantial book by which I am best known to the historical world. The reader may be relieved to find that the narrative at this point ceases to be a travelogue, and a no less picaresque series of emotional as well as physical journeys. From this point on there will be rather more history in this history of a history man.

Life was divided between King's College on the Strand and a handsome little detached house in an obscure part of south London called Honor Oak, up on a ridge above Peckham on the one side and Lewisham on the other. The oak of honour was a tree under which Queen Elizabeth I was supposed to have taken refreshment, on a hunting trip from Greenwich. The original tree had long been replaced, but the little park at the top of our rough little cul-de-sac, Honor Oak Rise, was still called One Tree Hill.

Down the hill on the other side was St Augustine's Church, which, with what was left of my parochial Anglican convictions, I insisted we attend, although it was a church where Liz's faith withered and almost died, like a palm tree in the Arctic. Some people called it St Disgustings. We more than attended. I ran the Sunday School and we looked after the missionary side of things, trying to make our fellow parishioners share the cosmopolitan view of the world which we expatriates had necessarily acquired in foreign parts. Students from many parts of the world came to us for Christmas, or stayed for a few days, or a week or two. One of our favourites was a Vietnamese journalist. He told us: 'I go to the British Council. They tell me to go to the Hyde Park Corner, where I will hear people talk up and talk down the queen. I go to the Hyde Park Corner. No one speak of the queen. Everyone speak of my country.'

Working with the British Council, we gave parties which mixed locals with our students. It was not yet clear whether 'coloured' people could be integrated into the congeries of villages which is south London. Our friend and fellow parishioner Herbert Eames, soon to be Conservative leader of Lewisham borough council, was asked only one question on the doorsteps. 'When are you going to get them out?' Strangely enough, the parish already had an interest in the Sudan (and that was

Herbert's doing); and presently a young engineer and his wife went out from Honor Oak to the Southern Sudan to build the cathedral in Juba. I had a good deal to do with the Church Missionary Society (CMS), in the days when it was led by that remarkable Africanist, visionary and poet, John Taylor, later bishop of Winchester. I was a member of the Men's' Candidates Committee, and Liz and I regularly had candidates for service with the CMS to stay, our job to decide whether they were right for that vocation, or were people living inside inverted commas, as John Taylor used to put it. I also served as the representative of the London Theological Faculty on CACTM, the body which oversaw ordination policy in the Church of England: an odd development, since I had been before CACTM as a candidate for orders ten years before. It was then that I discovered that bishops are human beings too.

No. 19 Honor Oak Rise had a bedroom with a deep window seat where, before we got around to buying furniture, we had all our meals, enjoying a view which extended from Millbank through Westminster to St Paul's, seen over the trees of Peckham Rye, almost as if London itself was a garden city. There was a spectacular cherry tree which was in full blossom when our first child was born in May 1962. The house cost us £5,500, free of mortgage, purchased with a small legacy which Liz had inherited. My modest superannuation from Khartoum bought the first family car. Apart from that we were skint. Very occasionally funds ran to the purchase of a bottle of Cyprus sherry, at 9s 6d a time (50p in modern money).

King's College was reached by the no. 63 bus, or more often by car, since there were no restrictions on parking; nor, for that matter, at the British Museum, which I would leave at lunchtime to walk down to the original Sainsbury's in Drury Lane to put the week's shopping in the boot before going back to the Reading Room. I was so lucky to be at King's in the 1960s. Those gloomy corridors, reminiscent of one of Her Majesty's rather older prisons, still have a genius loci about them which arouses deep emotions. I do not forget my first beginning of term service in that Byzantine chapel; nor Professor Tasker, about to retire from his chair, author of *The wrath of God*, mounting the pulpit to announce with great confidence his text: 'There was a man sent from John whose name was God.'

And here it has to be explained that on the Strand there were at that time two institutions under one roof: King's College London, a theological college which was part of the Church of England; and University of London, King's College, which was and on paper still is what it says. King's College was headed by its dean; University of London, King's College, by the principal. The principal when I arrived was an Aberdonian classicist called Noble, not I think very memorable, but he was succeeded by a more electrifying figure, General Sir John Hackett, a veteran of Arnhem, who had run the British Army on the Rhine and assumed that similar tactics would work on the Strand – and also a historian, with a particular interest in the crusades. Since the year was 1968, those proved to be interesting times. Hackett prepared for his new responsibilities by reading all that he could about *les évènements* in Paris and elsewhere. At King's he cultivated the more radical students, all six of them. They told him, over brandy late at night, that in the revolution he would be one of the first to be eliminated, since he was the sort to make the present system work. Or so he assured his staff in mandarin speeches in which he failed to mention whether our latest pay rise would ever materialize, and which were indeed a substitute for taking any real interest in those below the rank of professor. In the men's loo there were two sanitary metal devices above the urinals, which we all said were twin microphones, one connected to the dean's office, the other to the principal's.

As a Lecturer in Ecclesiastical History, I was formally part of University of London, King's College. But many of the students I taught were non-matriculated Anglican ordinands, studying for something called the AKC (Associateship of King's College); and since I was paid by the University of London, and so ultimately by the British taxpayer, it was arguable, and nowadays would be so argued, that I had no business to be teaching those people at all. Other students were candidates for the London degree of Bachelor of Divinity, an exacting course, with Church History a distracting and for many irritating diversion from the hard graft of Greek and Hebrew. One of my favourite students failed the BD, but went on to take a First in History at York, which perhaps tells us all that we need to know about those two disciplines. Another BD student was a certain Desmond Tutu, who, whenever I met him in other parts of the world, such as California, would both delight and embarrass me by crying out loud: 'But this is one of my teachers!'

I also lectured to historians from many of the London colleges, some of whom came all the way from Royal Holloway near Windsor Great Park on a Thursday afternoon to attend my not very competent lectures on the Ecclesiastical History of Western Europe, 1400–1700. (What did I know about Jean Gerson or Jacques-Bénigne Bossuet?) I also taught essay classes for the King's historians. But when I attended, by invitation, the first departmental meeting convened by my friend John Elliott as Professor of History, I was taken to task by my head of department, since I was responsible only to him, no part of the Department of History.

The historians were a solid bunch, and especially solid in the sense that none of them ever left to go anywhere else. There was Gerald Hodgett, a good social historian of the later middle ages, Charles Duggan, a learned medievalist, married to Anne Duggan, a great authority on Thomas a Becket; and Christopher Howard, 'Splendid Isolation' Howard, for that was his chosen topic, who made it his business to tell John Elliott, at that same departmental meeting, that his new ideas were all very well, but not compatible with tradition, let alone with preparing students for the public examinations of the University of London. The two most captivating teachers in the department, who lacked the King's staying power, were strongly contrasted historians of the seventeenth century: the Marxist Brian Manning, whose lectures were conjured out of thin air, and Garry Bennett, who prepared everything meticulously; later an Anglican cleric and Oxford don who was to die in circumstances still much discussed, after the publication of a preface to *Crockford* which was critical of Archbishop Robert Runcie. When I arrived, in April 1961, the Professor of History was a rather dull Tudor man called C. H. Williams, another Neale product, who his students unkindly called 'Charlie Hearthrug Williams'. He had been at King's for ever, but, Ancient Mariner like, never missed an opportunity to tell anyone, who included my wife at that annual summer curiosity, the 'Conversazione', how it was that he had come to succeed C. H. Hearnshaw, a more considerable figure. But Williams had his kindly side. He once asked me: 'Ever thought of getting ordained Collinson?' I told him that the idea had crossed my mind but had gone away. 'Going to find it difficult to get a chair, aren't you?'

The Faculty of Divinity had more weight, and the capacity to inspire. Its head within this Dual Monarchy was a remarkable man, Sydney Evans, the true pope of King's in those days, later dean of Salisbury. We shared an interest in the Boat Club, for I used to coach from the towpath between Putney and Mortlake on Saturday mornings, bellowing advice through a megaphone which no one, I'm sure, could hear. Sydney and I were returning on the tube from the annual Boat

Club dinner. 'What is to happen to you?', he asked, and I assumed that I had been found out, seen through. But what Sydney meant was that my professor, Clifford Dugmore, who King's had appointed to his chair in the late fifties, persuaded by the kingmaker in Ecclesiastical History of his time, Norman Sykes, was not up to much. And the Department of Ecclesiastical History consisted of Dugmore and me. Dugmore invariably introduced me as 'my assistant, Collinson'. I was a true sorcerer's apprentice. I was regularly despatched to the Borough Post Office in Southwark to purchase sheets of the latest stamps, for Dugmore was a great philatelist. And when the Dugmores moved from Thame to Surrey, I helped to move the books, as did a later 'assistant', Eamon Duffy, from the Strand to Puttenham, when Dugmore retired.

Dugmore had begun as an Old Testament scholar, but hard times had led to the sale of his Hebraic library and an interest in pig-farming, which he managed to combine with the post of Bishop Fraser Senior Lecturer in Ecclesiastical History in the University of Manchester, where he got on badly with the professor of that subject, the distinguished Methodist historian of the Lutheran Reformation, Gordon Rupp. (It was for that reason that Sykes sought the means to move him on.) Dugmore's inaugural lecture at King's had a revealing title: 'Ecclesiastical history no soft option'. But Clifford Dugmore is still a name to be inscribed in gold in the annals of that sufficiently hard option. It was Dugmore who launched the *Journal of Ecclesiastical History*, to this day the flagship periodical in its field, anywhere in the world. And it was Dugmore who invented the Ecclesiastical History Society, in face of the scepticism of other leaders in that field (Gordon Rupp, Owen Chadwick), and whose annual publication *Studies in Church History* has, like my marriage, outlived its forty-sixth year.

The other professors and lecturers in the Faculty of Divinity were men (almost all men, the exception to prove the rule, Morna Hooker, later Lady Margaret Professor in Cambridge) of real distinction: Christopher Evans, Professor of New Testament, Peter Ackroyd, Professor of Old Testament, Geoffrey Parrinder, the comparative religionist. And then the theologians: Denis Nineham, later Regius Professor in Cambridge, and, after that warden of Keble, who owed his vocation to a sermon preached in his school chapel by my wife's uncle, but who had a low opinion of Gordon Selwyn as a theologian; the Oxford high churchman Eric Mascall and his complete opposite, George Woods, an 'Honest to God' man (those were John Robinson's sixties), who died suddenly soon after his arrival on the Strand; Maurice Wiles, later an Oxford regius, with a shared interest in the missionary side of things; and the altogether unusual theologian and Old Testament scholar Ulrich Simon, a convert from Judaism and Marxism, whose detestation of nineteenth-century bourgeois culture knew no bounds, extending to regular denunciations of the music of Johannes Brahms, and provoking him into giving me his four-volume set of the Oxford sermons of John Henry Newman.

In 1967 we were joined by Gordon Dunstan, the first F. D. Maurice Professor of Moral and Social Theology. Dunstan was editor of *Theology*, the journal which my wife's uncle had founded, back in the twenties. He tried to persuade me to write a kind of 'Quest for Corvo' article, which would be a portrait of Gordon Selwyn by someone who had never known him, but most of whose colleagues had. When I found how negative the recollections of colleagues were (Mascall – 'the rudest man I ever knew'), the project was abandoned. But, married as I am to Selwyn's niece, I know both that there were reasons for that rudeness (his first wife had died in tragic circumstances in the war, and a son had been killed at Arnhem soon after), and that there was a very attractive side to the man which not everyone saw.

The extraordinary diversity of the King's theologians was the strength of the faculty. There was no 'line'. This bewildered many, and half the students who came as ordinands departed determined to do something else, while many others were convinced by the King's experience that they ought to be ordained. With the passing of their generation, the Church of England, as it was from about 1965 to 1995, is ceasing to exist. So far as I was concerned, these senior colleagues were immensely encouraging and supportive. So was Michael Howard, the military historian and later Oxford Regius; at that time a great power in the University of London. At last I came to feel that I had found my way into the right profession, and that I could hold my own after all.

What did I teach? The Reformation, of course, mainly to the theological students. The intellectual and bibliographical resources to sustain lectures on Luther and Calvin and all the other reformers were, so far as I was concerned, slender, and the in-depth, social history of religion in the sixteenth century was still in its infancy. It embarrasses me when clergy up and down the country (and it happens quite often) tell me what they owed to my lectures. I also held forth on 'Religious and ecclesiastical movements, 1789 to 1945' – and I loved doing it. There is nothing better than teaching outside your own period. I became quite deeply immersed in the story of the French church in the nineteenth century and beyond, the First Vatican Council, Christian Socialism (years later I would give the F. D. Maurice Lectures in King's), Darwinism and religion, religion and the First World War, the Ecumenical Movement. I taught a Master's course with set texts which included Pio Nono's Syllabus of Errors, *Essays and reviews*, Seeley's *Ecce homo*, some of the writings of the trendy Catholic Modernists of the early twentieth century, and Adolf Harnack's *What is Christianity?* I once had on my shelves forty or fifty life-and-letters biographies of English churchmen of the time. But they have all gone, to make way for more recent interests.

It was an important moment in my life when A. G. Dickens came to King's in 1962, to succeed Williams in the History chair. Geoff Dickens was already acknowledged to be the leading historian of the English Reformation, although his talents had been somewhat hidden under the bushel of the University of Hull, for which Philip Larkin rather than Dickens is famous, an institution of which Anthony Crosland, as secretary of state for education, claimed never to have heard. Up to that time Dickens had been known for a rather single-minded concentration on the history of religious change, and resistance to change, in the north of England. But in 1964 he published his general study, *The English Reformation*, which advised all those who needed to be so advised that the great revolution in religion which erupted in Tudor England was about more than Henry VIII's troubles in the royal bedchamber; that it was as much bottom-up as top-down, a genuine revolution in religion and society, not a mere coup d'état. The book was at once hailed by the leading authorities of the day as nearly definitive, not yet suspecting the 'revisionist' onslaught that would be mounted against its very premises in years to come. According to Dickens, the Reformation was an idea whose time had come. According to his younger and aggressive critics, it was either an idea in which no one was much interested or even not an idea at all. Rather a negation of ideas, or of practices and traditions to which 'most people' were still deeply attached. We are still trying to pick up the pieces.

The first edition of *The English Reformation* was dedicated, to the mystification

of many, to members of 'the Tudor Seminar': S. T. Bindoff, Clifford Dugmore, Joel
Hurstfield, Henry VIII's biographer J. J. Scarisbrick – and myself. What was this
'seminar'? A group which met annually in some Alpine resort to survey, as from a
peak in Darien, all that lay around us? No, we were merely a hardworking collective
which taught a Tudor Special Subject, week by week, for the University of London.
When Dickens was in the chair, this was a master class, but not perhaps how master
classes are meant to work. Some hapless student had no sooner embarked on a
paragraph on, as it might be, the Bible in the Reformation, than Dickens would cut
in with twenty minutes of his own great learning on that subject. The student paper
would never be allowed to finish.

Dickens was someone else who gave me a great deal of what is nowadays called
validation: most of all when he published a little textbook on the continental Reformation and said in the Preface, with extreme and uncalled for generosity, that it
was a privilege to have me studying and teaching alongside him. Presently, Dickens
left King's to become director of the Institute of Historical Research, and chose to
make his statutory director's seminar another master class in Reformation History,
now devoted to teaching those writing theses on the Reformation in, as it might
be, Ashby-de-la-Zouche, that there was more to life, and history, than Ashby-de-
la-Zouche. It was a privilege to sit alongside Dickens in those seminars and to add
my pennyworth on John Calvin, for whom Dickens had little sympathy. These were
the funds which I invested and which delivered good dividends when I got to the
University of Sydney and began to devote much of my time to lecturing on the
Reformation.

Another source of constant inspiration and encouragement, laced with the most
astringent of criticism, was Geoffrey Nuttall, the doyen of historians of English
nonconformity (who died in 2007, full of years), the candidate who really should
have got the London chair when Dugmore was appointed. Geoffrey was therefore
not at King's but up on the Finchley Road at New College, one of the last of the once
great dissenting academies. Geoffrey took a close interest in my work, but when he
attended a lecture I gave to the Ecclesiastical History Society he wrote the next day
to say: 'I thought your lecture was good rather than very good.'

Meanwhile work on the history of religion in Elizabethan England was making
progress, thanks to my mother, who did all the typing. Sir John Neale, now in retirement in Beaconsfield, where he was the neighbour of Enid Blyton, went through
the book of the thesis, *The Elizabethan Puritan movement*, line by line. It was
decided that the book should be published by the firm of Jonathan Cape, with which
Neale had had creative dealings for many years. The Neale philosophy, shared with
Michael Howard and Graham Greene of Cape's, was that scholarly works should
be published in the most accessible way, without the burden of footnotes. So it had
been with Neale's own famous biography of *Queen Elizabeth*; and readers of Garrett
Mattingly's classic *The defeat of the Spanish Armada* were given scant means of
knowing what his sources may have been. I managed to make a deal with Cape's
which enabled me to refer to my credentials in extensive endnotes. I needed to. As
I had told the interviewing committee in Liverpool, thirteen years before, I had no
'method'; only an omnium gatherum of materials culled from more or less every-
where.

The Elizabethan Puritan movement constructed out of many bits and pieces of
evidence a picture of how religion worked, and often failed to work, in Elizabethan
England. And there was an argument, even an overarching thesis, typical of the

kind of left-of-centre *Guardian*-reading man which I have always been. It was a long discourse on the theme of the moderate centre failing to hold under pressure from two extremes. Most Elizabethan Protestants began as well-intentioned reformers, who wanted to make good better. But when the episcopal leadership of Elizabeth's church was obliged, under political pressure, to impose on their clergy conformity to a rather peculiar religious settlement, including symbols of what many regarded as the 'popery' of the past, worms turned and demands for 'further reformation' became more strident. Extremists condemned not a few details in the Book of Common Prayer ('shells and chippings of popery') but the Prayer Book in its entirety. Soon the bishops themselves were seen as the problem rather than the solution. The radical anti-hierarchical ideology of Presbyterianism was born, which would eventually tear the Church of England apart, creating the dichotomy of church and chapel which was the secret of England's plurality and diversity, something which in the eighteenth century would greatly impress Voltaire.

But not then, and not yet. Moderation did after all prevail, especially in the aftermath of the reign of Elizabeth, the time of James I, when the centre largely held. My hero was Elizabeth's second archbishop of Canterbury, the moderate and pastorally sensitive Edmund Grindal, whose own career ended in disaster when the queen sacked him for standing on his Reformation principles to the brink of lèse majesté, but whose heirs were the pastoral, preaching bishops of the Jacobean church. Most readers, even critics, were, and continue to be, convinced. The book was published in 1967, and it was destined to hold its own for rather longer than many, perhaps most, historical monographs.

Neale's ambition was that the book would receive wide coverage in a domain more public than professional academic circles. 'Perhaps that clever chappy who writes in the *Evening Standard* – what's his name? Foot, Michael Foot. Perhaps he'll review it.' That was not to be. But I remember a cold Sunday morning in April in Cumbria, when I read Hugh Trevor-Roper's rave review in the *Observer*, as we stood on the platform at Ravenglass, waiting to catch the little train called the 'Ratty' up into Eskdale. It was a good start. And it meant that I was not too upset when A. L. Rowse dismissed the book in a contemptuous eight lines of the *English Historical Review*. 'It is well known that Mr Collinson has been engaged with this thoroughly rebarbative subject for some years, and we must all be grateful that he has finally got it off his chest.'

I published little else before the late 1970s, apart from a handful of 'learned' articles and essays. My total ouput by my fortieth birthday was ten items, including the big book, although I did a lot of reviewing, not only for academic journals but for the *Spectator*, my patron on that paper being Hilary Spurling. I went to few conferences apart from meetings in the summer of the Ecclesiastical History Society and the annual Anglo-American Conference of Historians, held every July at the Institute. My attendance on those occasions reminds me of what the character of Ogo Jones says in Dylan Thomas's 'The outing': 'I didn't really want to come at all, but I always go.'[1] But there was still the Institute and its weekly seminars, including the Neale seminar on a Monday evening, now, since Neale's retirement, somewhat nominally presided over by Joel Hurstfield. And there, whatever else happened,

---

[1] Nowadays this would have meant a non-career. My pupils and pupils' pupils, academic children and grandchildren, have to expose themselves, have to go to many more conferences and colloquia, and have to publish, or perish.

which was often not much, one met everyone working on England in the later sixteenth century from both sides of the Atlantic and even from the Antipodes.

What happened otherwise in those fabled sixties, the era of the Beatles and Carnaby Street, all of which passed me by, was the begetting and rearing of children. It was an old-fashioned lifestyle, nowadays almost unknown. Liz having given up nursing when we left Khartoum would not return to her profession until 1976, a gap of fifteen years. Four children in six years was certainly a full-time job in itself. I have very happy memories of our life in south London, Liz less so. Nowadays children are more often than not born to women in their thirties rather than their twenties, and they find that they get tired almost all of the time. Every afternoon there was the weary trudge down to the park, Peckham Rye, with, by 1965, three children in or on the pram. But of course those children were, and to this day are, our greatest joy.

Helen Hay Collinson was born on 17 May 1962. I was not a New Man, and although I was to be found at the Middlesex Hospital when the event happened, I was not present at the birth; rather, since it was a Wednesday, I was sitting in an adjacent room putting finishing touches to my Thursday lecture on the Hussite Revolution in fifteenth-century Bohemia. The night when Andrew Cecil Collinson made his appearance in this world was more disgraceful still. This was deep into the Long Vacation, so no excuses. It happened to be the birthday of the Indian doctor who lived across the road. His entertainment was so lavish that, when I went home to bed, the registrar at the Lambeth Hospital failed to reach me on the phone when Andrew was born, in the early hours of the morning. Of course in the days that followed I made frequent visits to the Lambeth Hospital. But Liz will not allow me to forget that those visits happened to coincide with the final Test Match of that series against the West Indies, only a few hundred yards away at The Oval. Helen and Andrew were as full of near-sibling rivalry as you would expect, being born only fifteen months apart. But, by the same token, they are very very close. To quote Bing Crosby, God help the mister (or missus), who comes between me and my sister, or vice versa.

Esther de Waal was Helen's godmother, and Jasper Selwyn, Uncle Gordon's son, her godfather. As parents we had everything to learn. On a holiday in the West Highlands, we left three-month-old Helen in the car while we went for a brief stroll, only to find that we were in danger of being cut off by the incoming tide and had to wade for it. In a little hotel on Skye, far into the night, we bought alternate rounds of malt whisky with the owner, not very good business for him. Soon there was every sign that this was affecting breast-fed Helen. And on getting back to London we were told off for not having already started mixed feeding. Somehow or other, Helen and her siblings made it out of infancy.

Almost their first steps were taken on the firm sands between ribs of rock at Marloes in Pembrokeshire, surely the finest beach in Britain, with views through the mist of the pounding surf to Skokholm and Skomer, the rock pools still full of little rocklings and blennies, the lane down to the beach glinting every few yards as it got dark with glow-worms. At Watwick Bay, just around the corner of St Ann's Head into Milford Haven, the beach slopes so steeply that you can dive in from a run down the sand. It must have been there that Henry Tudor and his little force landed in 1485. At three, Helen climbed the rocky hill behind Whitesands Bay at St Davids called Carn Hen. This was henceforth 'Helen's mountain', until Andrew climbed it too. In the evenings after dinner I used to swim from the steep rocks of the Old Deer Park at Martin's Haven, in and out of the caves, and once Liz saw four heads rather than one, the others belonging to Atlantic grey seals.

Those years saw two moments of terrible sadness. First came the news that Dick Marsh had been killed climbing on Dow Crag in the Lake District, together with his climbing partner, another clergyman. Dick had always said that he would never marry, since his lifestyle was too adventurous, too macho. But as warden of an outdoor centre in Wharfedale he had married the matron and at the time of his death they had two small children. I went up to Greenwich Park and walked up and down the hill from the Observatory all afternoon. And then we heard that Jock Morrison had been drowned in Hong Kong. He had moved to the Far East, and had married Betty, who like Jock suffered from a mild form of epilepsy. His doctors had told him that he could go swimming, but it was not good advice. We sat on the sofa and cried bitter tears.

Sarah Christina Collinson set foot on the world stage on 23 September 1965, late enough to be treated with extreme condescension, verging on contempt, by both three-year-old Helen and two-year-old Andrew. 'Oh Sarah!' they would exclaim at some fresh demonstration of her ignorance of this or that, little suspecting the academic prowess which this Cambridge Ph.D. would display in later life. Last of all came Stephen Selwyn Collinson, born on 5 November 1968 and destined to become a painter and musician, now known as Steve Rivers. When I told Professor Dugmore that Stephen was expected he said: 'You've got to lay off. You'll kill her.' Visions of drunken husbands returning from the pub and not even bothering to remove their boots. But Dugmore had a point. Stephen's birth was followed by an operation which went badly wrong. Liz was in hospital for some time, and it was necessary to organize emergency care for Stephen, and for the rest of the family. Nowadays we would sue. We didn't even think of it, settling for a letter of apology. It was tough on Steve, and even tougher when we took him to Australia when he was only nine months old, back to England, a place beyond his mental comprehension, at the age of five, Australia again at six, England, finally at seven years of age. But the kids have survived it all, Steve included.

By now the expectation was that I would either be promoted or would find a chair, or perhaps a readership, somewhere else. I hoped for rather than expected these better things. I was still earning only a little over £1,000 pounds a year and we had no other income to speak of. We had extended the house to accommodate the family but now could barely afford to live there. But promotion was apparently out of the question. The powers that be had for the first time applied to the University of London the national ratio of senior to junior posts, and London was badly out of line. You'll get no promotion this side of the ocean. But to cross the ocean was a last desperate throw. First there were interviews for senior posts on this side: a readership at Durham, the chair of Modern History at Exeter, the chair of Ecclesiastical History at Manchester. True to form, I handled all these situations very badly, and just as it had been in the 1950s, I came back each time with my tail between my legs.

In the early summer of 1968, with Stephen already on the way, I received a letter from John Manning Ward, who was apparently something called the Challis Professor of History at the University of Sydney, Australia. Did I know that following the departure from Sydney of Jack McManners (at first to Leicester and then to be Regius Professor of Ecclesiastical History in Oxford) there was a vacant professorial chair in his department? Could he come to see me at King's on such and such an afternoon at two o'clock to discuss the possibility that I be appointed? I replied saying that it was most unlikely that I could consider a move to Australia, and that I had to take the minutes at a meeting of the Faculty Board at 2.15. Ward replied saying that he had to come to King's in any case to visit a Canadian historian of things imperial called Jerry Graham, and suggesting that we talk for ten minutes. 'Nothing will be lost and much may be gained.' So I met, briefly, with my future colleague. It was the only interview I ever had for that Australian job.

Later that afternoon I drove to Liverpool Street Station to pick up my mother in the car and deliver her to Waterloo. I told her about my meeting with John Ward, only to amuse her. 'I think that you should go to Australia, and I'll come with you. It will be the solution to your problems and to mine.' So that was that, then. Liz maintains that she was not even consulted. The decision was much criticized within the Collinson family. How would my sister Marjorie manage without my mother? In fact she managed very well indeed (for all of thirty years before she was taken into care in her late eighties); and my mother had seen that it was better that way than becoming dependent on Marjorie, which would have been a distressingly asymmetrical relationship.

In the summer of 1969 we took emigration seriously. For that is what we were doing. No thought of coming back after a year or two. (Of no period of British history am I more ignorant than the years 1969–74, the Edward Heath years.) Two or three times a year, I had had to go to Heathrow to conduct nephews and nieces on to flights back to their missionary parents in Morocco. You had to wait around until the flight was airborne, so I used to go and get my hair cut. Every time the barber would ask: 'And what exotic part of the world are you off to this morning sir?', and I would answer 'Forest Hill', and he would say 'and very nice too.' But now the ritual changed and I told him that very soon I was off to Australia. He knew the country and warned me what to expect. 'At breakfast they don't ask you to pass the butter, they say pass the effing butter!'

Dugmore gave a little party for me at King's, and Bindoff and Hurstfield who came had fun wondering whether Neale would regard my chair as a real chair, since it was in the colonies. We sold everything that we were not going to take with us, including our neat little Honor Oak house, for which we got exactly what we had paid for in buying and extending it: £8,800. Now it must be worth at least half a million. On 14 August 1969, a few days after my fortieth birthday, the Jewkeses took all seven of us down to Southampton, where we boarded the Italian liner *Angelino Lauro* (sister ship of the *Achille Lauro* which would be hijacked a few years later) and set sail for the future. My mother celebrated her seventy-fourth birthday on board.

It was a ridiculous way to travel, considering that we could have flown to Sydney in a little more than twenty-four hours. The ship went into the Mediterranean to pick up the bulk of its passengers (Italians who really were migrants) at Messina, Naples (we went to Pompeii) and Genoa. The Suez Canal was still closed, so we sailed back out of the Med, past the Rock of Gibraltar, a week after we had first seen it. But I was paid my Sydney professorial salary the moment I stepped on board, and was still drawing my London salary until the end of September: for doing – what was that saying in the RAF? To save money, the *Angelino Lauro* spent as little time in port as possible: a brief visit to Tenerife, six hours in Cape Town. For days before we reached that port of call we were regaled with daily bulletins about the flora, fauna and history of South Africa. But we did have time in Cape Town to visit Jock Morrison's widow in a suburb where we went into a shop to find two customers, one white, one black, and two people serving behind the counter, one black, one white. Thirty years later we would be back in the new South Africa.

Life on board ship (First Class) was very tedious, all the more so since every night was supposed to be a special night, French, Spanish or whatever, with the usual ceremonies when we crossed the line. Children's meals were taken separately from the adults so that we were forever coming to or from the dining saloon. I was reminded of the Jesuits in seventeenth-century France who taught that you should no sooner leave the confessional than you should desire to return thither again. Everyone got ill with the bugs which were efficiently wafted around by the air conditioning. Stephen, 'Pasqualino' as the stewards called him, cried and cried. Again and again, a message would be brought to the saloon 'your son cry', and sometimes the son himself would be carried down. But between Cape Town and Fremantle, across the southern Indian Ocean, things became more interesting: a storm of Cape Horn proportions, seas that really were mountainous. People were flung across the width of the ship and cracked their ribs. Helen was in the cabin with a thermometer in her mouth when the ship went down on its side as if it would never come up again. When it did, the thermometer was nowhere to be seen. But at last, on a wet Friday afternoon, we came through the Heads of Sydney Harbour and under the bridge, five weeks after leaving Southampton. We left the ship at Darling Harbour, to be met by another new professorial colleague, Marjorie Jacobs, while our baggage, including all my books and papers, went on to New Zealand.

14

Sydney

Manning Clark, at that time the only Australian historian of whom any Australian had ever heard, told in the Australian equivalent of the broadcast Reith Lectures that he had once sat in Manchester trying to write the history of his native land. It wasn't working. So he came back to Melbourne and began to read the essential sources for Australian history: the Bible, Shakespeare, Dostoevsky. It was necessary to discover what a man is before placing him in that utterly strange environment. (Manning was apparently unaware that homo sapiens had contrived to live in that rather large desert island for tens of thousands of years, without the benefit of the Bible and the *Complete works of Shakespeare*.)

Now we too had to work out what it was to be human beings in Australia. Like so many convicts, we were put into 'staging flats' in a suburb called Drummoyne, huddling under the Gladesville Bridge, over the Parramatta River. It was not quite Brooklyn Bridge, but nor was it the glamorous Sydney Harbour of the brochures. The accommodation was very basic, and my mother, who was suffering from her chronic bronchitis and diverticulosis (intermittently diverticulitis), had to be content with a miserable little room, upstairs. One evening, a mining engineer, living above us, stepped out of his area of expertise to mend the plumbing, with the result that a deluge came down on all our things. Sarah had the measles, and ten-month-old Stephen suffered from an acute middle ear infection. There was no washing machine, only an old-fashioned copper and a wooden pole. Liz lost a stone in weight in a month. When I pleaded with the university finance officer, an unpleasant Ulsterman, to do something better for us, he made it clear that he regarded me as a relatively low form of life.

Helen and Andrew began to attend an inner city school, a steep climb up the hill to the Drummoyne shops for Liz, with heavy laundry bags hung on Stephen's pushchair. There the children were lined up on the playground as on military parade and were harangued through bull horns. 'Some of yez is putting yer lunch boxes on yer left side so when you turn left to go into class you trip over them.' Not surprisingly, children wetted themselves in class. Helen befriended a little boy to whom this happened, Nicky Cobbin, and brought him home. As he came through the door, there was Sarah. 'Gee you're the cutest!' he said.[1]

There were two major challenges: to find somewhere for all of us to live and for me to come to terms with the History Department of Sydney University. Let us take the university first, the university of Germaine Greer and Clive James and an iconoclastic student newspaper called *Honi Soit*. I was in an absurd position.

---

[1] The Cobbins/Porters (Nicky's mother Pip had remarried Barrie Porter) became our greatest Australian friends, and, seventeen years later, Nicky and Sarah would be living as partners, first in Sydney and then in Cambridge.

Sydney, founded in 1850, was the oldest university in Australia, older than all but five English universities. For its first thirty or so years it had had only three professors, twenty-four students, one faculty (Arts), and an annual grant of £5,000. But in the 1850s a stupendous range of Gothic Revival buildings had been erected on farmland on what was then the edge of the city (now an inner city location, on the Parramatta Road): a spacious cloistered quadrangle, a turreted gateway and a Great Hall which was a copy of the Great Hall of Westminster, two-thirds size. Schoolteachers used to bring their students to the Great Hall, so that they could see what the middle ages looked like. This was Australia's Oxford, to Melbourne's Cambridge, or, more appropriately, the other way round. The pride and joy of some of the older professors was the First World War Memorial, a carillon which rang out with 'Gaudeamus Igitur' at graduation and on other high occasions.[2]

The Department of History, which celebrated its centenary in 1991, was the best in the southern hemisphere, although of course Melbourne would dispute that. Its vice and at the same time its virtue was eclecticism. There was no Sydney 'school of history'. Everyone was allowed to do his or her own thing. Upwards of 1,000 students were taken in each year to study History, along with other Arts subjects, and many of those went on, from their second year, to take History Honours, which would occupy all of their time in the fourth year. (The model was Scottish.) In 1949 six members of staff had taught 1,400 students, mostly in crowded lecture halls. But in 1969 the staff, counting tutors of various kinds, numbered upwards of fifty and included many historians of real distinction. It was a golden age. The range of subject areas was impressive: Ancient History, Medieval History, Early Modern History ('Renaissance and Reformation'), many kinds of Modern European History (there were British, French, German, Spanish, Italian and Russian specialists), the United States, South Asia (four historians of India). Soon China and Indonesia were added to the menu. History was treated with enormous respect, which sadly is no longer the case in the early twenty-first century.

One curiosity of the situation in 1969 was that there was very little Australian History on offer: only one course, which had few takers, since the man who taught it found it hard to make much progress into the subject, rather as the original colonists of New South Wales had taken decades to find a way over the Blue Mountains into the interior. It was said that there had been a year when Duncan MacCallum got the First Fleet on to the high seas, only to discover that the manifest had been left behind, so that they all had to go back again. The ranking historians of Australia had been headhunted to other universities. There were several colleagues who knew a lot about the history of their own country, but they taught other things. There was a marking of time before the subject would be reinvented, in the 1970s and beyond. The History Department could not claim to be a major graduate school. The Ph.D. had been introduced in 1956, but by 1969 only six doctorates had been awarded. The traditional pattern was to take a local MA before proceeding to Britain or North

---

[2] Enoch Powell, Professor of Greek in the late thirties, had his room under the gateway, and used to rush out and shake his fist whenever the machine performed. There were many Powell stories in Sydney. Invited to a tea party on the North Shore, the ladies clustered around and told him how kind it had been of him to come. 'Yes, it was, wasn't it? Shan't happen again.' Stephen Roberts, Challis Professor of History, having published a best seller, *The house that Hitler built*, boasted about the languages into which it had been translated. Powell asked: 'But when will it be translated into English?'

America for doctoral research, returning to Sydney to teach but, in most cases, not to publish very much.

Why was my own situation absurd? I was from overseas, and therefore it was assumed that I was the fount of all wisdom and academic statesmanship. That was why I had been parachuted in, over the heads of more local contenders for my chair. And yet this was the first time in my life that I had been part of a real Department of History, unless you count Khartoum. (In London I had been attached to a Faculty of Theology, part of a two-man Department of Ecclesiastical History.) Two or three days after my arrival, I was summoned into the presence of the vice-chancellor, an English (or rather Cornish) economist called Bruce Williams, together with Marjorie Jacobs, a South Asianist who had been appointed to her chair a little after me. John M. Ward, who had been Challis Professor and head of department for more than twenty years, was supposed to be present. But his father had just died, and Marjorie and I faced the VC alone. At least Marjorie had been at Sydney for her entire career (since graduation in 1936), as had John Ward, Challis Professor since 1949. But Williams turned to me. What did I think ought to be done to (or was it 'for', or 'with'?) the History Department? I had absolutely no idea.

Fortunately I had arrived in September, in the third term, when the emphasis was on examinations rather than teaching. But come January, and the new academic year, I had to apply myself to my new responsibilities. Under John Ward's headship, the three professors carved up the empire between them. My bailiwick consisted of Medieval History and Early Modern History, eight colleagues, although I also had a general responsibility for the first year. The middle ages had been brought to Sydney in 1961 by Ian Jack, who had been joined in 1967 by a dynamic and inventive teacher, another John Ward, John O. Ward, an authority on the pseudo-Ciceronian rhetorical text, *Ad herennium*. I knew little about medieval rhetoric, or about Ian Jack's subject, which was the marcher lordships of England and Wales in the later middle ages. So I dealt with Medieval History as the Austro-Hungarian Empire dealt with Hungary, or Lord Lugard with Northern Nigeria, by indirect rule: hands on only in respect of my own period, the early modern. When Ian Jack told me that we ought not to renew the appointment of a probationary lecturer, Rodney Thomson, I did what he said. Thomson is now the most distinguished medievalist in Australasia. It was on my watch that he was denied continued employment in Sydney.

In 1991 a volume of *Centenary reflections* was published, to celebrate 100 years of History at Sydney. I read with interest a chapter on 'The department in the 1970s', written by Barbara Caine, at that time a junior member of staff and a committed feminist, now a weighty member of Australia's academic establishment. It is not often as a historian that you are able to bring into focus your own memories, an archive which you yourself have engendered, for the record of those years exists, part of it exhibited in the Fisher Library of Sydney University in 1991, and a secondary account of events written by a competent historian. According to Caine, the Sydney History Department which I joined in 1969, apart from being 'a very masculine place', was the seat of 'absolute professorial power'. That was indeed the formal situation. The department as such had no legal existence. Much was about to change, with the *ancien régime* challenged both by the student insurgency which had arrived two or three years after the events in Paris and elsewhere in Western Europe, and by discontent among the non-professorial staff, headed by the colonels and majors, so to speak, senior lecturers and associate professors, ostensibly democrats but certainly interested in a share of power. The Departments of Philosophy and

Economics were both in turmoil. The official history of the university, *Australia's first*, speaks of 'a prolonged crisis of identity and function'. The mini-revolution in History was more subdued, but it was a messy affair all the same, and in 1975 it projected me back from Australia to an English university, changing all of our lives yet again. It is understandable if I feel sensitive about the record of those events.

What is 'absolute power', and how do absolute systems operate? Who really called the shots in pre-revolutionary France? Under the Ward regime, the regime of a man who by training and temperament was a constitutional lawyer, there were no departmental meetings. But if this was despotism it was enlightened despotism. Ward dealt closely and sensitively with all of his colleagues, particularly those who were heads of courses. The first lesson I had to learn was that you should never interfere with a head of course, just as parents of boys at Eton have to learn not to go over the head of their son's housemaster to the headmaster. It is true that the three professors met for two or three hours a week behind closed doors, to discuss the affairs of the department as they sought fit. But that was no more nor less than their responsibility and duty under by-laws which acknowledged the existence of the Professors of History, but not of the department.

My first initiative was to attempt to introduce a new structure for History I, which I was supposed to be in charge of. In place of several courses in Ancient, Medieval and Early Modern History, I proposed the model of a 'core course', to be followed by a number of mini-special subjects, to be taken in the third term. The proposal fell flat on its face. It was resisted in particular by a colleague called Gwynne Jones, who taught Tudors and Stuarts. Gwynne, like the biblical Jacob, had laboured for many years in another Australian university, teaching Ancient History. At last, at Sydney, he had his own course, in his own period, and he was not going to let a mere professor get in his way. One consequence was that in all my five years in Sydney I never taught my own period and subject, Tudor and Stuart History. No Sydney student ever heard me talk about Henry VIII or Queen Elizabeth I, or the rest of all those fascinating Elizabethans. So much for 'absolute professorial power'!

Instead I became part of a team teaching a History I course on Early Modern Europe, so traditional in its emphasis on the themes of Renaissance and Reformation that everyone called it 'Theology I'. The tradition had been established by a fine scholar, devoted to the memory of Erasmus of Rotterdam, Bruce Mansfield. And although Bruce had left for a chair at Macquarie University, on the North Shore, no one broke the Mansfield mould. We were a strong team. There was Ros Pesman (Cooper), an Italian Renaissance specialist; Ken Cable, who was really an Australian historian but whose day job was teaching Henry VIII and all that; Graeme Harrison, an authority on sixteenth- and seventeenth-century Spain – but much more than that, an imagination capable of kindling other imaginations; Maida Coaldrake, an old Japanese hand, who looked after the Counter-Reformation; and, when she transferred to History from Economic History, Ian Jack's wife Sybil, whose domain was the economy and society of Tudor England; and me. Once a year, I devoted an entire lecture (thanks to Erwin Panofsky) to Albrecht Durer's 'Melancholia I': one slide on the screen for an hour.

In this large course, which enrolled upwards of 250 students and sometimes an evening class as well, the model of a core course for the first two terms and a mini-special subject in the third term, did come to prevail. I offered more than twenty lectures a year on 'Martin Luther and the German Reformation'. When I introduced a slot on the English Reformation, the brighter students said: 'Now you are talking about something that you really know about.' Someone who did know about the German Reformation was Bob Scribner, who had left the Sydney department just before I arrived, first to work with A. G. Dickens in London and then to become in due course the leading historian in the world of that great subject, in all its social and cultural depth, before dying prematurely in Harvard in 1999. Thirty years on, in 2003, I harvested my Sydney lectures in a little book on *The Reformation*, which has been published not only here but in the United States, Spain, Portugal, Brazil, Slovakia and Korea. It was Bob's widow, Lois, and fortunately none of the reviewers, who pointed out (privately) that my book enshrined a view of the cataclysmic religious changes of the sixteenth century now long since superseded, not least by Bob, whose great book on the subject was so sadly stopped at the check-out counter.

Otherwise, my efforts were invested in a Fourth Year Honours seminar which ran under the title 'Churches, sects and society'. It was a time when Sociology was seductive among historians. And since bright Australian historians are very good at the methodology and philosophy of the subject, this course was teeming with contentious and discussable issues. The idea was to bring a more or less empirical historical method to bear on sociological theory and taxonomy; as it might be the Troeltschian distinction between churches and sects, and the Niebuhrian suggestion that sects tend, especially in North America, to transmute into denominations. The course was catholic in the extreme. We took in the early Christian schisms and heresies, Donatism especially, medieval heresy, radical religion in the Reformation and the English seventeenth century, the so-called 'Weber thesis' about the supposed relation of the 'spirit' of capitalism to the Protestant 'ethic', Jansenism in seventeenth-century France, Mormons, churches and industrial society, modern sects and cults, the problematical issue of secularization. I had some of the ablest students that I would ever meet until I got to Cambridge, sixteen years later. And just as St Paul almost persuaded Agrippa to become a Christian, those students almost turned me into the kind of historian who ingests, and even produces, theory. It was a very superficial conversion.

What in the meantime had been happening to the rest of us? In the spring (autumn) of 1969 we were house-hunting in a city consisting of 350 suburbs, fifty miles from east to west and fifty from north to south. The house would have to provide separate accommodation for my mother, and the problem was that most of the affordable properties were built in the canyons ('creeks') typical of the Sydney topography, so that if there was a granny flat it was usually a dismal basement. The suburbs around the harbour and running up the Pacific Highway to the North Shore were beyond our means. But at last we found the right house in a place called Beecroft, to the north-west, beyond Epping and on the way to Pennant Hills, along one of the lines of road which had led the early colonists up into the Blue Mountains, via the Macquarie towns, Windsor and Richmond. ('Welcome to Richmond, Redolent with History', you were told as you entered that pretty little town.)

No. 6 Kirkham Street was a house of the 1920s, solidly built with floors of jarra wood from Western Australia and elaborately moulded ceilings, but gloomy. There was a large, level garden, and a cottage which had been a garage but which had been converted to house some elderly relation. It was all that my mother needed. There was still a broken-down old wheelchair, in which the children raced around the concrete paths. The house cost us $30,000, which some colleagues thought was far too much. But nowadays, with some improvements, it is worth well over a million, in a suburb which has gone up in the world.

Beecroft at that time was not smart, but it was full of trees, there was a park where the fruit bats flew above your head as you came from the station, past a Boer War memorial, and it was populated by people who valued education and were often religious. This was Sydney's Bible Belt. When we bought a secondhand bed from a neighbour, who turned out to be the brother of one of the professors who had failed to appoint me to a chair in Manchester, he said: 'You seem to be classical people.' There was no pub and no Catholic church.

We bought our house from a man called Kennard, a manufacturer of ladders and roof-racks, who was the leading Australian figure in the sect of Exclusive (or 'Closed') Plymouth Brethren. The worldwide leader of the sect, an American called 'Big' Jim Campbell, was in the last stages of alcoholism (the Exclusive Brethren drink), and its affairs were in the hands of an international commission, which included Kennard. The Kennards were moving out because God had told them to shift, with all their followers, to the south coast, D. H. Lawrence territory. My mother, who combined a devout belief in divine providence with a good sense of humour, said that the Lord knew that she needed that little cottage, which was why the Brethren were moved on.

It was an interesting experience, dealing with the Kennards. On the shelves to the left of the fireplace, where we would put our record player, were rows of volumes, containing all the teaching delivered in such and such a place on such and such a date since the days of the founder, John Nelson Darby. As with the Roman Catholic Church, this was a religion which attributed authority to Tradition. The Kennard children, and there were many, had to decide at the age of twelve whether to belong to the sect and conform to its exclusive norms or not. In the garden there were many small peach and nectarine trees which no one had planted. Our neighbours told us that the reason was that when there were religious meetings in the garden, young Gordon Kennard used to climb the jacaranda tree with a bag of fruit, make hooting noises, and throw the stones towards the worshippers. On one of my visits to the house to decorate (we were still waiting for our furniture to arrive from England), I found a dozen bottles of malt whisky and several half gallon flagons of sherry in the cellar. The Kennards turned up and said that they thought that they might have left something behind. I told them that I was just about to give them a ring. We parted on good terms.

We began to settle into a pleasant life in the mostly benign climate of New South Wales. The soil of Beecroft is rich, but the Kennards were Anglophiles who had imported many tons of superfluous topsoil to enable them to grow roses, azaleas and camellias. The native trees which we tried to encourage didn't like it at all. The citrus trees and the vegetables were looked after by Dominic Simonetti, a Sicilian by origin who had prospered as part of the Australian workforce, one of the most remarkable men we have ever met. As a child he had tried to murder his sadistic schoolteacher, rolling a boulder down towards the path which the teacher took every day to school. He became a dedicated communist, suspicious of all Australian governments, of whatever colour, and of his church, although he went devoutly to mass on all occasions. Dominic was looking after the garden before we bought the house and, thirty-seven years on, he is still working there. In a recent letter, written at the age of eighty-one, he told us, in his idiosyncratic English: 'Start on april 1969 for Mr Secil Kenned. Stedely every second Wed. travel to 6 Kirkham Street. Still the best Roses, Citros, Shrubs of the whole area.' I converted the large box in which our piano had been transported into an aviary, which we filled with Australian

38 The family on the steps of no. 6 Kirkham Street, Beecroft, New South Wales, 1973 – *back row*: PC, Steve and Helen; *front row*: Andrew, Sarah, Liz

parrots: crimson rosellas, eastern rosellas, galahs, Port Lincoln parrots. Soon we had twenty-four chickens ('chooks' in Australian), any number of guinea pigs and rabbits (strictly illegal), and a labrador collie cross called Jessie. When Jessie had eight pups I took a census: seventy-four pets in all. (The children were supposed to look after them, but of course didn't.) We installed a swimming pool, just across from my mother's cottage, so that she was able to keep a sharp eye on Stephen. But she was not sharp-eyed enough one Saturday afternoon to spot Stephen, not yet two years of age, stark naked, walking out of the gate. He made it across the busy main road to the local tennis club before being brought back.

Given our Drummoyne experience, we were wary of public education, and while Helen and Andrew began to attend Beecroft School we put Sarah into a little experimental school meeting in that indispensable ornament of any old-fashioned Sydney suburb, the 'School of Arts', where there was no enforced discipline and not much of a curriculum. The children would go on an expedition to the beach and would come back with specimens which would occupy them for the next week. But we soon learned that schools like that existed for the benefit of children (not to speak of their parents) who for one reason or another were disturbed. Soon Sarah joined the others at the public school, and we began to appreciate the quality of primary education in New South Wales. But if you didn't like the school's policy you could have your say at the Parents and Teachers Association. The protocol of these meetings was typically Australian. The men sat on one side and did all the talking. The women sat on the other and knitted. But Liz had a lot to say. Once a woman shouted: 'Mrs Collinson, you whinged before you came here, you've gone on whinging and you'll whinge after you've left.' Like most pommy wives, it took Liz at least two years to begin to feel at home in what was a strangely foreign environment. But she campaigned, with eventual success, to keep the school open for the community out of hours and in the holidays (apart from anything else a remedy for vandalism); and she drove around the factories in the western suburbs picking up raw materials for summer workshops held on the school premises.

It took time to get used to the Australian bush. At first we wanted to take a giant razor and clear the hilltops of all those scraggy trees. But then we found the hidden beauties of the creeks and gullies, pockets of rainforest with giant tree ferns and many pungently aromatic shrubs. We soon came to love the evocative calls of Australian magpies and currawongs (yes, and kookaburras too), the screech of rainbow lorikeets as they streaked overhead. And sometimes there was a lyre bird on the path.

We often stayed at a time warp: the Hydro-Majestic at Medlow Bath. There was no Bath and no Hydro: only a late Victorian hotel which might as well have been at Matlock, with walks laid out among what could have been Derbyshire rocks (but the trees were all wrong!) and breathtaking views out and down over the pastoral Megalong Valley; where, one Sunday afternoon, Stephen cut off one of his toes in the creek, only to have it sewn back on in Katoomba Hospital, after a frantic drive over miles of dirt road. In those Blue Mountains we began to undertake major expeditions (for the children at least): to the Blue Gum Forest on the Gross River, 2,000 feet down and up again, which five-year-old Sarah managed on her own two pins; the Grand Canyon of Blackheath; and the big walk out to Mount Solitary from Katoomba. Camping took over from the hotel. We caught crayfish ('yabbies') in the creek and boiled them in billies on the fire. And the stars! And yet, love it though we did, we were always conscious that this was a place very different from, say, the Lake District, and almost anywhere in Britain, where the landscape has been created by many centuries of human settlement and penetration. At best, the Australian bush tolerated our presence, and we knew that we had nothing to contribute to it.

Saturday mornings were frantic: music lessons, horse riding, tennis – and above all the weekly ritual of the Beecroft Sports Association. With the help of the mums and dads on the starting and finishing lines, an entire Olympic programme of athletic events was crammed into three or four hours. I cannot think that this was wise. Little kids were obliged to do 100 metre sprints with no chance to limber up. We had soon had enough, and even earlier Andrew had given up on soccer, intimidated by fierce Australian mums who shrieked at their small offspring from the touchline.

Throughout those years, we had a strong sense of living in a country which had its future before it, a good future, whereas in the England to which we gave little thought there seemed to be only the past. What could possibly go wrong with this young, dynamic, prosperous nation? We became involved in Australian politics, strong supporters of the Australian Labour Party. We had the same touching faith in Gough Whitlam as we had once had in Harold Wilson and would later invest, briefly, in Tony Blair. When Whitlam won his election in 1972, it was exciting. One or two seats in the outback had still to declare; the party caucus, which appoints the cabinet, could not be formed; and for several days we had government by daily press conference, Whitlam and his deputy, a Tasmanian called Lance Barnard. One day they recognized Communist China, the next they abolished university fees.

In the later months of 1971, it became clear that my mother was ill, and soon we knew the problem to be cancer of the oesophagus. She had enjoyed a good life in Australia, and had settled in better than the rest of us. She found the right sort of church, she was soon doing much of the secretarial work for the Australian branch of the Middle East General Mission, with which she and my father had been so deeply involved in the 1930s. Most days she wheeled Stephen up to the shops in his buggy, and an old gentleman used to put a chair out on the pavement for her to sit down. When we learned the diagnosis, I had a sense of bitter injustice. Why? But my mother wanted no surgical intervention, and was reconciled to what had to happen. After some time in hospital she came back to her cottage where she was nursed by Liz until very nearly the end. Her last two weeks were spent in a nursing home around the corner. We had all been to the cinema to see *The railway children*, had come back and gone to bed. Liz had some sort of premonition in the early hours of the morning of 13 January. It was four o'clock and pouring with rain, and yet she felt that she ought to put on wellington boots and go to the home. But of course she didn't. Mummy died at 5.45 a.m. I was full of guilt that I had not been there, and was not helped when the staff explained that was what they were there for, to look after the final fact of death without troubling the family. That too was Australia. The funeral was held the next day.

If my mother had lived for only two or three more years (she was seventy-six, but her mother and two of her sisters had died in their nineties), we should all still be in Australia. It would have been too late to bring back to England children by then of secondary school age.

My mother's death and funeral happened in the week when I was due to take over the headship of the History Department. I got a few days' reprieve, but was then plunged into a job not very different from being head of a large comprehensive school. These were to be the most arduous years of my working life. My teaching load was not reduced, and indeed there was a year when I taught evening as well as day courses, besides all the admin and innumerable boards and other meetings. I left home at six in the morning and was rarely back before eleven. In all our years in Australia, I was never away from the department for more than nine days, apart from study leave overseas. My successors interpreted their responsibilities differently, not thinking it necessary to live over the shop. They thought that the Sydney History Department existed for them, whereas I old-fashionedly assumed that I was there for it. But the future was with those successors.

Nor were my duties confined to the History Department. For most of my time in Sydney I was chairman of the Board of Studies in Divinity. This was a funny brief to hold. The University of Sydney was expressly forbidden by its foundation statutes to teach theology. But it awarded a BD degree on the basis of courses taught and examined in the various denominational colleges which existed on the edge of the campus, and which otherwise served as halls of residence for students from the country: St John's (Roman Catholic), St Paul's (Anglican), St Andrew's (Presbyterian), Wesley House (Methodist). But Moore Theological College, a bastion of the most conservative evangelicalism, whose principal normally went on to become archbishop of Sydney, held aloof and prepared its students for London degrees.[3] Those who taught for the Sydney BD, who for the most part were not members of the university staff, formed a Faculty of Divinity. But I taught some of the Church History myself. A good measure of collegiality was lent by a theological dining and paper-reading society called The Heretics, which dated from the 1920s. When the Catholics joined us and we held a meeting in St Patrick's Seminary in Manley, the nuns who served us dinner asked where the atheists wanted to drink their coffee. Towards the end of my time, Vice-Chancellor Bruce Williams found a bit of unnoticed money (fire insurance, cynics said) and used it to fund a chair in Religious Studies which, with a small department, still exists. So much for religion.

January 1972 was a landmark moment for the department. John Ward had been head for twenty-three years. Once or twice, when he went on leave, my predecessor Jack McManners had taken over as acting head. But now the succession passed to me. It was clear, whatever the university by-laws might state, that my style of governance would be very different from John Ward's. I practised collegiality, actively. Unlike the other professors, I always took morning coffee and afternoon tea in the common room; and Liz and I regularly entertained both staff and students. I organized a weekly staff-graduate lunchtime seminar on all topics whatsoever, from the era of Mithridates in Caucasian Asia to the literature of the Black South: sandwiches and a half-gallon flagon of wine. A colleague who was not one of my special friends has since remembered this as the only time when the department functioned as an academic community.

There was an expectation of change, shared even by Professor Marjorie Jacobs. So it was that the first ever departmental meeting was held, on 7 April 1972. The agenda, as hammered out on my vintage typewriter, is reproduced in *History at Sydney* (illustration 34). Item 3 consists of a deceptively innocent statement: 'To nominate and elect a Committee to assist the Professors of History in the planning of courses for 1973 and to discuss wider aspects of the structure of courses within the Department.' Hardly the Communist Manifesto. But in the biblical story of Elijah, the prophet's servant reported seeing in the far distance a cloud the size of a man's hand. This was that cloud.

One of Liz's Stubington aunts, Aunt Edie Radwell, died, and left to Liz her handsome house in Links Lane, Rowlands Castle. What to do with the proceeds? We still had no thought of ever coming back to England. We took our inheritance into the realms of fantasy, inspecting acres of rocky land far out to the west, where you would have had to prospect for water before thinking of building a house. While the children (and Liz) rode horses on Saturday mornings, under the watchful eye of a Germanic riding instructor in tight leather breeches, I sat in the car going through the property pages of the *Sydney Morning Herald*. But sitting in the arena at the Royal Easter Show of 1973, we found the place: a cottage on the water at Patonga, one of the tidal creeks feeding into the Hawkesbury River and Broken Bay, close to where we had broken down on a boating holiday, to find ourselves looking, stupefied, at the enormous head of a leatherback turtle, a reptile of hippopotamus like bulk of which we had never before heard.

---

[3] Once, Archbishop Marcus Loane shared with me his concern about the levels of crime in Sydney. Do you think, he asked, that the reason is that so many of our citizens now lack a British background?

So we knew Patonga: a sandbar, a jetty, two or three streets of well-matured houses, abandoned boats gently sinking into the mud, mangroves across the water with ibises, egrets, fish eagles, dense National Park bush behind. This was the last unspoiled place on the New South Wales coast. An American colleague, whose children called it 'Pat's Tonga', knew the Maine coast and said that the place was 'down eastern'. And far from needing to prospect for water, when we moved in, on the Queen's Birthday Weekend (June) of 1973, everything in the house, 6 Jacaranda Avenue, had been left there for us: radios, fishing rods, two or three boats. (And there were jacaranda trees all around the house, and, beside the water, coral trees which attracted flocks of honey eaters.) The next morning our kids and the Cobbins/ Porters were already out on the water in canoes. You could harvest your own Sydney rock oysters, go off in the boat with a couple of lemons, and wash them down with riesling on some deserted beach. I could never understand why Helen ate so many oysters, but was later told that she knew that they added cholesterol and gave you heart attacks, so she ate them to save my life. Sunday mornings were spent drifting up and down the creek fishing for a species called flathead. So it was that we heard on the radio that Margaret Thatcher had been elected leader of the Conservative Party: another cloud the size of a man's hand.

At the end of 1973, I was due for study leave, which would naturally be spent in London. Liz and the children left in September, to take advantage of a complete school year. Thanks to the help of our old friends, the London 'crowd', they found a flat in SE3, Blackheath. I would follow just before Christmas. In the meantime, we rented our Beecroft house and I lived at Patonga with Jessie, the dog, either driving all the way to Sydney or catching the train at Woy Woy, a place well known to the late Spike Milligan. Sometimes I was only back at Patonga for five or six hours, but it was always worth it. One morning there was a fish eagle on the mangroves opposite, lit up by vivid morning sunlight against the dark foliage: a vision to live with not just for that day but for ever.

I began to study the natural history of the creek, observing, for example, as David Attenborough would later observe, the tidal eruption of thousands of little soldier crabs, marching in tight formation across the strand. I imagined that this would be my Walden: that here I would live the life of Thoreau, devoting myself in retirement to capturing the spirit of the place. But what was that spirit? We were innocent of the fact that this was one of the last strongholds of the native peoples of that part of Australia. Along the shores of Patonga Creek were huge middens of shellfish. We thought that the people who had made those middens had just chosen to go somewhere else. But 'Dark Corner', a cluster of houses around the point, was not so called because it had no electricity, but on account of the fact that that was where the natives had made their last stand. Years later, in the San Gabriel Mountains behind Los Angeles, I would again have the chastening revelation that I was living and walking in dead people's space.

But in that spring of 1973 we had more immediate problems on our minds. There were many threatening bush fires, started, I believe deliberately, by someone who had a grievance against the National Park. When I joined the Volunteer Bush Fire Brigade, working a few feet away from the flames in temperatures in the high thirties, I felt at one with the local population for the first and only time in all our Australian years. The women came up the hill with ice-cold coke, and we stood around, briefly.

Shortly before Christmas 1973 I took Jessie to a kennels and boarded a plane for Bangkok and Hong Kong, where I stayed for a week with old friends of Liz, a jaunt which included a strange excursion to Macao and its casinos, all paid for by Stanley Ho, a fabulously rich and shady tycoon with whom Liz's old colleague's husband, Colonel Malcom Nares, had certain dealings. The original idea was that I would then take ship for Khabarovsk and travel westwards on the Siberian Railway, with a diversion from Irkutsk down to Samarkand and Tblisi. I even saw the Russian ship in harbour at Hong Kong which I should have boarded. This was the very trip later chronicled by Paul Theroux, and, if I had stuck to the original plan, I would have been immortalized along with that Russian fellow passenger who tackled enormous beef and jam sandwiches with a set of stainless steel teeth. But, fortunately, I decided that I needed to see my family, and on New Year's Day I flew straight back to London. And there they all were, having already lost the Aussie accents which had coloured the cassettes on which we had corresponded during our three months of separation.

Those early months of 1974 told us why we were so lucky to be living and working in Australia. Coming into London from Heathrow, the *Guardian* explained that Britain was no longer governable. We were soon plunged into the three-day week. The British Museum, where I was mostly working, closed early, to save electricity. To get back to Blackheath, you had to walk two miles from New Cross Gate. It was miserably cold, and people walked the streets all wrapped up within themselves, whereas in sunny Sydney they smiled and waved their arms. When I joined the Saturday morning excursions to a riding school in Kent, I could not believe that the glutinous mud could be that deep.

But what a treat it was to be back doing research, serious stuff in the archives for the first time for many years. In 1974 I did most of the work for my biography of Elizabeth I's second archbishop of Canterbury, Edmund Grindal, which would be published in 1979: an almost hagiographical account of a man sadly misjudged in the Anglican historical record, who just might have managed to prevent all the divisive damage which happened to the Church of England after his time, and far into the seventeenth century. And now I reverted to type, the type of a butterfly collector, for whom no fragment of information is irrelevant or without interest. One of my Sydney doctoral students, working on that great Victorian, William Whewell, who invented the word 'scientist', was living in Blackheath at the same time. He was shocked to discover how quickly I had jettisoned all that Sydney theory and model-building, to reveal myself as an unreconstructed London empiricist. But Richard Yeo and his wife, equally shocked to discover that Liz had never been to Paris, looked after our four children for a weekend in which we made up for the deficiency.

It was a good leave. The children had a successful year in their Blackheath schools, with the exception of Stephen, who fell into the hands of a truly awful teacher. In the spring we packed into a tiny car and went south to visit my brother Bernard and his family near Marseilles, on into the Alps, and under Mont Blanc to the Tecino of southern Switzerland, where we stayed with my sister Hilda and husband Jakob in a village above Lake Maggiore. Come the summer, we were back in Cumbria on our beloved Midtown Farm, our favourite place a deep, cold swimming hole on the upper Esk, above Brotherilkeld, and the bridge erected in memory of Dick Marsh.

I gave a couple of prestigious lectures. The first, at King's College on the Strand, was called 'Towards a broader understanding of the early dissenting tradition'. It contrasted the 'vertical' approach of traditional denominational historians ('Thy hand, O God, has guided / Thy flock, from age to age') with the 'horizontal', contextual understanding of religious history which modern historiography has made possible. It proved to be one of the more influential of my public pronouncements. The other, a special faculty lecture given in Cambridge, was on the subject of Queen Elizabeth's favourite of favourites, Robert Dudley, earl of Leicester, and it foreshadowed a substantially different approach to Elizabethan history, different that is to say from Neale's idealized Elizabethan Age.

As yet we gave little thought to the possibility of returning to Britain, or to the English academic scene. A seed had been planted in an anteroom at Sydney, where several of us were waiting our turn to make the case for the promotion of a colleague before the appropriate committee. 'So you've decided to settle for this?' said Archie Davies, a long-serving professor of Oriental Studies, and, like myself, a pom. 'This' meant facilitating and overseeing the work of others, not doing any original work of one's own. That was how Sydney professors were supposed to spend their time, and it was what I was doing. Something inside me said, 'No, I don't think that I am settling for this.' But for the time being the seed did not germinate.

Sir John Hackett invited me to meet him at King's College in the Strand. Clifford Dugmore was about to retire. Would I like to succeed him? I was not sure that my family could live happily or comfortably in London, and I doubted whether I was fit to profess Ecclesiastical History. (I know no Greek!) So the job went to the lecturer who had succeeded me, the admirable James Cargill Thompson. Two or three years later James dropped dead, returning to college from lunch at a pub, and once again I was urged to apply for the London chair. But once again, I held back. Meanwhile, in the summer of 1974, in a car park at Canterbury, where I was working on the cathedral archives, Roger Anstey, who had taught me in Cambridge and who was now Professor of Modern History at the University of Kent, asked whether I knew that UKC had a vacancy. The Professor of History, Leland Lyons, a major Irish historian and the abortive biographer of Yeats, had departed to become Provost of Trinity College Dublin. One thing led to another and I applied for the chair. But before the day for the interviews I had second thoughts and withdrew my name. No appointment was made, and they wrote to say that if I were to change my mind about Canterbury, I should get in touch. So it was that the University of Kent had to cover the cost of a plane ticket from Sydney, rather than a day return to Canterbury West from Charing Cross.

That was the result of what happened when we got back to Sydney in September. In my absence, John M. Ward had stepped back into his old role as acting head of department. Most of my innovations were dismantled. It would not be fair to say of John Ward, as of other restored monarchs, that he had learned nothing and forgotten nothing. What he did retain was an acute and constitutionally justified sense of what his place and responsibilities were as Challis Professor of History. I now resumed the headship. But within a week or two the three professors were visited with a manifesto and an ultimatum. The department must be turned into a representative democracy without further ado. The professors were 'to enter into negotiations with the sub-professorial staff to create a system of self-government in the Department of History'. (This was more moderate than a motion which it had replaced, which had called upon the professors 'to agree to transfer the powers which they now exercise to the Department as a whole'.) Thus ensued a whole year of endless meetings and negotiations, the resurrection of departmental meetings (now with a chairman who was not the head of department) and the creation of umpteen committees of this and that. It was not a recipe for happiness.

For myself, I did not so much blame the professors (and the three of us had little choice but to stand shoulder to shoulder) as my colleagues who had lit the fuse. I was sure that if they had only bided their time for a few weeks, I could have got things back to where they were before I went on leave. But, as it was, I walked out of one of those dreadful meetings without telling anyone where I was going, caught a plane to London, and was soon sitting before an appointing committee in Canterbury. This was not considered in Sydney to be a sideways move. Who had ever heard of the University of Kent at Canterbury? The University of Sydney was 125 years old.

In that ancient university, those eruptions and tremors were so many signs that the tectonic plates were shifting. The Professorial Board had become an Academic Board, and the chairman who presided over this change, which was important both instrumentally and symbolically, was John M. Ward. Soon Ward became vice-chancellor, and it was as vice-chancellor that he and his wife and one of his two daughters, along with other leading figures in the university, were tragically killed when a commuting train ploughed into the observation car of a steam train excursion.[4]

I almost forgot to mention that in my last year in Sydney I was elected a Fellow of the Australian Academy of the Humanities, an honour in which I take pride. In spite of all, our last year in Australia was happy. We had acquired a Toyota Land cruiser, a four by four vehicle built like a tank with which we penetrated deep into the bush. Patonga was sublime, I still believe one of the most beautiful places on earth: a tidal creek snaking up deep into the forest, luring us to the headwaters in our canoes, rocks, then mudflats and mangroves, a paradise full of birds and fish. (Back in England I dreamed of Patonga every night for a year, always waking up with a feeling of desolation.) In November we sold both our houses and Liz and the children boarded the Lloyd Triestino liner the *Marconi* on its last voyage. They were to cross the Pacific, visiting New Zealand, Tahiti, Fiji, Acapulco, and so through the Panama Canal to Curacao and the Atlantic: the journey of a lifetime. I stayed in Sydney to clear things up. Those were febrile days. I was wheeling my books out of my office and down to the car park, with a tranny perched on top, as we learned of the sacking of Gough Whitlam by the governor general. In the ensuing turmoil, even cocktail parties split into two, not the usual division of blokes and sheilas but pro-Whitlamites and anti-Whitlamites.

I left Sydney by plane in early December, spent a few days in Thailand, and arrived in an England enveloped in fog, to grope my way down to Canterbury and to begin to look for somewhere to live. After visits to Suffolk, the aunts in Hampshire and the crowd in London, I took another plane down to Malaga, where the *Marconi* was due to arrive on Christmas Day in the morning. I had a day or two in hand, went up to Granada and then, on Christmas Eve, took a day trip to Morocco. On a cliff

---

4   In October 1997 I went back to Sydney as the first J. M. Ward Memorial Lecturer, and spent a fortnight in an office on the corridor on which I had lived for five years, a quarter of a century before. Nothing had changed and everything had changed. Cruel financial constraints and a creeping postmodernism had converted the old History Department into something different: a much smaller School of (I think) Social, Cultural, Gender and Historical Studies. Collegiality was a luxury no one could any longer afford. A polemical Sydney historian (not a member of the department), Keith Windschuttle, published a book at that time called *The killing of history*.

south of Tangier, with eucalyptus trees against a brilliant sea, it was hard to believe that I had ever left Australia, or that that freezing fog was not just a bad dream. And then it happened, just as planned. The ship came in at breakfast time. Andrew saw me on the pier but said it couldn't be me since I was carrying a guitar. I had bought his Christmas present in the guitar street in Granada. I had already placed all my baggage, including piles of other Christmas presents, in the left luggage, and at once got the family on to a coach to go up to Granada and the Alhambra. But we had almost forgotten what day it was. Back in Malaga, the ship, which I was to board for the last part of the cruise, was due to leave, and no one could open the firmly locked luggage repository. I came on board with what I was standing up in, and borrowed a razor from Arthur Boyd, the famous Australian painter. The passengers also included Sir Keith Hancock, the biographer of Smuts, according to Liz a dreadful cheat at Scrabble.

We called at Malta, Messina and Naples before finally docking at Genoa. At Milan station some of the luggage was stolen, including Liz's camera and all the pictures of the great trip. Roger Anstey met us at Folkestone on New Year's Day 1976, took us to tea at his home outside Canterbury, and on to a truly dreadful little rented house at Herne Bay, the best that Roger had been able to do for us. This would be home for the next three months, and where we all went down with 'flu. There was one room for cooking, eating, homework, lecture preparation and TV watching. The owners of the house had moved across the street and observed our every move through net curtains. Herne Bay was a poor exchange for Patonga. Jessie, who had flown back from Australia in her own box and was now housed in quarantine kennels on the cliffs between Dover and Folkestone, was on the whole rather better off.

15

Canterbury and Sheffield

For some considerable time, it seemed to have been a mistake to have exchanged our pleasant life in Sydney (not to speak of Patonga) for Canterbury, and the University of Sydney for the University of Kent (UKC). For starters, my salary was now less than half what it had been in Australia, in real terms. And salary adjustments showed no sign of keeping up with rampant inflation, in those pre-Thatcher, Callaghan years. The university diary for 1976–7 contained this 'IMPORTANT' notice: 'KEEP TELEPHONE CALLS SHORT . TURN OFF ALL UNNECESSARY LIGHTS AND OTHER ELECTRICAL APPLIANCES. USE "SECOND-HAND" ENVELOPES FOR INTERNAL MAIL'. During this period of financial stringency, your co-operation is urgently sought in making every possible economy consistent with efficient working.' Marjorie Jacobs came down to Canterbury, trying to persuade me to go back to Sydney, where my chair remained vacant. Only an obstinate conviction that one never turns back led me to resist those blandishments. Remember Lot's wife.

As for UKC, it was an interesting experiment, an invention of the mid-1960s when brains no less powerful than those of John Henry Newman or Lord Lindsay of Balliol and Keele (they included the historian Asa Briggs who invented the University of Sussex) were asked what was their idea of a university. The Canterbury model was a version of the then prevalent pattern of campus universities, without a city wall. (More recently, with the upgrading of so many civic polytechnics, the urban university has taken over, and, like some flesh-eating bug, lays waste many a quiet suburb, since students must live somewhere.) Kent was created as an association of colleges, each headed by a master headhunted from the ancient and collegiate universities, and expected to reside in a pepperpot master's lodge (more like the lodge at the gates of a Georgian mansion), tacked on to the college proper. There were ambitious plans for a good many colleges on that windswept hill above Canterbury, where people had chosen not to live for 2,000 years. In the event, only four materialized: Eliot, Darwin, Keynes and Rutherford. To proceed from one to another was an undertaking, in wintry weather. 'Darwin in only twenty-four hours' was a newspaper cutting pinned to a noticeboard in Keynes. At first students were supposed to be back inside by ten o'clock at night. They could not own cars within twenty-five miles. Interdisciplinarity was the watchword. There were no departments: only faculties, again headed by seasoned Oxbridgians who were expected to stay the course, like American deans. Comparisons with more successful models, say, Warwick or York, would be instructive, but must await a comparative history of the Robbins universities.[1]

---

[1] But see Robert Stevens, *University to uni* (London, 2004), and Robert Anderson, *British universities past and present* (London, 2006).

Within a decade many things had changed. There was nostalgic talk of 'the founding fathers', and what had happened to their ideals. The masters of colleges had retreated to comfortable homes in the city or the surrounding countryside, leaving their lodges to be occupied by college managers. The old regulations had collapsed, and students came and went at will. Not having fridges, they hung their milk and other foodstuffs out of their windows in plastic bags, which may not have been what the architects of the colleges had in mind.

Above all, the grey heads of the still infant university deplored the demise of the noble interdisciplinary aims it was supposed to pursue. But to anyone arriving, as I did, in 1976, that was a Mark Twainish sort of death, much exaggerated. There were still no departments, only boards of studies, within that all-significant faculty structure. The Faculty of Humanities had begun life under an Oxford classicist, Guy Chilver, dismissed by Hugh Trevor-Roper in his diary as a 'fool', whose views on the crisis of 1938 he had heard with 'contempt and disgust'. But after a storm in the Kent teacup Chilver had retired from the scene, giving way to the eminent Shakespearean scholar R. A. Foakes, who urged us to 'think faculty', and if he found himself in a minority of one on the Faculty Board, as he often did, wondered aloud what his colleagues thought they were about. We historians were distributed among the four colleges, and I found myself in Keynes. When John Cannon from the University of Newcastle came to inspect History at the university on behalf of the University Grants Committee, he complained that there was no door labelled 'Head of Department' against which he could knock if he, a student, had a problem. He had a point, even if he obstinately failed to understand our ways of doing things. The role of professors was so undefined that the equivalent of a royal commission was established to determine what that role was. The report, like all such reports, gathered dust.

Not for the first or the last time, I had a hard act to follow, for Leland Lyons was a genuinely distinguished scholar, as were several of the original professors. My professorial colleagues were Donald Read, whose specialities included modern British politics and the press; and my old friend Roger Anstey, a serious Methodist, notable for turning received (and cynical) wisdom on the subject of how slavery came to be abolished in the British Empire on its head. It really was all down to Clarkson and Wilberforce and their friends, although they played a clever hand of cards in disguising the disinterested altruism of their motivation. As a devout historian, Roger believed that human affairs showed signs of steady improvement, thanks to the ameliorating influence of Christianity. I could not agree with that, sharing with Martin Luther a kind of Christian pessimism so far as the affairs of this world are concerned. But we agreed on most other things, including (the only area where professors had a role) which of our colleagues deserved promotion.

Roger died of a heart attack in 1978, not very long after his wife Averil had died of cancer. Geoffrey Templeman, the founding vice-chancellor of Kent, a Birmingham medievalist who boasted about his studies with Marc Bloch in Paris, was remote from his staff (he never lunched in college), unless there was something wrong with them, when he took a more than kindly interest. It was suspected that he was more involved in the local NHS Trust than in the university. Told that Anstey must have recovered from a nasty turn because he had just gone off to America, Geoffrey said: 'But will he ever come back again? That's what I want to know.' Unfortunately that was not allowed to be a joke for very long.[2] And soon Roger was replaced as Professor of Modern History by another Africanist, David Birmingham, whom I had known since he was a schoolboy.

Our chancellor in those years was the former Liberal leader, Jo Grimond. He had replaced the duchess of Kent, much to the disgust of Geoffrey Templeman, who had wanted another royal, and who never extended the hospitality of the vice-chancellor's residence to Grimond, so that on his annual visits to confer degrees he had to stay with a friend in the city. Jo enjoyed making speeches at the four or five degree-giving congregations, telling the graduands on one occasion that, if they were good listeners, they should think of getting themselves elected to the House of Commons. Soon after the loss of a son in a car crash in France, one of his speeches was all about death, to the bewilderment of his audience. After that it was put to him that he might like to make only one speech a year, the others to be delivered by some of the honorary graduands. Next time Grimond stood up it was to say: 'I used to make a speech at every one of these ceremonies, but clearly they haven't gone down too well, because now I've been told to give only one.' We found new delight in the distant view of Canterbury Cathedral, perfectly framed in the great window of Rutherford College, where these ceremonies were held. But Grimond was a good chancellor, ranking in my book with Fred Dainton, chancellor of Sheffield, a chemist who took an active interest in the affairs of the Sheffield historians.

For the teaching staff, Kent's structures held advantages. In the college common rooms we mingled with colleagues in many disciplines, which was something which never happened in rigidly departmentalized universities. (At Sydney, I almost never met my colleagues in Economic History, or English Literature.) And we taught together. The first year in Humanities was devoted to the twentieth century, and we shared classes and tutorials with philosophers and political scientists: which almost made up for the pain of having to ingest tedious paperback texts on what was still the Common Market – or was it already the European Economic Community? In the third term of the first year, our students embarked on what were called Part One Topics. It was a tonic to teach 'Childhood' alongside Mark Kinkead-Weekes, re-reading *The mill on the Floss* and *Father and son*, and to be guided by psychologists into the fallacies of Freud's *Little Hans*; while Hugh Cunningham almost persuaded us that the imposition of universal schooling on Victorian children was much like what happened to Africa in the nineteenth century. I enjoyed other topics: 'Religion and Science'; and, most of all 'Religion and the First World War', a course which I helped to invent, alongside the Jewish scholar and publicist, Dan Cohn-Sherbok.

The novelist Kingsley Amis coined a notorious phrase on the eve of the new university foundations when he said that more meant worse. That has been found to be a fallacy. But it has to be said that in the 1970s the majority of UKC history students were not up to much, and were not highly motivated. They were certainly not up to the standard set by the abler Sydney students taking History Honours, who, to be fair, would have been Oxbridge material in Britain. We taught in tutorials of two or three, and I note that until 1979 it was always 'Mr' or 'Miss' this or that.

[2] On another occasion, the brilliant legal historian Brian Simpson told the vice-chancellor that his mother-in-law was living at the top of a steep flight of steps in Hastings. 'Brian, if your mother-in-law falls down those steps, they will take her to St Christopher's Hospital, where they will do what they can.' 'Do you ever look at your stools, Gibson?' Templeman once asked the Professor of French.

Only then does my diary begin to use Christian names. The essays were scrappy, and totally lacking in the apparatus of footnotes and bibliographies which were drummed into our Sydney students from Day One. But that sort of thing was not encouraged by the Kent historians, who had mostly been educated at Oxford, where, apparently, you were supposed to write about, as it might be the English Civil War, as if your thoughts on the matter were entirely original, and no one had put his mind to it ever before: a bit like me, climbing the Cuillins in 1948, not knowing the names of the mountains, or whether anyone had ever bothered to go up them. There is a case to be made for this approach to the subject. In Sydney, people knew about someone called Christopher Hill, but almost doubted that the seventeenth century had ever happened. That sort of thing led to the creeping disease of postmodernism. There is ambiguity in the very word 'history'. Is it the past, or stories about the past? But to pretend that history is not mostly historiography would be like an archaeologist neglecting the stratigraphy of his subject. Paradoxically, the Oxford method was making that very point. Each undergraduate essay added to the stratigraphy. Surely no one supposed that this would be the last word on the subject.

These are some of the reasons why I sometimes wondered why I was in Canterbury. But I had some splendid colleagues, who taught me a great deal. And not just the historians. With Kate McLuskie, Marion O'Connor and Mick Hattaway from the English Board, I taught an MA in Elizabethan and Jacobean Studies which opened up new worlds; and Mick and I would take this genuinely interdisciplinary attack on the historicity of texts and the textuality of historical documents to Sheffield, where we would both be transplanted in 1984. Of some twenty historians, three were early modern Europeanists, covering France, Germany and Italy, and it was made clear at my first Board of Studies meeting that I was surplus to requirements, so far as they were concerned. So it was farewell to Martin Luther. And now I did teach a good deal of Tudor and Stuart history, in harness with my Welsh friend, Peter Roberts; and even more of the social history of late medieval and early modern England, sharing the teaching with Malcolm Jack, who, like the little girl with the curl on her forehead, when he was good was very very good; and a brilliant late medievalist, Andrew Butcher, whose legacy is invested in the students he taught rather than in the books he never wrote.

We launched a summer school for (mostly) American students, which I directed, and which should have been much more of a success than it was. We lined up an astonishing cast of lecturers and seminar leaders: Derek Pearsall and Elizabeth Salter on Chaucer, the elderly George Potter on Renaissance politics, the great Eugene Vinaver of Manchester who gave us the last lectures on medieval romances that he ever delivered. Vinaver had the grace to tell us that he had learned much from his students in the summer school. I found that hard to credit. I was once approached by a delegation of students who told me that they suspected that Professor David Aers, a radical student of late medieval English texts, was a Marxist. Well, well. Apparently they expected to get their money back.

And all the time, down at the bottom of the hill, was the cathedral, and its amazing archive. I was soon digging deep into the religious culture of sixteenth-century Kent, courtesy of the act books of the ecclesiastical courts, and the records of evidence given in court in thousands of litigations involving marriage, inheritance, slander and who knows what else: thousands of closely written folios, rivalling the proud claim of the *News of the World* that all human life is there. The defamation suits were especially rewarding, since these cases depended on the accurate reporting of the very words spoken. If a woman had been accused of 'going to the Ness to play the troll, as thou hast done before', you were told that the Ness was Dungeness, and that the woman in question, whose husband had been press-ganged so that she did not know whether he was alive or dead, had 'played the troll', that is had practised prostitution with the fishermen who came there in the season. The matrimonial cases were no less revealing. Agnes Butterwick, a Mistress Quickly-like figure, was a witness of critical importance in a matrimonial suit between two rich and powerful Canterbury families. A whole volume of evidence was devoted to Mistress Butterwick, who was by that time dead. Had she been a good woman or not? She had been midwife to many of Canterbury's crypto-Catholic families, so that their Protestant enemies were her detractors. We learn from one hostile witness that she had operated a brothel in Ashford for soldiers returning from Henry VIII's Boulogne campaign. Later she looked after a child reportedly fathered by a priest at Blean outside Canterbury (where our family went to church). When the vicar saw the baby he said that it was a fair Christian child. If it isn't, said Agnes, you're a Jew. Lodging with the widow of Alderman Starkey as a kind of companion, Agnes played a crucial role when certain 'rich men from the Weald' came seeking Mrs Starkey's hand. But her reward for playing the matchmaker was to be sent packing by the successful suitor. I was back in my butterfly-collecting element.

And soon I was involved with something more serious: the *History of Canterbury Cathedral*, which I co-edited and to which I added my pennyworth on the sixteenth and seventeenth centuries. What, after the Reformation, was a cathedral for? It was not a question to which I was able to give a very convincing answer. UKC under Templeman had turned its back on the cathedral, which was silly. All that was rectified under his successor, David Ingram, when congregations of the university for the conferment of degrees began to be held there, as they still are.

It was certainly a privilege to be living under the shadow of that remarkable church; although sometimes it seemed that my day job was taking one party or another of Australian or American friends around the place. We were there for the institution as dean of my friend Victor de Waal, Esther's husband; and soon for the enthronement as archbishop of Robert Runcie, who also became a good friend. In 1978 the Lambeth Conference was held for the first time at the University of Kent and I found that I knew many of the bishops from different parts of my life: David Sheppard from Liverpool, John Taylor of Winchester, who had become a friend in my CMS years, the Sudanese bishops, bishops whom I knew from Australia and, of course, Desmond Tutu, to whom we gave an honorary degree in the cathedral. My summer school was running at the same time, and we queued up with the bishops in the refectory at Darwin for our lunch.

And then came the excitement of the visit of Pope John Paul II in May 1982. Esther later told me that on that visit they saw a very human side of the pope. Overwhelmed by his first sight of the cathedral when he first arrived, the pope threw out the careful timetable prepared for him by his unwillingness to leave the Popemobile. On being told that he must take a siesta after lunch, he bowed and responded: 'Yes, in Canterbury even the pope obeys', as he went up the stairs. Blessing the de Waal family in the great drawing room of the Deanery (with no photographers present, so there is no record of this), coming to Thomas, the fourth son, who is six foot four, the pope had to stand on tiptoe to reach the top of his head, saying, with amusement in his voice, 'Benjamin, the littlest one.'

The public life of that strangely fragmented civic community which is Canterbury occupied me in various ways. One was the Canterbury Archaeological Trust, which was in the business of rescue archaeology, one move ahead of the developers to dig up, as it might be, and was, the theatre which had once packed in Roman audiences. The musical scene was especially divided; but all the better for that. Trevor Wye, when not teaching the flute in Manchester and London, produced remarkable results from bumbling amateurs, including my oboe- and bassoon-playing daughters, who used to double up as his cleaners. Trevor Pinnock's father was around, and my son went to Trevor's school, so we were able to see and hear Trevor on the keyboard from time to time. Under the gentle auspices of the Deller family, Alfred and Mark, the summer saw the Stour Music Festival, at Boughton Aluph church, near Ashford, where I first heard performances from Musica Antiqua Köln.

When Mark Deller's singing career was threatened by a worrying throat condition, Liz was in theatre for his operation. She had gone back to work after fifteen years away from the nursing scene. While assisting the anaesthetists, I believe that she saved one or two lives. 'Are you sure that you want to do that?' she would ask an inexperienced anaesthetist.

We lived in a very convenient house at the bottom of the hill from the university, built by a man with six children. It was a pleasant walk to work in the mornings, up through the woods and past two or three ponds. One delicious May mooning, the lower pond was full of newts, and there were two grass snakes, their heads raised from the surface, predating on the newts.

Our four children were happy in Canterbury, although it is interesting that they have never wanted to go back there. (But there are lifelong friends who date from that time.) Two of Reg and Doreen Jewkes's children lodged with us in turn, Helen and Rachel, while they did their sixth-form studies at the King's School. So we were usually seven at the evening meal. Our children were both beneficiaries and victims of the selective education system which still obtains in Kent. Helen, Andrew and Sarah all made it into the local single-sex grammar schools, where they received an education of varied quality, but came out of it well enough: Helen to read History at York, Andrew Medicine at Bristol and Sarah Anthropology, and later International Relations, at Trinity College Cambridge. But Stephen drew the short straw, 'failed' the eleven plus, and went to a secondary modern school a few yards away from our house known as the Archbishop's School. It was not the worst of the local secondary moderns, but Steve knew within a week or so of arriving that he was among a lot of no-hopers. When Bob Runcie asked him where he went to school, and said, 'that's my school', Steve said in all innocence: 'Oh, I never knew that you went there.' Steve was not a no-hoper. He took a degree in Fine Art, did some great paintings, but has since made his name in African music, in the interests of which he has changed his name to Steve Rivers.

The pace quickened, in ways good and bad, as we came to the end of the seventies, and Margaret Thatcher moved into Downing Street. In 1978 I was invited to give the Ford Lectures in English History in the University of Oxford which were delivered in the cold January and February of 1979. That is the best thing that can happen to a historian of these islands, and now it seemed that to have come back from Australia was not such a bad idea after all. I had hardly ever been to Oxford, and I had to ask my way to the Examinations Schools, where the lectures were given and where Hugh Trevor-Roper, as Regius Professor, conducted me to the rostrum. The entire Oxford faculty turns up to the first of those lectures, and other Ford lecturers have confessed that they hoped that they might be run over by a bus, crossing the High Street to reach that formidable audience. (But, as a stranger to Oxford, you have nothing to lose.) After that, numbers tend to dwindle, and you are in danger of being relegated to a smaller room, which I believe happened to Sir Geoffrey Elton, whose Fords became his famous account of Thomas Cromwell's enforcement of the Henrician Reformation, *Policy and police*, arguably his greatest book. My subject was various aspects of the English Church and religious life between the accession of Elizabeth I and the death of James I. The audience held up pretty well. The lectures were later published as *The religion of Protestants: the church in English society, 1559–1625*. My friend Sir Keith Thomas commended the book to the Delegates of the Oxford University Press, but then encountered me in the Bodleian Library to tell me what he really thought of it. Mostly his judgment was favourable, but he disagreed with my suggestion that if there had been no Archbishop Laud there might have been no Quakers. Who knows?

More validation followed in 1982 with my election to the fellowship of the British Academy. By then, I had spent a term as a visiting fellow at All Souls College, and so had got to know Oxford a little better. It was a strange and in some ways unnerving experience. Rodney Needham, Professor of Anthropology, was one of the few fellows who took any interest in us transient visitors. 'Tell me what you do. I probably shan't understand, but do try.' The rules at breakfast precluded the reading of anything so much as a letter, but allowed conversation, provided it had nothing to do with anything that mattered. On one occasion, Needham said: 'I've always wondered about the etymology of the word "shove".' James McConica said: 'I try not to think about it' – and never returned to breakfast. Nowadays I should probably have been happier at All Souls, which no longer inhabits a different planet. But what a treat it was, to look from that breakfast table through curiously wavery eighteenth-century glass at the Radcliffe Camera, and within minutes to be in Bodley. I spent my time in Oxford researching early English nonconformity, from the fifteenth-century Lollards to the seventeenth-century sectarians, the subject of a set of Birkbeck Lectures in Ecclesiastical History delivered in Cambridge later in the year. I was entertained royally at Trinity, which sponsors those lectures, little knowing that that would not be my last visit to Trinity.

But in the meantime serious things had been happening on other fronts. On 2 September 1980, soon after coming back from a holiday in the depths of Devon, and late in the evening and in the dark, I stepped off an already moving train as it left the station, fell over and over and slipped neatly between the platform and the track. (Thank God for 'mind the gap!') Two ladies saw what had happened and stopped the train. An interesting conversation ensued. Was there a man down there or not? I was unable to contribute. Taken to the Kent and Canterbury Hospital, I had two or three operations which left me without a left foot. I wrote a letter to the local paper, thanking the ladies who had saved my life. They came to see me in hospital, two or three days before they were due to emigrate to Argentina. I quite enjoyed those seven weeks in hospital. I had a room to myself, and taught my special subject and postgraduate students. Those who came to visit brought me books I would otherwise never have read, and I got to know my visitors better than ever before. The registrar of the University of Kent asked me whether I had insured myself against this kind of accident. I hadn't – but the University of Kent had. Soon he came to see me with a cheque which represented the price of a house. In a Dostoevsky-like gesture, it appeared that I had sold my left foot to pay for my children's higher education. I also had a visit from the railway police, who cautioned me and told me that I had committed two distinct offences: opening the door of a moving vehicle, and leaving a moving vehicle. On this occasion they would not prosecute, but next time they certainly would. The loss of the foot made very little difference to me physically. I could still manage the Snowdon Horseshoe, if at a slower pace, and in 1984 I did the 5,000 feet and the twenty-five miles up and down of Half Dome in the Yosemite.

Worse was to come in 1981. Andrew, our elder son, was beginning a gap year, working as an orderly in the National Hospital for Nervous Diseases in Queen's Square, where Doreen Jewkes was the senior anaesthetist. But for that, but for our old friendship with the Jewkeses, he would not be alive today, for he could not have survived what was about to happen if he had been dealt with in Canterbury. A lump under the arm was found, under surgery at University College Hospital, to be a tumour, and presently Andrew was diagnosed as suffering from a very rare form of non-Hodgkin's lymphoma. So rare that Mr Suhami, the brilliant oncologist in charge of the case, took some convincing. Few people had previously survived this form of cancer. But chemotherapy was just getting into its stride, and Suhami told us that he hoped that something could be done. That was on an afternoon when we had to go on to Cambridge for my first Birkbeck Lecture. Alan Hodgkin, the then master of Trinity, who knew something about these things, was very supportive. A little later, my GP in Canterbury told me that he was sorry to have heard about Andrew. I said, yes, we were worried sick, but the consultant had told us that he hoped that Andrew could be cured. I'm sorry, said Dr Buss, but that's not what the senior registrar told me. Now what are you to believe?

In the event, several doses of chemotherapy, which had to be stopped when Andrew's white cell count fell below an acceptable level, worked. Twenty-six years on, Andrew is himself a consultant physician (in paediatrics), and the father of three lovely children. We can never be sufficiently grateful to the NHS, collectively, and to Mr Suhami, personally. In the course of that painful year, Andrew took an A-level course in English, and gained an A, while he failed an exam in typing, the only exam he has ever managed to fail.

We will always take some convincing that Andrew's illness was unrelated to our Cumbrian holidays, many days on the beach at Drigg, near the nuclear complex of Windscale. In the early eighties public alarm about the latest rounds in the deadly game of Cold War deterrence (Mutual Assured Destruction) brought us into active membership of CND. We went on marches and demonstrations, and Liz became an active supporter of Greenham Common Women's Peace Camp. It was in that context that we became friends with Rowan Williams, now archbishop of Canterbury. We continued to be active peaceniks, opposing both the Iraqi wars, in letters to the papers, in vigils, and on the streets. Both Helen and Andrew did holiday jobs in Gaza and the West Bank, and we were strong supporters of the Palestinian cause.

Storm clouds of a different kind now moved in on the university scene: Mrs Thatcher's Savage Cuts. At the University of Kent we were told that the Faculty of Humanities had to shed a certain number of staff, but it was not clear how. There were a few gallant Captain Oateses, like Mark Kinkead-Weekes, FBA, an authority on D. H. Lawrence, who went out of the tent to be gone for some time, a quite unnecessary loss to the university of one of its best teachers and most dedicated public servants. Day after day, the vice-chancellor, registrar and finance officer interviewed staff, one by one, offering terms for early retirement. What happened to all the other things they were supposed to be doing? Alf Smyth, a learned Dark Age historian, with a command of classical languages, early Irish and Icelandic, who had tried to organize an exhibition of Anglo-Saxon jewellery to coincide with the pope's visit, was told that he seemed to be good at that kind of thing. Had he thought of making another career in fund-raising, an occupation normally reserved for retired rear admirals? I was seen three times, as a member of staff over fifty, as a historian and as chairman of the History Board.

Now for some very black humour. In the midst of this crisis a lecturer in English, Dr Shapiro, last of the old-style Leavisites, was murdered in a house just behind ours. He had picked up a boy at Dover who, on his own plea, had not expected the encounter to lead to what Dr Shapiro expected. And then a Lecturer in Philosophy, our next-door neighbour, committed suicide. Gerhard Benecke, our early modern Germanist, died in mysterious circumstances in China. We had almost reached our quota when another member of the English Board, and a very talented pianist, succumbed to the cigarettes he smoked all the time. I could have written a campus novel called *Unnatural wastage*.

But we had still not reached our target. So when the chair of Modern History at Sheffield was advertised, I decided that I ought to apply. I was interviewed and offered the job. Back in Canterbury I informed David Ingram, but said that I was not sure that I would be doing the right thing by my colleagues in leaving. 'Nonsense', said the vice-chancellor, 'you'll be doing them all a great favour.' So that was that. By October 1984 I was living and teaching in Sheffield. This was the first time that Mrs Thatcher moved me on, with a little bit of help from Dr Ingram.

Before that, at the age of fifty-five, I went on the first of eighteen visits (so far) to the United States: to a fellowship at the Huntington Library in San Marino, California, which was another way of taking me off the UKC payroll for six months. No one who has been privileged to spend time in that most remarkable archive and library, rich in resources for Shakespeareans and all other students of early modern English culture and history, is entitled to complain about anything. And yet, set among gardens of exceptional importance and beauty (the Australian garden and the desert garden each occupying several acres), the Huntington is almost too perfect. I went to a Saturday church fete in Pasadena and bought for a few cents a paperback copy of Samuel Johnson's *Rasselas*. And then I realized what the problem was. The Young Man is asked why he is unhappy in the Happy Valley, and his answer is that it is all that he has ever seen. But it was a very agreeable and fruitful six months. I began to take more seriously the interaction of politics and literature in my Elizabethan period, coached by such veteran scholars as Bill Ringler, and younger and up-and-coming stars like John King, now of Ohio State, who was my neighbour in the next office. I also did the work on the impact of Puritanism on English culture which led to such publications as *From iconoclasm to iconophobia: the cultural impact of the second English Reformation* (the Stenton Lecture given at Reading in 1985), and my Anstey Memorial Lectures for the University of Kent in 1986, *The birthpangs of Protestant England: religious and cultural change in the sixteenth and seventeenth centuries*.

The rhythm of life at the Huntington could not have been more agreeable, although the working day was short. An early lunch was obligatory, always to be followed by a walk through the grounds, led by Elizabeth Story Donno. The library closed at 5, which left no alternative to evening hikes along the trails in the San Gabriel Mountains, which rise to as much as 9,000 feet behind Pasadena. What memories of Strawberry Peak, above Strawberry Canyon, with slopes of ceanothus, 'Californian lilac'! There were rattlesnakes too. I fell in love with the Salton Sea and its fish and its birds, before it became hopelessly poisoned by agricultural chemicals; and with the beautiful Anza Borrego desert hills, between the Salton Sea and San Diego.

On Sundays I went to All Saints Pasadena, the largest episcopalian church west of the Mississippi, where liberal attitudes on such questions as women's ministry, nuclear weapons (vigils against the white train) and migration from Central America belied the huge wealth of its congregation. I got to know an elderly and lifelong Republican who was entirely convinced by a visit to Nicaragua of the justice of the Sandinista cause, and the iniquity of the US-backed Contras. 'Where is your family?' they used to ask, before Liz arrived. On Easter Sunday, Desmond Tutu preached one of the greatest sermons I have ever heard. After Good Friday, it was all utterly hopeless so far as Christ's disciples were concerned. (And you really need to hear Desmond pronouncing 'utterly hopeless'.) And so, still in 1984, with South Africa. Within a few years, all was to change, and Desmond had a prophetic vision of that change. He ended with a prayer in Xhosa. 'Don't worry. He understands.'

Liz and the boys came out for a holiday. We went to the Olympics, and we were in the stadium when two women sprinters (Zola Budd and Mary Decker) became entangled with each other, the major 'incident' of those Games. Being in the stadium, we saw less than if we had been watching on television. A little boy sitting behind was concerned that not all the events were being won by Americans. 'But Johnny, you have to realize that some of these little countries are very good at sports.' We drove up that dramatic coast, from Malibu to San Francisco, past the nature reserve at Point Lobos, with its sea otters, sea lions and brown pelicans. Steve and I climbed up to 11,000 feet on Mount San Jacinto above Palm Springs. We went to Sequoia National Park (and were silent before those unimaginably immense trees), King's Canyon, the Yosemite. Andrew got to the top of Half Dome on his twenty-first birthday. And then to San Diego, to see Andrew off on an adventurous holiday in Mexico. California is one of the most beautiful countries in this world, even while it sits on a tectonic time bomb and uses far more water than it has or should: one of those ancient and vanished civilizations which there may or may not be archaeologists to uncover in 2300: Hollywood aka Machu Picchu.

In my last weeks in Kent, three of us spent a morning with Ted Heath in Albemarle Street, a policeman outside the front door, a mug of something on the windowsill. 'What can I offer you: brandy, bacon and eggs, coffee?' We settled for coffee. Heath had us in the palm of his anti-Thatcherist hand for two hours until it became clear that his idea of a university was some white-coated technological outfit in Japan, not, above all not, the University of Essex. Year in year out, Heath was blackballed for an honorary degree at Kent by the kind of Conservatives who dominated its governing court (another Templeman legacy). A particular opponent was Robin Leigh-Pemberton, who at about that time was made governor of the Bank of England. Goodness knows why. Leigh-Pemberton came to Canterbury to give a town and gown lecture which deployed many mysterious mathematical formulae. When asked, over dinner, what these magic numbers might mean, the great banker said: 'Oh don't ask me about that. My people do all that for me. I'm a humanist.' Does that tell us all that we need to know about what was rotten in the state of Denmark in the 1980s? Eventually Heath got his richly deserved honorary degree, with Bob Geldof honoured in the same ceremony.

I arrived in Sheffield in October 1984 and for the first year lodged with Mick Hattaway, who had moved in at the same time. (Liz and Steve were still in Canterbury.) We instantly became heads of our respective departments (History and English

Literature), which until then had had little to do with each other. I enjoyed life at 26 Elmore Road, with Mick and his then partner, Sue Widdowes. I learned that professors of English Literature have to read over breakfast the novel they are supposed to teach that day. I became good friends with little Rafe, who called me 'Professor La La', and when Max was born, Liz was there to help. It is just too too bad that Rafe was killed (and Max injured), snowboarding in the Alps, just before Christmas 2005. Presently Liz and I bought a house in the university suburb of Broomhill, built by a manufacturer of saws in about 1850: the most handsome and spacious home we have ever owned. In the four years before we sold it, it went up in value from £45,000 to £145,000. Liz found interesting employment in the Charles Clifford Dental Hospital and the Weston Park Hospital for cancer patients. As for Stephen, he found himself in the sixth form at King Edward VII School ('King Ted's'), which though by then a comprehensive still had the character, and reputation, of a first-class grammar school: a rather drastic sea-change for Steve.

The Sheffield History Department was one of the best in the country, and destined to get better. As some index of that improvement, I would be succeeded as Professor of Modern History by Sir Ian Kershaw, doyen of historians of Nazi Germany. He had quite an easy act to follow. I taught the so-called 'new' Social History, in harness with splendid colleagues, John Stevenson and Anthony Fletcher, the best teacher I have ever known. Other early modernists, Mark Greengrass and Linda Kirk, looked after the European side of things but allowed me walk-on parts. They were some of the best colleagues one could wish for. I ran a Special Subject, 'Catholics, Lollards and Protestants', which was never very successful in recruiting students. They told me that if I had called it 'The Reformation' it would have done better. Most of the Arts subjects were (and are) housed in the Arts Tower, a sore thumb of a mini-skyscraper where you make your way up and down to the various floors by one of those fearsome paternosters, which (in the Birmingham version) feature dramatically in one of David Lodge's novels. But we historians were accommodated in a large Victorian house, I think a former doctor's surgery; and for the first time ever I was able to house the whole of my library in a very large office.

The humanities at Sheffield University were on the cusp, beginning to find that being redbrick was not to be inferior. In my first year, two firsts in History were awarded, the first for many years. My predecessor, George Potter, used to say that people who get firsts don't go to Sheffield. And even the great William Empson, whom my colleague in English Literature, John Haffenden, would brilliantly bring back to life, had thought mickey mouse lectures on some canonical author or other, dealing with the basic facts of his or her life and output, were appropriate for Sheffield students. But by the mid-eighties no one any longer patronized or underestimated Sheffield undergraduates.

Some of the things that happened to me in Sheffield were a repetition of events in Sydney, ten years before. On the retirement of my immediate predecessor as Professor of Modern History, Ken Haley, the department, collectively, had reconstructed itself and the syllabus. New, and in some ways quite radically new, elements were introduced: a compulsory course on 'World civilizations, AD 900–1900' which we all had to teach, and which had me up at five in the morning year after year, trying to relearn the rudiments of Indian History; and a course in Historiography, devised by the brilliant Michael Bentley, in which we were all equally obliged to take some part. The idea was to leave the students after one term convinced that they knew nothing, and then to patiently reconstruct their knowledge in the second term.

What was supposed to happen to the brains of their teachers was not, I think, a question ever addressed. Ken Haley, as one of the last of the old-style professors, deeply disapproved. They should have waited for me to arrive to propose my own courses.

The world had moved on from Haley's day. This was that blissful dawn between old-style professorial tyranny and the new and much worse rigours of top-down imperatives, driven by money and considerations of industrial productivity, a different style of management. The new Sheffield syllabus was indicative of a view, almost an ideology, of where the historians stood, collectively and in relation to the university, which matched what my Sydney colleagues had demanded in 1975. The politics of these matters concerned the headship of department. I was that thing, as Professor of Modern History, for all but one term of my four years in post. The revised Statutes of the University allowed the office to be held by sub-professorial members of staff, so that my colleagues were insistent on their right to elect my successor. We had many departmental meetings, discussing appropriate procedures. David Luscombe, Professor of Medieval History, took part in these deliberations; but then reminded us that under the terms of his appointment (many years before mine) he, unlike me, was entitled to resume the headship of department, turn and turn about. David, a medieval intellectual historian of distinction, Fellow of the British Academy and soon its publications secretary, was not power-hungry. He believed that the old rotation was necessary to preserve the threatened interests of Medieval History. Even his medieval colleagues were of another mind. A little later, with Rees Davies, then president of the Royal Historical Society, I would be summoned to Trinity College Dublin to adjudicate on whether a recently vacated chair, previously dedicated to things medieval, should stay that way or be opened up. The issue was the same.

What I may call the Luscombe question ground on, indeed, until a bit after my time. And meanwhile, elsewhere in the University of Sheffield, there were stresses and strains, like the creakings and groanings of a ship caught in the Antarctic ice. As head of History, I had to negotiate the merger of several history departments: Economic History, Ancient History and Archaeology. It didn't all work out according to plan. And the university at large, in those Thatcher years, had to decide whether it would retain Physics or Earth Sciences. Earth Sciences lost out, being reduced to a small service department of five from an outfit of twenty-five. Overseas students brought in desperately needed money, and in one of the more bizarre ventures of that time, the university (through the agency of my friend and colleague Mick Hattaway) bought a job lot of Syrians to read for an MA in Elizabethan and Jacobean Studies. It was not a successful experiment. The only man in the group was also the most competent and literate in English, and a Muslim of fiercely orthodox views. In one of our classes, it was suggested that an episode in the Jacobean play *A woman killed with kindness* was an echo of the biblical story of Abraham having his hand stayed as he was about to kill his son Isaac. 'Excuse me, but it was not Isaac. It was Ishmael.' 'Oh yes, I'm sorry. I do know that your Quran tells us that it was Ishmael who was to be the victim.' 'Yes indeed, it happened at Mecca in the Hejaz. It is historical fact.' When the Syrians failed their examinations, as most did, there were legal consequences which probably cost the university more than it gained from the investment. We were not very popular.

When Professor Bill Carr, our only modern Europeanist, retired, it was touch and go whether he would be replaced. Only advice from Professor Graeme Davies, who had such a great future before him, advice which resembled the casuistry of the unjust steward in the Gospels, outwitted an unsympathetic registrar and saved the department's bacon. To be fair to the then vice-chancellor, Geoffrey Simms played with a straight bat and was a considerable help. I was continually fighting my corner, contending against senior colleagues in other departments with whom I would probably have been on the best of terms if we had got to know one another in happier times. However, there were no hard feelings. Sheffield later gave me an honorary degree, as, for that matter, did the University of Kent.

And now Sheffield jumped on the bandwagon of the new IT technology. We had in our care the astonishing archive amassed in the seventeenth century by one Samuel Hartlib, an intellectual wheeler and dealer. Hartlib and his many corre-spondents were interested in everything, and we shared those interests. Three of us, Mark Greengrass in History, Michael Leslie in English and myself, landed the first ever British Academy award for a group research project.

Just outside Sheffield, improbably close, was the Peak District. You could leave the city centre and be deep in the Derbyshire hills within twenty minutes, sure that several red grouse would fly low over the road in front of your car. We soon learned to love those hills, which explains why, between 1989 and 2005, we chose to live there, in the village of Hathersage in the Hope Valley, a stone's throw from where George Potter and his wife Rae used to live. The early winters were severe, perhaps the last severe winters the Peak District will ever experience. On one excessively adventurous Sunday, Liz and I went up Kinder Scout from Edale, and across to Kinder Downfall. The whole thing resembled a wedding cake, shining with ice, and on the Downfall people were climbing the ice as if they were in Scotland. We had no ice axe or crampons and were lucky to get down in one piece.

It would prove hard indeed to leave our Hathersage house. Sitting in bed in the morning, drinking tea, you looked straight out over the pleasant valley of the Derwent to Offerton Moor and Eyam Moor (with the famous plague village of Eyam on the other side of the hill). It was exactly how Renaissance and Enlighten-ment gardeners planned the human environment: the domesticated garden (and we had a beautiful garden), the rustic scene of animal husbandry beyond, and then, behind that, the untamed wilderness. An illusion, of course, since every detail of the English landscape, including our Derbyshire moors, is man-made.

In May 1987 I went to St John's College Oxford to read a paper to the under-graduate historians. I chose to present a rather savage critique of the latest book by Sir Geoffrey Elton, Regius Professor of Modern History at Cambridge, *The parlia-ment of England, 1559–1581*. It was the only time in my life and career that I chose to tackle Elton head on. Back in Sheffield, Liz indicated a rather fat envelope which had fallen on the mat in my absence. It proved to be a letter from Mrs Thatcher, telling me that she wanted me to succeed Elton as Regius Professor.

This was a great shock. It would never have occurred to me to have applied for that post, if it had not been in the gift of the crown and, like most jobs, had been publicly advertised. Did I want it? Could I live up to it? Could I afford to take it, since I would suffer a drop in salary of £2,000 or £3,000: something American colleagues find hard to believe, as well they may. My salary was to be a little over £30,000, rather less than police constables or primary schoolteachers now earn. Well, bishops of the Church of England have long since come to terms with those uncomfortable differentials. Should we pay our professors what we pay our bishops? It seems not. Seventeen years on, the median professorial salary in Cambridge is £57,000. Good luck to my successors. However, others who have been in a similar position will know that the real question was this: if I were to say no, could I face going through the rest of my life knowing that I had turned down the most prestigious post in History in the whole country and not being able to tell anyone?

I also had to consult my children, so it was two or three days before I rang up Downing Street to tell Robin Catford, the patronage secretary, that, yes, I would be pleased and honoured to accept the appointment. Well, said Catford, there's a snag. The prime minister has just called a general election, and that means that she cannot advise the Palace on this matter unless she is returned to power. If the election changes things, the new incumbent of No. 10 might have other ideas. So nothing could be breathed about the Cambridge job for six weeks. Catford was worried, because he knew that I had discussed the matter with my children, and that one of them was an undergraduate at Trinity. This, of course, was a bit silly, since everyone in the History Faculty must have known that I had been nominated.[3]

I did not want Mrs Thatcher to win (my weekly commutes between Sheffield and Canterbury in 1984 had been through cordons of police, containing the miners' strike). So I hoped that Neil Kinnock would come in, get around eventually to asking what was happening to that job in Cambridge, and decide to leave things where they were. I would then have had two letters to frame and hang in the loo. But in the event Maggie was back. And I am told that the first piece of paper she signed on returning to Downing Street from Finchley that Friday morning was the letter recommending my appointment; and that that was also the first thing that the queen did on the advice of the newly elected administration. So this was the second time in my life when Maggie Thatcher moved me on.

---

[3] Something to be said in favour of crown appointments is that nowadays they often involve wider consultation than is possible under electoral protocols. The most encouraging thing about this unexpected and alarming elevation was the knowledge that my future colleagues must have wanted it.

16

Trinity

I would be returning to Cambridge after an absence of thirty-six years. I was both surprised and excited by the prospect of becoming the next Regius Professor, succeeding the famous Tudor historian Geoffrey Elton, who had followed Owen Chadwick, and a long line of historians who were household names, at least in some households: Herbert Butterfield, G. M. Trevelyan, Lord Acton. Somewhere back there was Charles Kingsley, whom Elton had called 'the last of the absurdities'. Was there now to be another absurdity? My excitement was not widely shared. The *Cambridge Evening News*, learning that my daughter was an undergraduate in Cambridge, ran a little story under the headline FATHER NAMED FOR TOP POST. I made two paragraphs in 'Peterborough' in the Daily Telegraph, thanks to an old friend, author of *Does accent matter?*, the late John Honey. The headings were: Rise of Left-Winger (an improbable appointment for Mrs Thatcher to have made), and Few Signs (that is, few signs in my earlier career of this apotheosis). Honey was paid £30 for these fairly mischievous lines, but he sent me the thirty pieces of silver 'to devote to your favourite left-wing charity'. Pinker than pink, I was miscast as a leftie, and I spent the ill-gotten gains on a few drinks. Some years later, as a visiting professor at the University of Richmond, Virginia, I was introduced to an audience as 'not everyone's idea of a Regius Professor'. Not mine either.

Cambridge is a collegiate university in an absolute sense, in that it is practically impossible to function in Cambridge without a collegiate affiliation. Most university teachers are also fellows of colleges, while many college fellows hold no university post. It was not always so. At the governing body of one college, the bursar demonstrated that they would all have been better off for the past 300 years if assets had been invested in gilts rather than land (or was it the other way round?). One fellow said: 'Yes, but the last 300 years have not been at all typical.' So with the collegiate system, the last four or five centuries were not at all typical. Before that, colleges had been so many incidental extras to the life of the medieval university. It was in the fifteenth and sixteenth centuries that, thanks to founders and benefactors, many of them royal, Henry VIII in the case of Trinity, their numbers and substance expanded. It was then that the turreted gatehouses still to be seen at Queens' or Trinity were built, resembling the fortified great houses of the later middle ages. They admitted, or denied admittance, to a cloistered world. By the seventeenth century, it was possible to receive most of the essentials of a Cambridge education without going outside those gates, to the schools of the university. The vestiges of that tradition persist.

Those who have not been part of it find this little world hard to comprehend: the fact that the university and the colleges have distinct statutory existences and employ individuals, often the same individuals, separately and on different terms. The fact that, eleven years into retirement, I am no longer a teaching officer of the university but remain a Fellow of Trinity also takes some explaining to people in the outside world. The collegiate structure of the university inevitably places constraints on its capacity to expand. The other university in Cambridge, Anglia Ruskin University, already has more students than the senior body. So the twenty-first century may well see non-collegiate and expanding universities like Warwick leaving Oxbridge behind, unless we go back to the position before the last untypical 400 years. But this may be absurdly pessimistic. In October 2006 Cambridge was listed in an authoritative source as the second best university in the world (after Harvard and in front of Oxford).

The immediate relevance of all this for me, due to arrive in Cambridge in October 1988, was that I had to find a college willing and able to elect me to a professorial fellowship. Contrary to popular belief, a fellowship at Trinity does not go with the job of being Regius Professor of History. Henry VIII made no such provision. My chair was the invention of King George I in 1724, and the History Regius Professor, unlike his Henrician opposite numbers in Greek and Divinity, has nowhere to automatically hang up his hat. No one advised me on how to proceed, or how I might be proceeded with; whether to be reactive or proactive. There was some expectation that I would return to my undergraduate college, Pembroke, where I had been so happy between 1949 and 1952; and, if I had had a past as a fellow of Pembroke, that would probably have happened. But from Pembroke there was not a squeak, not even a letter of congratulation on my appointment. Meanwhile, I received an offer from the president of New Hall. I replied, politely declining the offer, not knowing that under rules which no one had told me about, only New Hall, which in its relatively brief existence had never had a professorial fellow, was entitled to make such an offer. That was why I had heard nothing from Pembroke. The master, the late Lord Adrian, was currently vice-chancellor, and he was a scrupulous man. Thanks to my colleague to be, John Morrill, I also received an offer from the master of Selwyn. Without doubt I should have been very happy in that society, graced as it was, and is, not only by John but by the best of recent Cambridge historians, and one of my predecessors, Owen Chadwick. But the redbrick buildings resembled one of those I had inhabited at school in Ely, and they put me off.

In 1987, I was acting as an external examiner in Manchester. (I had done the same job in several universities over the years, including Edinburgh, Lancaster and York. We all do it.) Walking across to lunch, an African historian, John Lonsdale, asked me whether I would like to come to Trinity, where he was and is a fellow. Another Trinity historian, Boyd Hilton, was behind the suggestion. So I was soon more or less committed to Trinity, which bent the rules in offering to elect me. It was an embarrassment when I went to a college feast at Pembroke and was told that everyone was expecting to welcome me back. It would have been nice to have been told. I wrote a letter of polite apology to Lord Adrian, offering the rather lame excuse that there were family connexions with Trinity. (They were sufficiently remote. The daughter of Mrs Humphry Ward, Liz's great aunt, was married to G. M. Trevelyan, a former master, while another great aunt was the first wife of Leonard Huxley and the mother of Aldous and Julian, step-brothers of Sir Andrew Huxley, who was master in 1987.) Richard Adrian, who had been brought up in the Master's Lodge at Trinity, wrote to say that he understood that there are all sorts of advantages to being a fellow of that college. And indeed there are. So it was, in early October 1988, that I was admitted by Huxley, who had succeeded his fellow

Nobel laureate Alan Hodgkin, in somewhat embarrassing circumstances. It was the luckiest break in a very lucky life.

For Trinity was, and is, very heaven. It is a heavenly experience to step out into a deserted Great Court early on a summer morning, or to look across Neville Court to that beautifully proportioned masterpiece, the Wren Library. And as for the contents of that library, a whole stack contains nothing but Aldine editions in Greek, many of them incunabula, printed in Venice before 1500! The choir under Richard Marlow was one of the best in Cambridge, and the college seethed with musical talent. Rachel Podger, now an internationally famous violinist specializing in Bach, joined with her brother in inventing something called Trinity Baroque. In my twenties, when I first became devoted to J. S. Bach, it was not possible anywhere in the world to hear performances which approached in quality and authenticity that undergraduate ensemble. There were times when the Puritan prig buried inside me rebelled against so much privilege, but the feeling was not difficult to suppress.

In a college like Trinity, there will always be internecine, C. P. Snow-style feuds, dislikes as well as likes, although, perhaps mercifully, we don't elect our master. Some memoirs of this kind would be full of little else but college politics. But I have found such things of marginal interest. I was a johnny come lately, and something of an outsider, as professorial fellows often are. I remember an occasion when I was a newly elected member of college council. Dr Anil Seal asked me at lunch, when I was entertaining guests from outside Cambridge, what had been decided in a certain matter of some delicacy. I replied that I didn't care to answer his question in public, and in the presence of my guests. He said that if I had been a fellow of the college for rather longer I would know that there was nothing which could not be discussed at lunch. Dr Seal would say that Trinity is all about 'candour'. Maybe so. Exceptions aside, I have always found Trinity a place of exceptional friendliness. And the college servants, from the Great Gate porters to the catering staff and the 'bedders' could not be nicer, more helpful, more friendly. Of the various college committees on which I served, the most memorable was the Livings Committee. Trinity presents to no less than fifty-three parochial livings in the Church of England. The dean of chapel, John Bowker, took this responsibility very seriously indeed. Where his predecessors, such as Bishop John Honest to God Robinson might have plucked a name from the air, there was now a prolonged search process, culminating in a series of interviews held in the master's study, to which Andrew Huxley would devote an entire day. His question was always the same: 'I, as you probably know, am an agnostic [after all, his grandfather, Thomas Huxley, had invented the term], but my mother used occasionally to attend the Unitarians. I should like to know whether you consider Unitarians to be Christians.' While the candidate reeled in his chair, Dr Bowker would come in with his question: 'What happens when I die?'

I respected, and liked, the four masters of Trinity I have known, not to speak of their remarkable wives. Heads of houses in Oxbridge are on a hiding to nothing. If they are not criticized for doing too little, they are censured for doing too much. It is sometimes said that the only master of Trinity in living memory of whom everyone approved was 'Rab' Butler, who had been parachuted into the college by Alec Douglas-Home. Butler was master at the time of the 'troubles' of the late sixties. At a tumultuous meeting held in the hall, someone at the back shouted out: 'Let's burn down the whole fucking college!' Butler said: 'I seem to have heard a motion. Does it have a seconder?' Andrew Huxley's successor was the best mathematician in the world, Michael Atiyah, who combined Trinity with presidency of the Royal Society, as does the current master, the astronomer royal, Martin Rees. After Atiyah came that very remarkable person, Amartya Sen. It has been one of the privileges of a Trinity fellowship to have known these towering figures.

My memories of the vice-chancellors in my time are less distinct, except for the admirable Sir David Williams, who having served two terms of office within the old dispensation, under which the vice-chancellor was a head of house, elected for two years, became the first executive vice-chancellor under new arrangements. With Richard Adrian of Pembroke I was deputed by the Council of Senate to expedite this change. David Williams was somewhat alarmed to learn that the only other vice-chancellor in history to have served for three terms, Dr Henry Butts of Corpus Christi College, had committed suicide on Easter Day 1632.

And what of our beloved chancellor, Prince Philip, duke of Edinburgh? Good stories abound. My favourite concerns a speech after lunch when the chancellor had conferred an honorary degree on a notable benefactor of the university, who had endowed our School of Business Studies:

> There's Mr Judge! He bought his degree. I can see some other wealthy people in this room. If you play your cards correctly, you too could get degrees. As for the academics who have been honoured, they are Welsh, and they've only got their degrees because the vice-chancellor [David Williams] is Welsh.

It fell to one of the Welsh honorands, Sir Keith Thomas, to graciously respond. (Strange to tell, one of the things which had precipitated Henry Butts's suicide had been the criticism he had received in the university for conferring too many honorary degrees on unqualified courtiers.) In 1989, which marked the two hundredth anniversary of the French Revolution, the chancellor blackballed President Mitterrand for an honorary doctorate, saying that he could not honour the head of a state which had executed its king. We had to give it to Richard Cobb of Oxford instead, a leading historian of the Revolution, who no doubt was more deserving. Lord Harewood was also blackballed, on the grounds that the chancellor could not confer a degree on a member of his own family who had been divorced, which appeared to limit rather severely the members of the royal family who could be so honoured. Incidents like that made the university a little restive. Soon Sir Alec Broers, David Williams's successor as vice-chancellor, went to Buckingham Palace to discuss the future. Philip came into the room. 'Ah, Broers, I think I'll give it another five years.' That was much more than five years ago. These delicious if thoroughly malicious anecdotes should not obscure the fact that Prince Philip has undoubtedly done the university much good, in ways not always so public.

In the past, the wives of Cambridge dons often led, on their terms and in their perception, miserable lives, not welcome in their husbands' colleges except on occasional ladies' nights. It was said that the late Dr Sheila Lambert, wife of my predecessor, Geoffrey Elton, for all her own scholarly credentials, was never happy in Cambridge, although she made up for that by entertaining Geoffrey's students on Sunday evenings in Millington Road. By my time, things had changed to some considerable extent. 'Spouses' (for now there were female fellows with husbands or partners) were welcome as guests at lunch or dinner, provided this didn't happen too often, which would have been against the 'good custom of the college', a vague formula to which one had sworn a solemn oath on admission to the fellowship. Liz was not unhappy in Cambridge. It was at this point that her working life in nursing came to an end. But she enrolled with the University of the Third Age (invented by my Trinity colleague Peter Laslett), where she found fulfilment in art, French and, for a time, bridge (fortunately that came to an end), as well as being a good friend and support to my students.

It was necessary to find somewhere in Cambridge to live. Prices were high (and have continued to climb at a steep rate ever since), so we decided not to put all our eggs in that basket but to maintain a comfortable family home in the Sheffield area, which in 1989 became Hathersage. So the two Cambridge houses we were able to afford, serially, were in unfashionable parts of town and small. Nevertheless, we kept up the tradition of entertaining students and colleagues, which we had taken from Honor Oak to Sydney to Canterbury to Sheffield. With the postgraduates there was no problem. The more the merrier. It was a little more awkward when we entertained senior and weighty figures in the university, not to speak of their wives, who were often rather large, making it difficult to squeeze through and behind with drinks and trays of canapés.

Beyond the college, there was the university and the Faculty of History. I hated the pride and joy of my predecessor, the faculty building on West Road designed by Sir James Stirling. But so did all my colleagues, so that we barely made use of our offices in that building, but came and went to give our lectures. This meant that there was no congenial faculty life, no common room culture, which was perhaps just as well. The economists comprised a deeply divided faculty, as they do every-where (ideology), but they all got on well in their faculty common room, or so I was assured. The Faculty of History, in my time, without the lubricant of coffee, was a scene of an almost unreal peace and tranquillity. The days of the warring titans, Geoffrey Elton and his many enemies, were well and truly over. (Some of those dinosaurs I never even met. Sir John Plumb and I lived in the same town for several years without ever being introduced. I was post-titan. Again, no regrets.) The almost comatose consensuality which I have sought and promoted all my life seemed to exist without any effort on my part. When, towards the end of my time as regius, we began to appoint a number of professors with a reputation for combativeness, it was almost a relief. Normality was returning.

The Statutes of the University told me that I could but was not bound to give lectures. However, it was generally assumed that the Regius Professor, like other teaching officers of the Faculty of History, would devote forty hours a year to university lectures. But what kind of lectures to give? Many undergraduates, and not necessarily the brightest, made a point of not going to lectures, relying on their weekly encounter with a supervisor, essay in hand. It seemed to me absurd that people who had made it to Cambridge, and to the most star-studded faculty in the world, should choose not to be exposed to so many truly excellent historians, and to be taught, as in some eighteenth-century mansion, by a private tutor. But so it was, especially in Trinity, where I did my own share of supervising. Just as I had gone through Cambridge without ever coming across G. R. Elton, so these Trinity under-graduates passed up the opportunity to be instructed by Quentin Skinner on political thought, or by John Morrill on the seventeenth century, or by Bob Scribner on the German Reformation, or by Keith Wrightson on pre-industrial English society.

Should I offer lectures of startling originality, which might attract the cognos-centi, or bread and butter lectures as tripos fodder? I am not the most charismatic of lecturers, and I never resolved that question to my own or anyone else's satis-faction. I decided, from the outset, that my lectures for Part One of the Historical Tripos would not consist of all that you ever wanted to know about the Tudors (most of our students had done them for A Levels). And, by the way, by changing universities I was again squeezed out of what I had been doing for the last four years. Social history, along with economic history, had its own specialists. I was deemed to be a political and constitutional historian. (That was where religion, my speciality, apparently belonged.) These were distinct papers in the Tripos, which itself was a nonsense. My solution was to offer a course of lectures on 'Problems in Tudor politics and literature'. The topics included Henry VII's poet laureate, John Skelton, Wolsey's biographer George Cavendish, the martyrologist John Foxe, Spenser, Sidney, Shakespeare. The first lecture was called 'Macbeth and Manchester United'. Now, did I choose that title because Elton would never have done so?

At first all went well. Among my audience was Lisa Jardine, and I went to her lectures in the other faculty on 'Reading Shakespeare historically'. I was happy to share with Lisa what she called a raft, made up of the historicity of texts and the textuality of historical documents. But then my lectures tailed off until I was meeting with a tiny conventicle in a small room in the faculty. Students wanted to know what the connexion was between what I was talking about and the examinations they would have to sit. 'I have heard', one of them said, 'that we may get a question about something called literacy. Is this relevant to that?' I had to say, not very, and I didn't see him again. A safer course of lectures on religious dissent, from the fifteenth to the eighteenth centuries, fared rather better.

There was widespread dissatisfaction with the structure of courses offered for Parts One and Two of the Cambridge History Tripos. There always had been. Tripos reform was the longest-running show in town. Earlier debates and resolutions, which had reached the higher levels of the decision-making process within the university, had opened up the Tripos to many new subjects: Africa, South Asia, Latin America, to the despair of diehards like Elton who not only believed in the centrality of English History, but defined English History somewhat narrowly as the development of its governmental laws and institutions. But these reforms had left unchanged an arguably unreformed relationship between a two-year Part One followed by a one-year Part Two. Many believed that students were bored by Part One, its combination of survey lectures and college supervisions, often traversing the same ground already covered in the sixth form. At the sixth-form level, the better taught students had already learned how to deal with original sources, which in Cambridge were an arcane mystery reserved for the intensive study involved in a Part Two Special Subject. And some of them had been encouraged to think about the nature of historical knowledge and practice in ways not always acknowledged in the Cambridge syllabus. But to alter the ratio of Part One to Part Two would have been inconvenient for directors of studies in the colleges. In a notorious vote in Faculty Board on St George's Day 1988, shortly before my arrival, the proposal to create a one-year Part One and two-year Part Two was defeated. And then, a year or so later, proposals for a radical reshaping of Part One, voted through the Faculty Board nem con, were effectively vetoed, or at least weakened, by those same directors of studies.

Part Two was more fun for teachers as well as for students. I devised a Special Subject on historiography, called 'Perceptions and uses of the past in sixteenth-century England'. It attracted some of the ablest undergraduates, and it was a steep learning curve for me as well as for them, since I knew precious little about the subject when I first began to explore it. (It's always best that way.) Neil McKendrick of Caius (later master of that college, but before that the most skilled of all

Cambridge historians in operating the system) decided that I was a good thing and sent me some of his stars. Now (remembering what George Potter had said of Sheffield students) people who get firsts did go to Caius. Three of those who took the course (but only one of them a Caian – Caius graduates tend to head straight for the city) are now lecturers in the History Faculty. There was always a great feeling of esprit de corps in those classes. One year the students hired a minibus and we all drove down to the National Theatre to see Ian McKellen's *Richard III*, which was one of our texts. That experience took me back to Canterbury, for my UKC colleague Marion O'Connor had done postdoctoral work on the influence of Shakespeare on Brecht, and this was a very Brechtian version of the play, close to *The resistible rise of Arturo Ui*.

If the Philippian Christians were for St Paul 'my joy and crown' (Philippians 4.1), my jewels were my postgraduate students. Before returning to Cambridge, I had supervised a total of eight or nine doctoral students over a period of twenty-five years. But now I had as many as a dozen at one time. And what a talented bunch they were! Some of them are now scattered among universities on both sides of the Atlantic: Fordham (New York), Portland (Oregon), Simon Fraser (British Columbia), Exeter, King's College London, UCL, Warwick. It was one of the proudest moments in my life when in 1998 eleven of these Collinsonians presented me with a Festschrift entitled *Belief and practice in Reformation England*. And what gave me particular pleasure was what the editors, Susan Wabuda and Caroline Litzenberger, found it in them to say about my very unacademic wife:

> We all share in our appreciation for the friendship extended to each one of us by Liz Collinson. She was a constant source of reassurance and support. She opened not only her home, but also her heart, to us all. In the turbulence each of us felt in his or her own way (as students do), as we worked toward our degrees, she was our 'anchor to windward'.

Those Collinsonians were part of a much larger body of postgraduate students researching for doctoral theses on all conceivable aspects of British and European History in the same period. Those with mainly British interests, and in the sixteenth century, made up a seminar which I inherited from Geoffrey Elton. Elton, for as long as he physically could, came to the seminar, and did nothing to make my life and role difficult; until, that is, one day when the visiting paper reader, Dr Glyn Redworth of Manchester, said, two minutes before six o'clock, that he had a few final points to make. Geoffrey could not tolerate papers that overran, and he got up and stomped out, saying: 'Really, this is preposterous.' The chattering classes had their own explanations for this outburst. Perhaps it had been provoked by the fact that Redworth had twice referred favourably to Dr David Starkey.

Those later years were not happy for Geoffrey. His contribution to meetings was almost always negative. But he was not well, and he wondered whither the country he had so enthusiastically become part of in 1939 was heading, under first Wilson and Callaghan, and then Thatcher. His last book, *Return to essentials: some reflections on the present state of historical study* (1991) was an embarrassment to many. The substance of the book consisted of lectures given in the University of Michigan. They were off-the-cuff, polemical and at some points outrageous, and Michigan was reluctant to publish them. But Cambridge University Press, through loyalty and long association, felt bound to do so. Elton took apart what he called 'erring colleagues', and they were numerous: 'Croce and Collingwood were utterly wrong.'

Nonsense always sounds better in French. 'When I was younger I was often accused of judging the Tudor century by the standards and criteria which it itself employed.' 'I frankly cannot think of a more flattering comment.' His principal target, especially in the inaugural lectures included in the volume, was Marxist or Marxist-influenced history, Christopher Hill and 'that very good man' R. H. Tawney. 'With great regret I am coming to think increasingly that there is not a single work which Tawney wrote which can be trusted.' This was a different Elton from the man who had said, in conversation with a number-crunching historian whose methods were very different from his, that there were many ways of making sense of the past, all equally valid. But the consistency in Elton was not only his unwavering insistence that 'the reality – yes, the truth – of the past exists', but in the selfless generosity of so much that he did for the profession, and for individuals within it – even women. As Elton's successor, I rode on the back of a discipline which he had redefined.

There were other seminars, all concerned with aspects of that interval between the medieval and the modern which historians of the period, to the mystification of the rest of mankind, call 'early modern': John Morrill's seventeenth-century seminar (with which we Tudors later merged), Keith Wrightson's social and economic seminar, Bob Scribner's seminar, which was self-consciously avant-garde, devoting whole terms to the theme of 'the body', Quentin Skinner and his fellow intellectual historians. On Monday evenings, under the benign patronage of Lisa Jardine, there was a seminar run by the postgraduates themselves, in which the presence of senior members was tolerated, so long as they knew their place. It was all so wonderfully different from the lonely experience of the very few doctoral students working on these topics in Canterbury or Sheffield: a truly critical mass. But not even the Monday seminar was immune from a kind of disease which afflicts flourishing graduate schools in which there is already an anticipated competition for research fellowships and the small number of academic posts likely to be available at the end of the line. The more confident, and even aggressive, students (not necessarily the very brightest), whether they mean it or not, tend to talk down and humiliate those suffering the desperate lack of self-confidence and even alienation which is often part of the postgraduate experience.

One of the best things to have happened in those years was the invention by the English Faculty of a Master of Philosophy course in Renaissance Literature. It was a rigorous course in palaeography, textual criticism and contextual studies, its rigours largely due to a remarkable fellow of Trinity, Jeremy Maule. Jeremy had a degree in History from Oxford, but taught Literature, and was equally able to cope with, and teach, Classics, or Theology. He had a marvellous nose for undiscovered sources. Towards the end of his life, for example, he found in Lambeth Palace Library hitherto unknown writings of Thomas Traherne. There is a grave danger that Jeremy will be forgotten, since he published almost nothing, apart from *The Oxford book of classical verse in translation*, which he co-edited with his Trinity colleague, Adrian Poole. The M.Phil. course was the best formation that Cambridge had to offer for anyone wanting to proceed with research into the civilization of England in the early modern period. Several of my Special Subject students went on to that course before coming back to work with me on their Ph.D.s. The disciplinary frontiers between History and Literature were being breached at many points, and often it was not easy to be sure where this or that young scholar was coming from, or where they were headed. All this owed little to the American fad of so-called 'New Historicism'.

When Jeremy Maule died, tragically and prematurely, on 25 November 1998, it almost marked the end of a golden era for early modern studies in Cambridge. Lisa Jardine left for London; Marie Axton, who had helped to sustain the M.Phil. course, retired; Bob Scribner had gone to Harvard, where he too would soon die before his time; Keith Wrightson was off to Yale. Not that it needed to make a great difference, I myself had retired in 1996. Under my successor, Quentin Skinner, arguably the most famous and influential student of political thought and discourse in the world, the faculty, or that portion of the faculty, took a distinct lurch towards intellectual history.

Of necessity, the sheer pleasure of sharing in all this intellectual vitality had to be balanced with public and administrative chores. I did my stint as chairman of the Faculty Board. For three years I was overburdened with meetings: the Council of Senate of the University on Monday mornings, Faculty Board or the Degree Committee of the faculty on Tuesday afternoons, College Council on Friday mornings. I don't remember that Wednesdays and Thursdays were free of meetings. I served for three years on the so-called Ad Hominem Committee of the university, which determined which of our colleagues in all disciplines should be promoted to the rank of professor or reader: a humbling experience, since Cambridge was overstocked with leaders in all kinds of subjects, not all of whom could be advanced. Back then, we were not able to do the proper thing by the world's leading authority on cephalods. But it was a very fair committee, in spite of the venomous criticism later levelled against it by Professor Gillian Evans. In all these various fora, it was a lesson which I had to learn, and Barrie Dobson too, who had come to the Cambridge medieval chair from York, not to speak of the way things were done elsewhere, which clearly had no relevance. And emerging from the holocausts which were UKC and Sheffield in the eighties, it was sometimes hard to understand why Cambridge thought that it had problems. But one learned to bite one's tongue.

Beyond Cambridge there were other public commitments. I served on the Council of the British Academy and chaired the section of the academy devoted to early modern history. I did two stints as vice-president of the Royal Historical Society (and later was made an honorary vice-president). For three or four years, I was the representative of the British Academy assisting a major project on the origins of the modern state, sponsored by the European Science Foundation. This took me to Strasbourg, Rome, Lisbon, Paris and even Istanbul. Taking third or fourth turn in expounding my ideas in a meeting in Paris, speaking my best French, the chairman remarked, as he had not done to those who had gone before me: 'Of course, we are all free to use our own language.'

Twice I served on the History Panel of the Research Assessment Exercise (RAE). This involved 'reading' (in a manner of speaking) some hundreds of publications in eight or nine weeks, since I covered Ecclesiastical History as well as Early Modern British History. For this one received remuneration which amounted, in total, to a little over £1,000. It was noticeable that those who were involved in this exercise again and again tended to go native, and to believe in its value. But I parted from any involvement in the RAE, deeply sceptical about its rationale and likely effects, at least so far as the Arts and Social Sciences are concerned. It is the symbol of the application to the Humanities of a model of productivity which may make sense in the laboratory but which ultimately derives from industry and business. I can even regret the penetration of our world by the word 'research'. Whatever happened to something called 'scholarship'? The RAE may have rekindled a few spent volcanoes and have persuaded some drones to become busy bees. But at what a cost. Who needs, and who will read, the books which today's academics are obliged to write, if their careers are to survive? The Royal Historical Society has recently conducted an investigation into the future of the monograph. Does it have one? Meanwhile, the RAE, and the fact that such a large share of the public funding of universities is earmarked for research, has had a distorting and deleterious influence on the recruiting of staff and their career development. Appointments go to candidates with two or three books already published or in the womb, who are then given generous research leave, their places as teachers taken by a new proletariat of temporary and untenured lecturers. At the very time when students, or their parents, are paying through the nose for their education, and getting into debt, there is a deliberate policy in some universities of reducing the hours spent in teaching in favour of research.

More agreeably, I continued to serve, as I had for many years, as chairman of the Advisory Editorial Board of the *Journal of Ecclesiastical History*. 1992 saw the foundation of the Church of England Record Society, its object 'to advance knowledge of the history of the Church in England, and in particular of the Church of England' by the publication of original source materials. This was the brainchild of the then Librarian of Lambeth Palace, the late Geoffrey Bill, who found some money under the bed to set the new venture in motion. Geoffrey Elton attended the meeting when it was decided to create the society, but said that it would never work. Fortunately he has been proved wrong. 2007 has seen the publication of the fifteenth volume for the Church of England Record Society. I am proud to have been the first president of the Society, serving until 2001.

Altogether more taxing was my involvement in the British Academy Foxe Project, as chairman of the committee which was supposed to keep an impossibly ambitious enterprise on the road, and on schedule. The aim was to produce, initially at least in electronic form, a scholarly edition of the *Acts and monuments* of John Foxe, the sixteenth-century martyrologist, popularly known as 'Foxe's Book of Martyrs'. This had not only broken all records for the longest book so far published in England, it changed its shape and character through four editions in Foxe's lifetime: 1563, 1570, 1576 and 1583. Our edition was to be a variorum edition of all four versions, replacing a very bad and often misleading Victorian edition. The Book of Martyrs took over Foxe himself, lock, stock and barrel, turning a witty and charming man into an abstracted recluse. It threatened to do the same for its modern editors, headed by the director of the project, David Loades. But fortunately we were able to recruit as principal research officer Tom Freeman, who knows more about Foxe, and everything to do with Foxe, than is decent, or credible. A facsimile of the 1583 edition, based on my own copy, is now available on line, and so is the first tranche of the critical edition which will be complete in 2011.

What in the meantime had happened to my own, I suppose I have to say, research? A lot was going on. A project which took far too long was a history of Emmanuel College, Cambridge, which I wrote in harness with my friend Christopher Brooke, Dixie Professor of Ecclesiastical History, and Dr Sarah Bendall. It is perhaps the longest and fullest history of any Oxbridge college. Why, people wondered, should I have bothered to spend so much time on the history of a college with which I had no connexion? (And the history of Trinity, admittedly a far more daunting prospect, remains unwritten, a bit of a scandal.) Ah, but there was a connexion. Emmanuel, founded in 1584, became the storehouse and seedbed of the Puritanism which I had studied for most of a lifetime. I took huge pleasure in uncovering its early history, and tracing its strange transmogrification into a quite different thing, in the mid-seventeenth century and beyond, as high churchmen and Cambridge Platonists thrust aside the stern Calvinism of the early years.

Alongside that I collaborated with my former student John Craig in editing a collection of essays on the subject of the Reformation in the English towns; and with John Craig and Brett Usher in producing, for the Church of England Record Society, some of the prime documentation for the history of Elizabethan Puritanism, on which I had first laid hands more than forty years before. I edited a volume on the sixteenth century for the Short Oxford History of the British Isles. And I contributed essays on religion and historiography to a number of door-stopping encyclopaedias.[1]

By this time that colossal undertaking, *The Oxford dictionary of national biography*, was taking over. I served on the Supervisory Committee, edited one of the sub-sections, and wrote twenty-seven articles for the *Dictionary*, mostly on my godly and not so godly old friends, the Elizabethan Puritans and bishops, but also articles on the twentieth-century Tudors, A. F. Pollard, J. E. Neale, S. T. Bindoff and G. R. Elton. My 'Elizabeth I' was, I'm told, at 36,000 words the longest article in the *Dictionary*. By the time I had finished with that, I was inclined to be finished with her, and I withdrew from a contract to write a full-scale biography for Blackwell. But in 2007 my *ODNB Elizabeth* was published by Oxford University Press as a separate paperback.

Long before this, since the mid-1980s, my various interests in the social history of the sixteenth century, its intellectual life and its politics and religion had come together with something it is not too much to call a conviction, the conviction that accounts of government and politics which neglect their social and intellectual integuments are impoverished and inadequate. Insofar as this conviction was directed against anyone, or any tendency, it had in its sights the limitations of Geoffrey Elton's narrowly 'constitutional' approach to these matters, expressed, for example, in his insistence that sixteenth-century parliaments were not political events but law-making machines; J. E. Neale's fixation on his beloved 'Lizzie' as both the prime mover and the object of what Elizabethan politics was about; but, most of all, the idea that there was something called a Tudor Despotism, a discredited notion, at least for the reigns of Henry VIII's children, but which Joel Hurstfield had tried to revive in the 1970s. These were some of the issues with which I engaged in my Cambridge inaugural lecture, delivered on 9 November 1989: '*De republica anglorum*: or, history with the politics put back'. My title tilted at another windmill. G. M. Trevelyan had famously defined social history as 'the history of a people with the politics left out'. The politics can never be left out of any situation or process of social interaction. And politics is always in itself social. I suggested that a new agenda might be 'to explore the social depths of politics, to find signs of political life at levels where it was not previously thought to have existed, and to disclose the horizontal connexions of political life at those lower levels as coexistent with

---

1   *Companion to historiography*, ed. Michael Bentley (London, 1997); *A companion to English Renaissance literature and culture*, ed. Michael Hattaway (Oxford, 2000); *The Cambridge history of the book in Britain*, vol. IV, ed. John Barnard and D. F. Mackenzie (Cambridge, 2002), in which I collaborated with three of my postgraduate stars, Arnold Hunt, Kate Peters and Alex Walsham; and *The Cambridge history of early modern English literature*, ed. David Loewenstein and Janel Muller (Cambridge, 2002).

the vertical connexions which depended upon monarchy and lordship'. It was a programme soon to be adopted by some of Keith Wrightson's postgraduate students, such as Professor Steve Hindle, of Warwick.

But what was I doing myself to advance this cause? *De republica anglorum* was the title of a book written in the 1560s by Sir Thomas Smith, an active politician and public servant, which offered to explain (to a French audience) how affairs were managed in England. The fact that Smith could define the English polity as an absolute monarchy and yet call it a republic set me thinking. At a seminar in Canterbury in 1983, I asked Quentin Skinner whether he thought we could speak of a monarchical republic, and he said that he thought that we could. Later I would come to understand better that the sixteenth century could find no incompatibility between the idea of a 'republic' or 'commonwealth' (the terms were interchangeable), and the institution of monarchy. In the following century, Algernon Sidney would write that 'all monarchies in the world which are not purely barbarous and tyrannical, have ever been Commonwealths'. The Muscovy of Ivan the Terrible was sufficiently barbarous and tyrannical, yet the first English book on the subject was entitled *Of the Russe Commonwealth*.

There were several reasons why the England of Elizabeth I was especially conscious of being a republic, a monarchy containing not only subjects but active citizens. One was the education in the Greek and especially Latin classics which was the common inheritance of anyone in this age of the Renaissance educated to at least grammar school level. (Think of Shakespeare.) Everyone knew and was fond of quoting the dictum of Marcus Tullius Cicero: a man is not born for himself alone, but for his family, and for his children, and for his country. Another was the heightened sense of responsibility for one's actions associated with first and second generation Protestantism, and the fear of the other, Catholicism, which accompanied that sense. But most important of all was the fact that the queen, by failing to marry and produce an heir of her own body, or to allow the matter of succession to the throne to be discussed, let alone resolved, threatened her people with a dangerous vacuum in the event of her death. There would be no need of an assassin (a popish assassin, of course). A fish bone stuck in the throat, or the micro-organism which carries smallpox could have done it. (It was a mole, or rather its molehill, which would terminate the life of William III.) A speaker in the parliament which met in 1567 said: 'If God should take her Majesty, the succession being not established, I know not what shall become of my self, my wife, children, lands, goods, friends or country.' 'I tell you, Mr Speaker, that I speak for all England.' Even the second person in the land politically speaking, William Cecil, Lord Burghley, envisaged a situation in which 'all England' might have to look after itself as a republic, almost in the modern sense; although of course Cecil was not a republican in our modern sense and intended the emergency measures he proposed to lead as soon as possible to securing a legitimate, acceptable, and male monarch.

I explored these insights in my inaugural lecture at Sheffield, and in a Neale Memorial Lecture in Manchester in 1986: 'The monarchical republic of Elizabeth I'; and, later, in a Raleigh Lecture for the British Academy, also delivered in Sheffield, in 1993: 'The Elizabethan Exclusion Crisis and the Elizabethan polity'. It was Mary Queen of Scots whom most Protestant Elizabethans wanted to see excluded, and it set them in a kind of opposition to their queen, right up to and beyond the moment when Elizabeth signed the fatal death warrant.

As the Bible says, from something as small as a mustard seed a tree can grow large enough for birds to perch and make their nests. Rarely has so much arisen from a casual conversation in a seminar room. In 2007 a collection of essays appeared, edited by John MacDiarmid, commemorating the twentieth anniversary of my invention of the term 'monarchical republic'. And Quentin Skinner was among the contributors. The essays develop, qualify and further problematize my original idea.

It is said that rolling stones gather no moss.[2] But this rolling stone gathered quite a bit of moss. The Historical Association awarded me their Medlicott Medal. There have been honorary doctorates from Canterbury, Essex, Oxford, Sheffield, Trinity College Dublin, Warwick and York. In the Sheldonian in Oxford my false left foot tripped on those tricky stairs as I ascended to grasp the hand of the chancellor, Roy Jenkins. 'You didn't put a foot wrong', said a kindly Keith Thomas. The TCD event involved our first visit to the Republic of Ireland. The occasion was the four hundredth anniversary of the foundation of the college and I was there to represent Trinity College Cambridge. Within hours of landing in Dublin, I found myself processing up the nave of St Patrick's Cathedral, past the hubristic tomb of the earl of Cork, along with Mary Robinson, the then president, the two primates, the lord mayor of Dublin, and, for good measure, Perez de Quella, former secretary general of the United Nations. This proved to be the first of many visits to Ireland. Year upon year, we went to uttermost Connemara, to cottages on lonely and beautiful strands, looking out to the sanctified island of Inishboffin, and beyond to Clare Island, the hills of Mayo, and Achill Island, with the Twelve Bens always a backcloth in the other direction. I have been honoured by no less than three *Festschriften*. First came *Religion, culture and society in early modern Britain*, edited by two esteemed old colleagues, Anthony Fletcher and Peter Roberts (1994), and carrying an excessively kind tribute from a Cambridge colleague, Christopher Brooke. My old teacher from Ely, Muriel Arber, was present in the Cambridge University Press bookshop when the volume was presented. Then came an Australasian volume, *Protestants, property, Puritans: godly people revisited*, a special number of the journal *Parergon*. Now Parergon is the journal of the Australian and New Zealand Association for Medieval and Early Modern Studies, a society which had its beginnings in a conference held in Melbourne soon after my arrival in Australia, and organized by my dear friend, the late George Yule, the first of many such meetings. And then in 1998 there was my postgraduates' *Festschrift*, already mentioned, *Belief and practice in Reformation England*.

Soon after arriving in Cambridge I was made a Commander of the British Empire. There are not many bits of that Empire left to go round, but I thought that I would choose to command Rockall. A Trinity economist kindly remarked that these things come up with the rations, and of course he was right. Surprise was expressed, not least within my own family, that I, a more than closet republican, should accept such an honour from Queen Elizabeth II. My response was to say (as is usual) that it was an honour not so much for me as for my office, and for the profession; and that insofar as the queen was and is head of state, I was happy, and proud, to receive it from her. It was how any of my sixteenth-century monarchical republicans would have responded. I was advised by the Palace of various dates when investitures were to be held, but was told that I could, if I preferred it, receive the CBE from the lord

---

2   And here I cannot resist recounting what happened to my colleague John Morrill when, on a lecture tour in Japan, he was surprised to be confronted with questions about the Rolling Stones. It finally dawned on him that he was being asked about the famous historian Lawrence Stone.

lieutenant of my county. Now the then lord lieutenant of Cambridgeshire was my old Pembroke contemporary and captain of boats, James Crowden, so I jumped at the prospect of being done, at his hands, in Trinity. It was a quaint little ceremony in what we call (even quainter) the Private Supply Room, attended by family and friends from various bits of my life. John Lonsdale said that it was a very English occasion. The snag was that I had to pay for the champagne.

But of course Falstaff has the last word on such honours, Robert Browning's 'just for a riband to stick in his coat': 'What is honour? A word. Air. Therefore I'll none of it, honour is a mere scutcheon' (*Henry IV Part I*, V.ii.). And honour doesn't pay the mortgage. There was never any question of Browning's 'handful of silver'.

17

The Glacis of Retirement

'That time of year thou mayst in me behold / When yellow leaves, or none, or few, do hang / Upon those boughs which shake against the cold' (Sonnet 73). By now, eleven years into retirement, that's how it begins to feel: shaking against the cold, and against that black night which Dylan Thomas urged us to resist. A still better metaphor might be that of the Atlantic salmon in the last phase of existence: the kelt, which, having spawned, in a wasted state drifts back down the river towards the wide sea whence it came.

Yet in the first five years or so the yellow leaves hung on. Retirement for an academic historian is not to fall off a cliff but to descend a quite gentle glacis. Less than five years into it, I'm impressed by the number of things I was still doing, and the amount of travelling undertaken, in the years immediately before and after retirement. Twice I went back to Sydney, the first time to take part in the largest historical conference ever held in Australia (and I also lectured in Melbourne and Perth); the second as the first J. M. Ward memorial lecturer, honouring my old colleague who had died so tragically. Twice we went to New Zealand, each time for me to lecture and to take part in conferences in Wellington; but, on the second visit, to take time out for a two-week drive around a landscape of astonishing beauty and variety: South Island in winter. Doubtful Sound on a wet day (every day on Doubtful Sound is wet) was awe-inspiring. I was a frequent visitor to many parts of the United States, mostly to the Huntington, and to the Folger Shakespeare Library in Washington, but also to Claremont California, Massachusetts, Oregon, Pennsylvania, Utah, lecturing, participating in conferences and running summer research institutes. In 1993 I went to the States three times. I lectured in Geneva and Zurich, and indeed in three continents, on one of my hobby horses: the relation between the disciplines of History and Literature, a tale of two cities and how it might best be regulated. (For that relation this was indeed the best of times and the worst of times.) In 2002 I wrote my little book on *The Reformation* in three or four weeks. It has been translated into Spanish and Portuguese (both the Portuguese of Lisbon and the Portuguese of Sao Paolo), Slovak and Korean: disturbing in a way, since it conveys a vision of the Protestant Reformation which was up to date in the 1970s, when I had last taught and had known anything about the subject.

Andrew and his family were now in Kwa-Zulu Natal in South Africa, where he was the senior paediatrician in a large black hospital. The effects of Aids were already being felt. Two or three children a day were dying. At the Bristol Children's Hospital, where Andrew had been working, it had been two or three a year. We went out for a long stay, and did a tour of the province, up to the dramatic Drakensbergs and back, via various game parks. And then we took a long drive through the Transkei and the Ciskei to Cape Town. So much natural beauty; but the images which have had the longest staying power are of all those homesteads scattered across the barren

Transkei veldt, and people displaced from the townships and dependent on mini-buses they could hardly afford to take their children to clinics like those which Andrew conducted. 'I need to see this child next week', he would say, knowing full well that the fare to come back could not be afforded. We loved Cape Town, and the vibrant scene around the Waterfront. But on the other side of Table Mountain were those sprawling, crime-ridden townships, where we got bushed one Sunday morning, losing our way to the airport. We went to St George's Cathedral in Cape Town, and I hoped to meet up with Desmond Tutu, but he was busy with the Truth and Reconciliation Commission in Pretoria.

A year or two later Andrew was doing his MD research in the Gambia. The family spent three years in that strange little ribbon of a country and we went out to stay with them two or three times. This was when Steve, too, was regularly in the Gambia, learning the art of playing the drum known as the djembe, from which he makes his living. At Keneba, up-country, where the Medical Research Council is based, the infant school children sang 'London's burning'. On the river, we saw ospreys which might next turn up at Loch Garton. On our last visit, Andrew broke his neck falling from his surfboard on to hard sand. That man has more than a cat's nine lives and, after a few months in a 'halo' (a kind of cage) he emerged unscathed, to start the next part of his career in Tyneside. We found their house in a street close to the marvellous beach of Tynemouth (Syon Street – you can't get away from the Percy dukes of Northumberland in that part of the world), where Andrew soon resumed surfing. He wrote a piece in the British Medical Journal: 'My life as a hat stand'. In a greengrocer's shop, he had been told: 'I hope that you're not going to cause any trouble.' He hadn't thought of that.

In March 2001 we went to Tucson, Arizona, where I gave the annual town and gown lecture for the great Heiko Oberman, director of an Institute of Medieval and Reformation Studies. Heiko was weeks away from death, and knew it. I did the last ever seminar for his postgraduates from a patio overlooking the lights of the city. The only difference between you and me, he told his students, is that I know when I am going to die. It happened two or three weeks later. Heiko was a very polemical scholar who took no prisoners. But he was also a devout minister in the Dutch Reformed Church. To lose Heiko and Bob Scribner within a couple of years was a severe blow to Reformation Studies.

Before that, in January 1999, I had set out for Virginia, for a semester as the Douglas S. Freeman Visiting Professor at the University of Richmond. It was a strange and not entirely satisfactory experience. I had proposed a series of classes on the history, and self-discovery, of the British Isles in the sixteenth century; but the course had been poorly advertised, and I found on arrival that I had just five students, one of whom, the only historian in the bunch, was on secondment from Queen Mary and Westfield College London. The Department of History was deeply divided, as departments in liberal arts colleges often are, by an issue involving the denial of tenure to a promising young medievalist. There were two corridors, one not speaking to the other. No wonder that I sometimes asked myself what I was doing in Richmond. But to spend those months in the Commonwealth of Virginia was a great treat. We drove down to Jamestown, listening on the car radio to the endless impeachment proceedings against Clinton, and up to Jefferson's Monticello and the Blue Ridge. As a seventeenth-century settler wrote: 'This country which had a mean beginning … is become a place of pleasure and plenty.'

In October 2000 I began a three-year appointment as an honorary visiting professor at the University of Warwick. This was better. I used to tell people that Sidney and Beatrice Webb could have had Warwick in mind rather than the Soviet Union when they said in 1930: 'We have seen the future, and it works.' It was no accident that Bill Clinton chose to make his last speech in office on that campus. I went to Warwick three or four times a year, to lecture or to be involved in a seminar. And usually I arrived at lunchtime, to spend the afternoon talking to the early modern research students. It was my last contact with those up and coming generations, and I miss the experience.

In June 2002 Liz and I decided to go to Arctic Norway, which was to revisit the Cambridge Expedition of 1951, and my holiday in the Lofotens with Esther in 1958. We worked out a brilliant itinerary, which included two or three days in and around Tromso, with a visit to Norway's Switzerland, the Lyngen Peninsula; and then a week in a rented cottage in Lofoten, with, thanks to all those new bridges and tunnels, a hired car to take us back to the most beautiful place on earth, Reine in Moskensoy.

It was downhill all the way after that, although good things still sometimes happened: like the opportunity to give the annual Creighton Lecture for the University of London in November 2002: 'Elizabeth I and the verdicts of history'.

We began to think that we should make a move away from Hathersage, where the winters, when they happened, were hard to cope with, and the house and garden too much for us to manage. Life in Hathersage had consisted, in large part, in keeping the flag of the rest of the world flying. We ran the local Christian Aid operations and were active in efforts to promote Fair Trade in the Hope Valley. Perhaps the time had come to climb out from under those increasingly taxing commitments. Family consultations went on for two years.

By the early months of 2005, we had come to a decision. It was our cleaner, the lovely Sue Johnson, who gave us a shove. 'You've got to move.' Devon seemed to be the right destination. Two of our four families were already there: Andrew (now a consultant in Exeter), Debs and their children; Sarah and Jeff and the two boys, about to become three. And soon Helen and Julian and the two girls would move from Tottenham to Coleridge's town, Ottery St Mary. As Adolf Hitler might have put it, our patience was exhausted. The Collinsons were about to annexe Devon. By the later months of 2005, most of our family and all eight biological grandchildren were within easy reach of the South Devon coast, leaving only Steve and his wife Nicky (who were married in August 2004) in Sheffield; and Anna, our grandchild by a different route and in another sense, still in London, with her mother Elaine.[1] But to pull up your roots and to downsize, in your mid-seventies, is not easy.

The move, and, before that, the choice of a house to move to, could hardly have been more fraught. We had just come back from a holiday in Jordan: Petra, Jerash, snorkelling at Akaba, the Wadi Rum. (We couldn't do it now.) Liz arrived in Devon in late March 2005, to help with the latest baby, but she promptly had a heart attack

---

[1] This reference to Anna requires an explanatory note. While our daughter Helen was in a relationship with Elaine Ginsburg, Elaine decided to have a child by donor insemination. Anna was born in 1989. Helen is not officially a co-parent, but she has been much involved with Anna's upbringing and development from the day of her birth. Now that Helen and her partner Julian have two daughters of their own, Maya and Zoe, Anna is a loving sister to both the girls, and a popular cousin for the children of our other families. We love her dearly and are proud of her progress towards a career in Animation. As for Elaine, she is very happy to have this relationship with our family.

and, following the insertion of a stent, a small stroke. Since then life has changed considerably for both of us. It is slower, and less gets done.

Liz was in hospital when I, *faute de mieux*, had to do the house-hunting. There are lots of pleasant places to live in Devon, but most of them are hilly and involve tiresome treks up or down to the village or the town centre to fetch a litre of milk. So forget about Totnes, Ashburton or Stoke Gabriel. I (and perforce we) settled on Shaldon, a village which also has its hills, but at its heart consists of two or three level streets, lying behind the tidal River Teign, just before it meets the open sea, across the water from Teignmouth. (You get there by the oldest working ferry in England, unless you want to drive over what was, in the early nineteenth century, the longest bridge.) The French burned the place down in the late seventeenth century, so the older cottages, built of 'cob', record a little renaissance in the 1690s. Later, there was a prosperous trade with Newfoundland, the merchants living across the Strand from their warehouses, which are now replaced by little gardens. Nowadays most of the cottages are holiday homes, or second homes, empty for much of the year. It makes for a quiet life, except for the ever-present and vocal herring gulls, which get going at four o'clock in the morning. Gone for ever, it seems, are our third world interests and activities. Devon is very happy with itself, thank you very much, and it's too bad about the rest of the planet. Liz has never much liked our Shaldon house, which she didn't choose. Much of 2007 was spent in extending and improving it, thanks to a modest mortgage from a little known bank called Northern Rock.

But our grandchildren make sense of our declining years. Sarah's boys, Will, born profoundly deaf but coping very well with the benefit of an implant, Matt and Jack, who live close to Haytor Rocks on Dartmoor, descend frequently. I must not say that they are so many Assyrians, coming down like the wolf on the fold. Grandchildren are the greatest imaginable joy, but it is a joy which needs to be carefully rationed. Andrew's three are older, and one can have sensible conversations, especially with eleven-year-old Tom, who has inherited his father's and grandfather's passion for the natural world, and for fishing. And unlike his grandfather he has a satisfactory sporting life: captain of his rugby team. Helen's two girls, Maya and Zoe, are also great and effervescent company. Maya finds walking from A to B boring. She performs endless cartwheels all along the street, or on the prom at Teignmouth. And she is an enthusiastic footballer. Five-year-old Zoe told her teacher: 'I think that that is a painting by Claude Monet.' How good it will be to go along with all of them, into later childhood and teenage, if only we manage to survive for just a few more years!

Cambridge is not forgotten. I shall hold a Trinity fellowship until the moment I drop dead. No other Oxbridge college provides lifetime fellowships. That decision in 1987 has paid off. I go back to Trinity as often as I can, to confront the bulk of my library in my room in Angel Court. 'Where have you been?' the books ask, and I feel like Moley going back to his neglected little home in *The wind in the willows*. Out of my window, as I write this, are the exotic chimneys of Alfred Waterhouse's Caius, and beyond that the astonishing skyscape of King's. Most years I take part in the annual election of research fellows, pretending to understand what the mathematicians and physicists have to tell us about their candidates, and wheeling and dealing, with variable success, to get the best historians elected.

So life goes on, even academic life. I have often thought about giving up on history altogether and devoting myself to, say, fishing. But I find the cruelty involved in catching the poor things repugnant. And, drawn back to my desk, I am challenged by the example of Leopold von Ranke, the father of modern history, who at the age of eighty-three embarked on a kind of universal history, and managed seventeen volumes of it.

In October 2007 we both spent two or three weeks in America. I launched a new lecture series at the Jesuit University in New York, Fordham in the Bronx, with a talk about Mary Queen of Scots. I told the Jesuits that it was very ecumenical of them to choose for this role someone who is not only a historian of Protestantism but a Protestant historian. That this happened owed everything to a former pupil, Susan Wabuda, now a professor at Fordham. I took in a monster conference in a hotel in Minneapolis, and gave a talk at the Folger Library: the main theme for me on these occasions my hobby horse of the Elizabethan monarchical republic.

It is perhaps a pity that I shall no longer research and write a book about what happened to Liz and her parents in Kenya in the early 1930s. I ought not to attempt that without going to that part of Kenya, and it is perhaps too late for that. But I am glad that Liz went there in 1997 to make a programme for the BBC, and to trace her parents' graves. One of the unexpected results of Liz's visit was a friendship with Bishop Stephen of Kitale, a Pokot who explained (he often came to stay with us in Hathersage) what it was to be a Pokot. Stephen told us that he was the neighbour of Kaitobok, one of the men who had been beaten under Liz's mother's ever watchful eye, back in 1934. In such ways, the world shrinks and time contracts.

Much of this memoir has verged on the solipsistic, as if the world outside of my own little life scarcely impinged. That is in the nature of the genre and it gives a false impression. The early mornings find us glued to the BBC World Service and the Today Programme. As what George Bush Senior called the new world order becomes ever more disorderly, the inevitable reaction is impotent, especially as we contemplate, forty-six years on, the Sudan, and especially tragic Darfur, which Esther's son Alex de Waal helps us to understand a little.

We were on the delectable beach of Ballyconneelly in Connemara on the last day of our holiday in 2001, with Sarah and Jeff and baby Will, the only problem being a very dead whale around the next headland. Three days later, it was September the Eleventh, Nine Eleven, and Jeff was in a plane bound for Washington. Susan Wabuda had rung up from New York when the first plane struck, and we were in front of the television when the South Tower was hit, and for the rest of that day; except for frequent phone calls to United Airlines, hoping for news with which to reassure Jeff's parents, who were worried sick. (Jeff had been taken hostage in Somalia a few years before.) At five o'clock they told me that the plane would land in Canada. That's interesting, I said. The latest on TV is that all Canadian airspace is closed. 'Thank you for telling us that, sir.' As Jeff's plane came back to Heathrow, the passengers, having been informed of a small navigational error, were still filling in their immigration forms. There was some anger, and no one was told what had been happening until they were back in the terminal. In October 2007 we paid our respects at Ground Zero.

Since Nine Eleven we have observed unfolding events with a concern verging on despair. We actively opposed the invasion of Iraq, talking to our MP, a benevolent backbencher called Tom Levitt, in candle-lit vigils in Hathersage, and in that great march in London. It was at the height of excitement about dodgy dossiers that I met up with John Humphreys of the Today programme in Warwick in July 2003, where we were both given honorary degrees. Then came Seven Seven in London.

I had lived for two years on the other side of Tavistock Square, where that bus was blown up, and Cedric Lazaro and I had jogged every morning around the statue of Mahatma Gandhi in the middle of the square. On that day Sarah was on her way to Great Ormond Street with Will, but only got as far as Paddington Station before heading back to Devon. With the mobile phone system down, it was Jeff's turn to be worried sick. And then, in August 2006, came the grossly disproportionate response of Israel to Hezbollah in an assault on the people of the Lebanon and their livelihoods and infrastructure which exceeded anything we have seen before, outside Chechnya. And our government looked on with something close to approval.

Without doubt, the intellectual and moral failure of 'the international community', meaning the United States and its hangers on, a failure to understand how the world looks from a standpoint in Nablus, or Gaza, or Baghdad, or simply, to anyone with any sense of history, how it ever works, is largely to blame for a regression from a so-called War on Terror (in itself a deeply flawed idea) to something which may indeed turn into a kind of war of civilizations. As the son of various missionary enterprises, aimed at the world of Islam, and as a veteran of Khartoum, I naturally have my own angle on these developments. I don't know the answers to the questions, but I think that I do know what the questions ought to be.

That may prove to be the least of our fears, or rather, not our fears but those of our children, and especially grandchildren. When we go to Widecombe-in-the-Moor to pick up Will from school, we sometimes chat to Will's great friend Wilf, and to Wilf's father, Pen Hadow, the polar explorer. Pen assures us that by the time Will and Wilf are grown up there will be no ice left in the Arctic. Climate change and global warming will reduce all other crises and conflicts of the twentieth and twenty-first centuries to what Sir Herbert Butterfield, referring to the Renaissance and Reformation of the fifteenth and sixteenth centuries, called 'mere internal displacements' in European history. It is the old man's lame excuse to say: 'Well, we shan't be here to see it.' (That's clearly inexcusable, especially if one has nine grandchildren.)

Liz and I, born in 1929, were part of the lucky generation. We lived through the Second World War, but not as combatants. We benefited from years of full employment; and from the Great Peace which was the Cold War. Our children were educated, right up to graduation from their universities, at virtually no cost to ourselves. My pension is adequate, and secure. We are not rich but we manage. In our time the world was our oyster, still a place to be enjoyed, in all its richness, and in our twenties we were adventurous tourists before the tiresome days of tourism. It was good to have seen Abu Simbel before the High Dam, and to have wondered at the great falls of Tissisat with no one else around to disturb us. I very much fear, indeed I am sure, that the times in which our grandchildren will grow up and make their various ways will not be so benign. Cynics will point out that similar sentiments are to be found in the cuneiform of clay tablets in ancient Mesopotamia. But it must have been soon after that that Noah's Flood happened. It is hard not to feel guilty, since the good times recorded in this memoir will be paid for by the next two or three generations.

Index

RECORD SERIES

OTHER PUBLICATIONS

Suggestions for publications should be addressed to Professor Stephen Taylor, General Editor, Church of England Record Society, Department of History, University of Reading, Whiteknights, Reading RG6 6AH, or at s.j.c.taylor@reading.ac.uk.